CHARLIE'S PLACE

CHARLIE'S PLACE

The Saga of an American Frontier Homestead

By Michael S. Malone

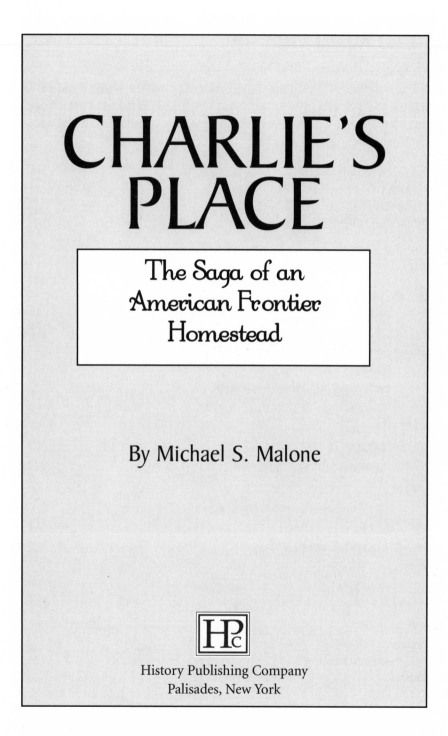

History Publishing Company
Palisades, New York

Published in the United States by
History Publishing Company LLC
Palisades, NY
www.historypublishingco.com

ISBN-10:1-933909-41-2
ISBN-13: 978-1-933909-41-7

LCCN: 2012933159
SAN: 850-5942

Malone, Michael S. (Michael Shawn), 1954-
    Charlie's place : the saga of an American frontier
homestead / by Michael S. Malone.
    p. cm.
    Includes index.
    LCCN 2012933159
    ISBN 9781933909-40-0 (pbk.)

1. Pioneers--United States--Biography. 2. Frontier
and pioneer life--West (U.S.) 3. Oklahoma--History--
Land Rush, 1893.   I. Title.

F596.M35 2012   978'.092'2
                         QBI12-600039

Table of Contents

FOREWORD

THE STORY OF THE CHEROKEE STRIP LAND RUN, AND THE SETTLING OF WHAT would become the great State of Oklahoma, is the extraordinary story we tell at the Cherokee Strip Regional Heritage Center in Enid, Oklahoma. Unique from other states, the majority of Oklahoma was settled by land run. Beginning in 1889 through 1895 a series of seven land runs were held opening up vast expanses of prairie and rolling hills to settlement. The Cherokee Strip Land Run of 1893 was the largest land run in American history with over six million acres opened for settlement and over 100,000 eager runners competing for approximately 45,000 plots of land.

Those would-be pioneers came from all walks of life with dreams as big as the Oklahoma sky to a land with enough space and opportunity to make them come true. Many were from other lands determined to break the chains of tyranny and have something to call their own.

It is the people of this amazing story that make us proud to be called Oklahomans. No doubt, it is because of our unique beginnings that our heritage is so rich with people of feisty spirit, warm hearts and forward thinking. People like Charlie Hasbrook who made the run and handed down a legacy of ambition, determination and entrepreneurship through generations of Hasbrooks evident today in his great-great grandchildren.

9

Being an early pioneer on a waving sea of open prairie was not for the faint of heart. It took strength, hope, courage and no small amount of fortitude to carve out a life ... and a home in this beautifully wild place and "prove up" a claim. Settlers learned early on that the only way to survive was to work hard and to help each other. As sure as the red dirt beneath our feet, those traits are the benchmark of Oklahomans yet today.

Charlie's Place offers readers an insider's view to one of the most significant events in American history ... the great Cherokee Strip Land Run. A tale of adventure, joy, tragedy and optimism ... as American as they come.

> —Andi Holland, Director
> Cherokee Strip Regional Heritage Center
> Enid, Oklahoma
> February 8, 2012

INTRODUCTION

A Door in the Earth

THIS IS THE STORY OF A FARM.

Not a particularly remarkable farm—at least not by Eastern, or even Oklahoma—standards. Certainly, it was undistinguished when it was created; merely one of thousands created in the course of a few years in the 1890s during the several Oklahoma Land Rushes.

But as the decades passed, and it endured long after its neighbors had all-but disappeared or been replaced, survival itself made the farm ever more interesting. And then, a century after it was built, thirty years after it was abandoned to the weather and roaming cattle, the farm suddenly became singular, even unique.

As the restorers studied the great sagging barn, with its unlikely cupola, they saw the bones of a structure with few equals in that part of the Great Prairie—a palimpsest of a type of construction about which there was little record. And though the house, with its collapsed porches and stair treads snapped by the weight of curious cows, had little to distinguish it, even it had a story to tell about construction, location and survival on the harsh frontier.

But most evocative of all was the little cave, dug out of the creek bank, with its arched walls and ceiling, the scraps of rotting muslin still hanging on the walls, and the sad little brick chimney . . . it told a story about the hardships of pioneer life better than any written description could ever capture.

11

And when the abandoned car was towed away, and the weeds mown, the mud dauber wasp nests cleared out of the barn and the great black bull snake driven out of the crawl space under the house, when the crane arrived accompanied by a phalanx of pick-up trucks, and the hammering and trenching and pouring and stripping began, the farm suddenly gained an importance, even a celebrity, it had never known before. Incredibly, at the culmination of a most unlikely chain of events that stretched from tiny Bison, Oklahoma to the nearby city of Enid, across the globe to Morocco and Germany, then on to Washington, D.C, and finally, and perhaps most mysteriously, to California's Silicon Valley electronics industry, history had come full circle back to the farm. Crimes would be rectified, losses restored, and even murders redeemed.

At the brink of oblivion, the farm would be saved, reclaimed, made shiny and new again—and sent out into the new century as an emblem of what had been lost, a survivor of a different world, a lesson about who we were and what we had become.

But as much as this is the story of a farm, it is just as much the tale of two people—like the farm, equally undistinguished on first glance, but whose accomplishments have grown over time, and whose lives seem more remarkable by the year. One was the man who pioneered the homestead and built the farm—it is this man for whom this book is named. The farm is Charlie's Place, and it always will be, whoever lives there or holds the deed.

Charlie Hasbrook created the farm, mostly with his own hands, ran it for forty years, and then lost it. No one felt that loss more than the second figure in this story, his granddaughter and my mother, Nadiene Malone. And though it took her sixty years—longer even than Charlie owned the farm—his granddaughter never forgot, never gave up hope. In the end she regained and restored everything that had been lost.

These are only the only major players in this tale. Not surprisingly, in a tale that begins in the 19th century, the beginning of this story is filled with many of the stock characters of a Victorian melodrama, the evil stepfather, the blushing bride, the orphans of the storm, the amiable hired hand, the righteous lawyer. Then, when the story moves forward to the Great Depression, the figures seem right out of the Socialist realism of the era: the exploited farmer of the Dust Bowl, the calculating and greedy banker, the bootlegger and the campus football hero. But in the end, as befits our post-modern age, none of these players prove to be quite what they seem, their figures much more complex, nuanced and even contradictory when seen in three dimensions against the backdrop of history.

What does remain through it all is the farm itself. Refuge, home, last defense, birthplace, career, object of envy and theft, squatter's hovel, abandoned shack, construction site, historic place—the farm has taken on many roles, and many looks, but it has never changed. No more than the creek that meanders through it, nor the deer than wander among its cottonwood trees.

It is Charlie's Place. Because Charlie Hasbrook found it, sacrificed everything for it, and made it his own. Not even death, or the evil intentions of others, could take that away from him. It is Charlie's Place, because his granddaughter loved him, and he taught her to love the farm. And because his blood made her as quietly indomitable as he was; with the same iron will—so that near the end of her own long life, in yet the third century of this story, she would finally fulfill her unspoken promise to him, thank him, and honor his memory forever.

＊ ＊ ＊

I have written this book in my fifties, in a new century, when most of the figures in the story are gone. But looking back, I realize I began to investigate this story more than thirty years ago, in my early twenties, at an age when many young adults discover, for the first time, that they have a family history; that they are just the latest chapter in a very long tale.

I was just out of college, starting my career, and I had stopped by one evening to visit my parents. My father was home, recovering from his most recent heart attack. He was starting to feel better—and, as always, was bored and driving my mother to distraction.

More as a way to keep herself occupied than anything else, my mother decided to organize the family scrapbooks and keepsakes. She was carefully unfolding and folding an old quilt that I'd never seen before—an aging blanket made from little squares of polka dots and flowered calico that was oddly incongruous in the Danish modern living room of an Eichler glass home in the heart of Silicon Valley. "What's that?" I asked. "This was made by your great-great-grandmother Woodley," my mother said. "Her son was your great-grandfather Hasbrook."

My father put down his newspaper. "Oh yeah," he said, "I remember her. Wasn't she the one who had two husbands murdered?" Then he glanced at me and arched his eyebrows knowingly, "And both times *she married the hired hand right afterwards.*"

"Oh Pat, that isn't true," my mother said indignantly. "They never found the murderers."

"Of course not," my father said, returning to the newspaper for dramatic effect. "She always gave them an alibi." Behind the paper I could hear him chuckle.

My mother frowned. "Now, that just isn't true."

"True enough," my father said from behind the newsprint, "The rest we'll never know."

That had my attention. I pressed my mother for more information about Grandma Woodley, whose named I had heard no more than once or twice in my life.

Reluctantly, for she knew her men well enough to know where this was heading, my mother searched through the oldest scrapbook and produced a photograph, perhaps the most iconic in our family's history. Taken in 1919, it was captioned in a cursive hand "Four Generations" and featured four figures, evenly spaced across the human lifespan from old age to infancy. Picture right was my Aunt Alliene, the oldest and most aristocratic of the sisters, as a baby, held by her grandfather, Charlie Hasbrook, unmistakable with his square face, kind eyes and shock of thick white hair. Behind them, stood my grandmother, Theresa Collins, looking both unexpectedly beautiful and infinitely weary. And at the absolute center of gravity, sat my great-great-grandmother Emeline Woodley. With her lantern jaw, tight frown and formidable bust, she looked like a 200 pound Carrie Nation; every man's nightmare mother-in-law.

"Ah, there she is," said my father peering over my shoulder, "What man wouldn't commit murder for such a delicate beauty?"

"Hush," said my mother. "Both of you just stop."

"What do you think they saw in her?" I asked.

"A farm," my dad laughed, "And lots and lots of life insurance money."

"I said, *hush*," my mother demanded. But she was laughing too.

* * *

I visited the Hasbrook Homestead only once during my childhood.

It was the summer of 1963, and we had stopped in Enid to visit family along the path of our move—following my father's retirement from the Air Force and his assumption of a new job with NASA—from Virginia to California. On the last day of our visit, we drove our new T-bird out of the city, south on the main road, running alongside the old Chisholm Trail, down to tall grain elevators of the tiny hamlet of Bison. Then we turned east, left, on a dirt road and made our way across the flat plain, a rooster tail of bright orange-red dust trailing behind us. We drove for miles through endless corn and wheat fields, punctuated by occasional lonely farmhouses and barns, and broken only by regular lines of cottonwood trees that demarcated the tributaries of Wolf Creek, itself a tributary of the Cimarron River.

I only knew we were driving to some farm; yet another dusty drive on a miserably hot and humid day. My father, by comparison, was hugely excited: his was a life of tearing down side roads in search of new experiences, and he knew that at the end of this drive lay many of the answers to the questions he'd long had about my mother's childhood and the man she admired most in the world.

My mother, whom I thought should have been excited—I too had heard stories about her childhood summers on the farm, the playing in the great barn and wading in the creek—was strangely silent. I assumed she was concentrating on the road, looking for the narrow bridge and the quick backward-turning access road. But it was in fact something much more; memories and resolutions were playing in her mind that I wouldn't fully understand until she was an old lady and I was a middle-aged man.

We drove through the old gates and down the along the face of the line of trees, the creek and woods on our left, the wide expanse of farm—with its noisy oil pump—on our right. We passed the stand of aging apple trees planted a half century before by my great-grandmother Mary . . . and then before us stood the old farmhouse, and beyond, the immense, bleached-silver barn.

My parents had not phoned ahead—indeed, I'm not sure anyone in my family would have had the number. Instead, my father as usual depended on his charm and gregariousness. And, as it had with everyone from Cornish girls during the War to violent revolutionaries in Marrakesh, it worked. The wary farmer and his wife met us in front of the house, talked for a moment with my father—my mother stayed in the car—and then nodded.

I remember only snapshot images in my mind of that visit. For example, I know we didn't enter the house, but I don't know if the farmer or his wife kept an eye on us as we walked around. Knowing what I do now, I assume they did.

What memories I do have aren't really trustworthy. I seem to recall that the farmer and wife were rather unfriendly. And that the light was slanting and golden, suggesting it was now early evening. But those recollections too may be colored by what I learned later. I do remember the barn, but only the big doors on the front, which were open, and the vintage farm machinery resting in the shadows inside.

But what I most remember, as vivid today as the moment I saw it, was the cave-like dugout. It impressed me not because of the extraordinary emotional resonance it carried for everyone else in the Hasbrook family—I knew little about that, other than the incredible fact that my grandmother had been a baby there—but for the sheer oddness of the place. It was just a door, flanked by stacked river rocks, *in the creek bank*. I not only had never seen anything like it, I didn't even know such places existed. It was like something out of a musty old fairy tale—and when my father managed to yank the creaky door open, exposing the arched vault and boxes of root vegetables inside, it was as if I was looking into the center of the earth.

In the years that followed, the house and barn and creek faded away, but the cave remained, in my mind the very symbol of the farm itself. I didn't realize just how true that was. And in school, as I studied the opening of the West, and the Oklahoma Land Rush, any mention of pioneer homes or prairie 'soddies' immediately brought to mind the dugout cave and its incongruous little door.

* * *

It would be forty years before I again looked through that doorway, now stripped of its door and bearing only a broken and silvered frame. I was a gray-haired, middle-aged man now, a journalist in search of a story. The farm had been abandoned now for more than twenty years—and it was as if the photograph that had been stored so long in my memory had been tossed onto the red dirt and left to be bleached in the sun, smudged with mud and rain and been covered with weeds.

It took me a long time even to find the dugout. The flood bank had become so overgrown with trees and brush that it seemed part of the woods lining the creek—and only when, ignoring the ticks and the likely snakes, I plunged down the back into the undergrowth, did I finally find the little threshold of dirt—compressed by feet for so many years that it was still too hard for anything to grow—did I at last find the hidden doorway.

So much had changed. Yet so much remained. Above me, to the right, the farmhouse still presented its familiar silhouette, but without the veil of the leaves between, it was in fact a shattered wreck, its windows and doors gone, its porch roofs collapsed into splinters. To my left, the great barn with its cupola still loomed, a dark wall against the cerulean sky. But the once ruler—straight line of its roof had begun to slump in the center, a prelude to its pending collapse.

Most of all, before me was the doorway, the portal that had haunted me my entire life. Inside, in the dim light, I could see the faded, whitewashed rear wall and the curve of the vault, surviving scraps of muslin hanging down like pale tendrils. The floor was a foot deep in rotting leaves. What long trail of events had brought Charlie Hasbrook to this remote and lonely place? And what had brought me here as well?

Warily, four decades after I last stood in this doorway, I stepped across the threshold for the first time.

PART ONE

THREE MURDERS

Starting Line: The Cherokee Strip

CHARLIE HASBROOK PULLED HIS HAT DOWN LOW OVER HIS EYES AND cinched up the strap tightly under his chin. He reached down and patted Old Prize on the neck.

The old race horse was skittish, but—unlike most of the thousands of horses up and down the two mile line that were also pacing and fretting—this was good news. Old Prize had known many standing starts in his racing career; and if this one was infinitely bigger, it was still familiar; and the horse was ready to run.

Charlie leaned forward and looked left and right. The line seemed to go on forever, almost from horizon to horizon, and composed of every possible vehicle. There were solo men, like Charlie and his old friend from the railroad days, J. W. "Will" Neel, who were on horseback. But there were also buckboards, Conestoga wagons, livery carts, even elegant landaus and other carriages.

And the people manning this odd assortment of conveyances were an equally odd mix. There were old sodbusters who had tried and failed on the prairie before, big city swells in tight jackets and bowlers, whole families stuffed into carts with babies wailing, army veterans still wearing bits of their old uniforms.

There were even solitary women: down the line Charlie could see one woman sitting astride a horse like a man and talking to a young fellow beside her; and nearer, a young but very hard-faced woman gripping the reins of her tiny carriage. Did they really expect to make it out there in the tall grass and hot sun?

Charlie shook his head. The air was filling with tension and desperation; it seemed to vibrate in the heat. The nervous, twitching horses only made things worse. He glanced back at Will, who appeared to be making his own appraisal of the crowd. Charlie raised his eyebrows; Will nodded: this wasn't going to be as simple as they had thought.

The realization had begun to dawn on Charlie the day before when he saw the vast tent city that had sprung up near the starting line. And then there were the trains, the longest passenger trains Charlie had ever seen, even in Chicago, all of them jammed with anxious pioneers. Back in Kansas, when he had thought of this stretch of the Indian Territory, Charlie had remembered standing at almost this spot and, besides the other men in his grading crew, not seeing another living soul from one end of the world to another. They had gone weeks before encountering a single Comanche hunting party. It had been as if they were the only people on Earth.

And now that same untrammeled plot of prairie was being churned up by thousands of hooves and boots and iron-rimmed wheels, cooking fires and latrines. And in a few moments, this vast, tightly aligned clump of one hundred thousand souls would burst out across seven million acres and carve it up into forty thousand farms and ranches.

To Charlie, and every other thoughtful person in the crowd, it had been apparent for many hours now that there were a lot more people waiting at this and the other starting lines than there were plots of land waiting to be claimed—more than two-to-one, in fact. And that meant this wouldn't be a land run, as some in the past had been, but a Land Rush. They wouldn't be competing for the best claims, but any claim at all. And there would be a lot of disappointed, angry and desperate people at the end. That in turn meant the worst kind of race: a long-distance sprint—broken axles, overturned wagons, and horses dying of exhaustion—and at the end, the prospect of having to fight to defend one's new land from legions of claim jumpers.

The prospect of all this made Charlie's mouth go dry. But he didn't go for his canteen—there might not be enough time. And besides, he would need it later. Instead, he patted Old Prize once more, and retightened his own chin strap.

He knew that the cavalry troopers had been ordered to fire at this, the Hennessey start, like all of the others around the Cherokee Strip, at noon. But when exactly was that? The only watch that mattered was in the hand of the commanding army officer, and Charlie didn't even know where he was positioned. But it had to be soon; just moments away.

The crowd was growing quieter and tenser by the minute. The only sound now was the whinnying of horses and a low murmur of anxious voices. Shoulders rubbed against shoulders, horses tails switched in the heat, and men were looking at other men on either side and measured their competition. It was becoming almost unbearable.

Then a shot rang out. The crowd roared in shock and surprise. Seventy thousand heads turned and craned so see the source. . . and one poor soul, assuming the Run was on, spurred his horse and took off across the Prairie. Behind him, half-dozen troopers took off in hot pursuit. There was another roar from the crowd, half cheers and half insults. Charlie stood in the saddle to better see as the riding man, hellbent for leather, raced over a low rise a quarter-mile away. Look back, you damn fool, Charlie said to himself, as he saw the troopers narrow the distance and draw rifles out of scabbards.

But the man never looked back. There was a puff of smoke, followed by a crack of report, and the rider flung out his arms, and then tumbled forward and off his horse. There were screams and groans in the crowd. The riderless horse raced on, while the troopers rode in a tight circle around the crumpled figure in the dust.

The crowd was agitated now, and not least Charlie Hasbrook. He had never seen a man shot dead in cold blood before, not even in Deadwood, and now his heart was pounding. He made a quick glance over at his friend: Will's face was pale and set.

Charlie turned back and stared out at the long prairie before him. The troopers were loading the body on one of their horses. Don't think about it, he told himself. Think about your future instead. About what's out there.

He looked down the line and prayed that his strategy was the right one. That Old Prize was the sturdy runner he had once been—and if not, that Will was a true friend. Charlie knew that this was his best shot at freedom, even happiness. He had been in flight since he was a young boy. Perhaps today he would finally land.

The crowd was still trying to recompose itself after the terrible event, when, in a sudden shock, the remaining troopers raised their pistols and fired with a loud crackling sound into the air. And the Oklahoma Land Rush was on.

Charlie Hasbrook clenched the reins, tucked his head and spurred

Old Prize forward. But the horse had recognized the signal and was already surging ahead.

THE LAST RIDE

There is a photograph, perhaps the most famous action photograph of the 19th century, which shows the sheer chaos of horses, men and wagons at the start of the Run. At the center of the photograph is a small man in a duster, hunched over as he anxiously spurs his gray horse forward. For a long time, I've fantasized that the man might be Charlie Hasbrook.

However there is some disagreement whether this photograph was taken at the start of the Run that began at the Kansas border, at Chilocco, or whether it is from the more famous start, Charlie's Run, in Hennessey. Either way, it is probably a pretty accurate representation of what Charlie experienced that day as he raced through the crowd, whipping Old Prize forward, trying to get ahead of the crowd.

Writes a modern historian: "[T]he signal was given, [and] the crowd burst over the line with a roar. Horsemen were unseated, wagons overturned, pedestrians trampled. There were cries of angry men, neighing of panic-stricken horses, shouts, curses, clatter of hoofs, and the rattle of wagons. It was truly pandemonium." Wrote a memoirist of the Run, "They broke with a yell and at first you couldn't see a thing for the dust that was raised where the grass had been trampled away along the starting line. In this blinding cloud, the wheels of gigs locked and there were spills at the very start . . . "

One of the reasons the Cherokee Strip Run still captures our imagination is that it seems to compress forty years of the pioneer experience, the entire history of the opening of the West, into a matter of weeks— ultimately into a matter of minutes. The Indians and the cattlemen rule the region one day, and disappear the next. Then, in a single afternoon, the pioneers arrive, spread over the landscape, stake their claims and settle down. It is as if the complete story of America's expansion in the 19th century is recapitulated on a single afternoon at century's end.

The Oklahoma Territory had been home to native tribes since prehistory. But the arrival of the Cherokee tribes from Georgia and the

Carolinas—first in 1817, and then driven there by the U.S. government along the "Trail of Tears" in the 1830s. In the years that followed, the Cherokee were increasingly pushed into the northeast corner of the territory.

By now, the Cherokees were among the most experienced Native American tribes in dealing with Washington, D.C. In 1835, they concluded a treaty with the U.S. government giving them hegemony over their lands. Later they successfully negotiated for a 6 million acre parcel of land—the so-called "Cherokee Outlet"—for hunting and even habitation.

Still, by the end of the century, the Outlet was mostly unused and empty . . . and so the Cherokee were willing to entertain offers for its use. Their first clients were the cattlemen, and the Cherokees were happy to lease grazing and easement rights for their land to the large cattle companies—and then taxed their cattle at 40 cents per head. This led to the creation of the great Chisholm Trail—which led five hundred miles from central Texas to the railhead at Abilene, Kansas; and from there to the slaughterhouses of Chicago to feed a hungry America. By the 1880s, most of the Outlet was regularly being grazed by hundreds of thousands of cattle.

For its part, the United States was diligent about enforcing the treaty, even in the face of growing calls by so-called Boomers for "Free Land/Free Homes." Thus, when various attempts were made by groups of settlers to move into the Outlet—including one by Davy Crockett's cousin—they were driven off.

But this state of affairs couldn't last forever. Populations were on the move; immigrants were arriving on America's shores by the millions. In Washington, lobbyists for both farmers and the railroads relentlessly pressed the case for opening up the region.

In the end, the pressure proved irresistible. On March 2, 1889—even as Charlie was driving railroad tracks across the region—in one of his last acts as President, Grover Cleveland signed a bill providing for the opening of Oklahoma's Unassigned Lands, including the Cherokee Outlet. As one might imagine, the Cherokees were not entirely happy with the arrangement. They had been leasing their lands to the cattlemen for $3 per acre when the U.S. Congress voided the deal at set the price at $1.25 per acre and newly-elected President Benjamin Harrison ordered the Outlet closed by the U.S. Army.

What came next was a lot of hard dealing. The Feds went around the Cherokees to the other local tribes, such as the Cheyenne and Arapaho, and cut separate deals for money and private plots to force the Cherokees' hands. But the Cherokees, for their part, knew they held the key plots, and held firm.

In the end, they struck a deal: the Cherokee Tribes agreed to sell the Outlet for $8.6 million, or a little more than $1.40 per acre. It made them rich, but as they watched the settlers line up to own their old lands, no doubt the Tribesmen and women must have been thinking about those lost cattle leases.After that, things moved fast. In a series of six land openings between April 1889 and April 1892, vast regions of Oklahoma Territory were made available for settlement. Most of this territory was awarded by allotments to bidders; but two were made available through land runs. These runs proved to be chaotic, corrupt, and very nearly disastrous. As a result, the Federal government decided that any future "run" would have to be much more organized.

That next (and final) run, for the "Cherokee Strip", as it has been known ever since, was announced for September 16th, 1893.

All of America noticed this announcement. Even at the time, the run for the Cherokee Strip—immortalized in America's collective memory as the Oklahoma Land Rush—was recognized as the last great act of pioneering in the country's history. That very year, Frederick Jackson Turner would famously announce the closing of the Frontier (" . . . the frontier has gone, and with its going has closed the first period of American history.") and the Land Rush would serve forever as the concluding act.

Even to our jaded modern eyes, accustomed to mass gatherings of human beings, the statistics relating to the Land Rush seem fantastic. The Cherokee Strip was essentially a deserted, unfenced rectangle of prime farm, pasture and hunting land the size and shape of Massachusetts minus Cape Cod—or Connecticut, Delaware and Rhode Island combined—226 miles east to west, 58 miles north to south.

With the Indians bought out and the white settlers driven out, the only signs of human habitation in this vast expanse was the Chisholm Trail itself, a line of wheel ruts in the red earth which nearly bisected the

Strip north to south; the Rock Island railroad line following a comparable path twenty miles to the east; and a single 30 foot long, L-shaped building—the only permanent structure on the Strip—at the Enid railroad stop. This building was the Land Office—soon to be, for a single day, the most popular building in the world. The building also had a single office set aside for a post office, soon to be almost as popular.

The strip itself had been thoroughly surveyed in the years since Charlie had first passed through working for the railroad. It was now divided into seven counties, each designed by a letter from K to Q. Enid's county was O. The counties were in turn subdivided into thousands of sectional (640 acre) plots, each corner of which was designated either by a rough sandstone marker standing six to eight inches high (for forested or bare earth areas), or a small pit surrounded by four piles of earth (for open prairies).

According to the rules of the Land Rush, settlers were allowed to claim a single 160-acre quarter section (native Indians could only purchase as much as 80 acres). All that a settler had to do was buy a registration ticket—ranging in price from $1 to $2.50 depending upon the quality of the nearby land—with its attached ownership ribbon. These tickets were available at one of the nine registration booths located in the Oklahoma Territory and in Kansas towns around the perimeter of the Strip, such as Arkansas City, Kiowa, Stillwater and Hennessey. Then the settlers merely had to ride to an unclaimed plot, plant the ribbon, record the boundary marker numbers and ride to the nearest Land Office—in Enid, Perry, Alva and Woodward (the last three little more than tents) to stake their claims. Once the claim was filed, the land was theirs . . . after they could prove that they had lived on it and cultivated it continuously for a span of three years.

There were an estimated 45,000 such plots. How hotly they would be contested depended upon how many people would show up on September 16th. By mid-Summer it was already obvious that a struggle of historic proportions was about to unfold. This, after all, was the year of the Great Panic, an economic disaster comparable in American history only to the Great Depression. People now were not just fighting for land, but for their lives. Charlie knew this, and that's why, some time near the end of those two lost years, he bought Old Prize, a horse he thought would get him into the heart of Strip ahead of most everyone else.

By the first week of September, the nine towns bordering the Strip began to swell with people, doubling and tripling their size, crushing their infrastructure under the strain. They became overnight—and short-lived—boomtowns. Hardest hit was Arkansas City, Kansas, a small new village less than a dozen years old, which grew overnight to a population of nearly 30,000.

A Mrs. Florence Howe who, like Charlie, was departing from the Hennessey line, wrote in her journal:

"We waited among hordes of people, and with the open saloons there was much hilarity, gambling and fighting." The registration process was a nightmare: "Three lines at a time, a quarter of a mile long, people stood shoe-mouth in dust and heat . . .water ten cents a glass, colored red from the dust and dirt."

According to a report in the *Kansas City Times*, the competition for places in these lines was so great that people were willing to pay considerable sums just to move up a few places. One such person in Hennessey, the paper reported, was a liquor dealer from Kansas City, Missouri named Niblock: "Niblock had paid during the day $25 in $5 installments to advance himself in line, and was about to spend $5 more for a place near the door of the booth when he dropped dead with the money in his hand." Charlie would have seen them carry Niblock away.

Meanwhile, in Guthrie and Oklahoma City, counterfeit certificates were being sold to suckers in for a nasty surprise.

Worst of all was the apprehension. Most of the multitude was farmers, but few had experience surviving in the wilderness or living in tents or dugouts or plowing and cultivating virgin prairie. With nothing to do but wait and worry, Mrs. Howe listed all the things she feared about her future life on the Cherokee Strip: " . . . hostile Indians, outlaws and cowboys, rattle snakes, tarantulas, centipedes, cyclones and tornadoes . . ."

Wrote one correspondent:

"Tonight, thousands of people are camped along the line and their campfires make an almost unbroken chain along the boundary. The weather today, while it is hot, was cool by com-

parison to that of the last few days. But the wind blowing from
the north stirred up the dust in choking, blinding clouds."

The next morning, September 15th, the crowd of pioneers, now estimated at as many as 150,000 people—perhaps the largest non-military
or governmental gathering of human beings in North America to date—
moved up to the brink of the various starting lines. They spent that day
and night jockeying for position in the front rank. It was a mob scene
that threatened at any second to turn into a melee. Only the presence of
armed soldiers—there not only to maintain order, but also to arrest or
shoot anyone who jumped the starting line early—forestalled disaster.

Inside the Strip, U.S. cavalry patrolled for any devious souls who had
tried to sneak in before the Run with hopes of quickly staking a claim in
the inevitable chaos of the first few hours. These were the now-famous
"Sooners", the classic kind of low-grade criminals who are later adopted
by descendents as a badge of their own roguishness [hence the choice of
the name for the University of Oklahoma football team.] Just how many
Sooners there were in the Strip is a matter for endless speculation; but
probably a few hundred, perhaps a few thousand.

In the weeks before the Run, the Cavalry had set a number of wildfires in order to clear the underbrush and expose the boundary markers.
Unfortunately, some of these fires—along with others set by Sooners to
add to the confusion—were still burning when the Run began. Thus,
depending upon the prevailing wind, many of the homesteaders found
themselves at the starting line looking out into menacing, and acrid,
skies filled with smoke. During the Run itself, one woman, trying to save
her team of horses, would burn to death in one of the fires.

On the morning of September 16, those with registration tickets settled into their spots on the starting line and waited. Thousands of others were still arriving. One hundred boxcars filled with people arrived
on the railroad from Arkansas City to the northern starting line; forty-
two cars rode out of Orlando, Kansas to the southern line. The train out
of Hennessey, Oklahoma Territory, carrying Charlie, Will Neal and their
horses, had pulled 39 cars jammed to the roof with people—and the two
men got to see firsthand the ultimate test of their grading skills.

As they moved up to literally toe the starting line, among the thousands of pioneers could be seen every age and nationality . . . and, according to historian John Edward Hicks, almost every form of contemporary transportation, including men and women on foot, bicycles, horseback, sulkies, 2-wheeled carts, and light buggies:

> "Farmers were there with heavy wagons and plodding teams. There were even the old-time prairie schooners, one with this legend on its canvas: 'White-capped in Injianny, chinch-bugged in Illinois, secloned in Newbrasky, bald-knobbed in Missouri, Oklahomy or bust.'"

Adding to the confusion were thousands of tourists, newly-arrived from distant towns and cities, who had come out merely to look at the insanity.

Somewhere in this sea of humanity, Charlie Hasbrook had lined up atop Old Prize. Next to him rode Will Neel, probably on a horse of comparable speed. Like many of the younger men, they had pushed their way up to the front of the mob in order to toe the starting line. Elsewhere in the crowd Miss Lillie A Gibson, in her carriage, had done the same.

Lillie wasn't the only solo women joining the run—elsewhere in the crowd was Laura B. Crews, her skirt rakishly divided, astride a horse and ready to ride with her brother Will. Like Lillie, Crews would be one of the few participants who would live to celebrate the 75th anniversary of the Run.

MELEE

For a few endless seconds after the starting guns, the noise and dust, shouts and screams were horrible and disorienting.

Finally, Charlie broke out of the mass and into the clear. He had open track before him. Now he would have to ride the dozen miles to reach his target: the grove of cottonwood trees at the bend of the little creek flowing into the Cimarron River.

Charlie took a quick glance back. All was chaos, boiling in a vast, roiling cloud of red dust. But Will had made it through as well, and was now riding just behind him. Old Prize had found his stride now, too. So far, everything had gone as planned. Now it was time to ride like hell ...

Marquis James was a contemporary of my grandmother, and her most famous schoolmate. Born in Missouri, he would grow up in the Cherokee Strip and go on to win two Pulitzer Prizes in the 1930s for biography. By then he was a cosmopolitan New Yorker. But he never forgot his extraordinary childhood, and late in his career (1945) he wrote a memoir entitled "The Cherokee Strip: An Oklahoma Boyhood" that recounted his father's story of riding in the Land Rush.

With its first-hand accounts, the book is one of the best-written sources on that remarkable day. Better yet for our purposes, Marquis' father's experiences are remarkably similar to Charlie's—he too bought a racehorse and started the Rush from Hennessey, perhaps just a few yards down the line from my great-grandfather—and so his recollections capture neatly what Charlie must have faced that afternoon.

Writes James:

> "[My father, Houston James] asked me to think of four or five horses lined up at the post at the Fair Grounds. They break and are away. Well, sir, in this race there were thousands of horses and thousands of riders and drivers, and they stretched in a line across the prairie as far as you could see. Papa asked me to look to the east and look to the west and imagine all those horses strung out ready to break. Most of the horses were under saddle. The others were hitched to every kind of rig. Light rigs—buckboards, spring wagons and sulkies—were the best. But there were covered wagons, lots of them, and even people on foot."

One memorable figure was the amusingly named (by modern lights) Ben Clampitt, a "lean old Texan" who had rigged out his buckboard as if it was a racing sulky, complete with leather stirrups. Sitting behind him, like a hoplite behind a charioteer, was one of Clampitt's hired hands. He carried a pitchfork, and as the race took off and the melee erupted, he jabbed at riders on either side of him to clear a path for his boss.

Charlie and Neel (and Houston James as well), by getting a quick start on fast horses, escaped the chaos and confusion that exploded just behind them. Within a few yards they, and a few hundred others, were already out of the melee, on fresh grass and in open air. Now they had to find the quickest path north.

Most were headed to Enid, towards the smaller plots within the town limits. These were considered highly valuable—especially by city folks who had little interest in farming. But others too, including Charlie, took the path to Enid because the old Chisholm Trail offered the smoothest path into the heart of the Strip. The alternative was to head directly across the countryside, cutting the distance by a third or more.

Both routes had their risks. The cross-country rider faced prairie dog holes, hidden roots, raging wildfires, and steep creek banks. But the Chisholm was no picnic either: deeply rutted from a generation of cattle and chuck wagons, in some places it was as wide as a modern freeway, but in others as narrow as a hallway.

Writes James:

> "The riders took the lead, mostly, with the fastest driving horses and lightest wagons next. And on they went. There were no roads, mind you, except the Trail, and no bridges. You got down and up draws and across creeks and ravines and gullies as best you could. Or you headed them. Wagons stuck in the streams and stalled in draws. Rigs broke down from the rough going. By and by the horses that had been ridden or driven too hard began to play out. Horses that had started slower began to edge ahead."

The distance from Hennessey to Enid was nineteen miles, as the crow flies. For the riders, even those on the Chisholm Trail, the real distance was closer to 25 miles—about three hours for a smart rider on a good horse dealing with flat out runs across open meadows and careful, slow negotiations of creek banks and streams.

Pat Wilcox was the young assistant postmaster at the Enid post office, working in the shorter wing of that town's solitary, L-shaped building. Sometime after noon, he ate a quiet lunch, washed his dishes, then, curious, climbed to the roof of the building for a good view. Focusing his binoculars on the crest of distant South Hill, Wilcox waited . . . and became the lone witness of one of the most remarkable sights in American history.

As he watched, the blue sky above South Hill suddenly showed a thin brown haze that grew thicker by the minute. Then, as the haze became a cloud, Wilcox noticed a single rider tearing down the front of the hill towards him. This was Walter Cook, a 22 year-old cowboy from the Chickasaw Nation.

Cook, thanks to his tough little pony, had taken the lead early and had held it the rest of the way. Now, as Wilcox watched, Cook crossed the city limits of Enid . . . and rode right past the building. Instead of taking a small city lot, the young man had decided to go for the gold ring: the single most valuable property in the entire Strip, the 160 acre quarter section adjoining the town square on the North side. The cowboy wanted to be king.

Wilcox swept the binoculars back to the south. Now fifty, now one hundred, more and more riders cleared the crest of South Hill. Ben Clampitt, bouncing through the air over ruts and mounds, was among them. So was at least one Sooner, who appeared out of nowhere and disappeared into the crowd. This group, trailing a thick dust cloud, also raced straight through town, equally ignoring the city plots—and, also ignoring Cook's markers, one after another drove their stake into the same quarter section. By nightfall, three hundred claim jumpers had staked Cook's claim.

Had there been three claim jumpers, Cook might have had a chance. He could have run them off or, justifiably, shot them. But with three *hundred* he had no chance. Within hours, the shrewdest of the claim jumpers had organized all the rest, subdivided the quarter section into town lots, named the place Jonesville and presented a united front to the government. The claim jumpers also offered a sizable number of the plots to Cook as a consolation prize—and to keep his mouth shut—and the young cowboy should have taken their offer. Instead, in the weeks and months that followed, he continued to fight, through hearing after hearing, for the whole claim. In the end he lost it all.

Said angry Houston James years later, "Walter Cook, who had won fair and square the greatest horse race in the world, never got a thing."

Meanwhile, from his rooftop aerie, Pat Wilcox watched now as the main body of the Land Rushers—hundreds, and then thousands of riders, on horseback and a growing number of wagons—poured over the Hill and rolled in a wide wave towards him. Within minutes, the exhausted multitude had swarmed over every available lot in the town and its environs. Soon thereafter, tents were erected, fires built and men began to form long lines outside the door of the Land Office. Pat Wilcox climbed down from the roof and went back to work. With so many already writing home to tell their good news, tomorrow would be a busy day.

In Enid, at least, the great Cherokee Strip Land Rush was over. As one historian wrote: "At noon the town had four inhabitants and one wooden building. At 3 o'clock it had had 12,000 [citizens]. By night it had a hotel and several restaurants."

A FATEFUL TURN

But Charlie Hasbrook wasn't there.

Even though he would one day be credited with founding the city of Enid, and though the water barrel he had sunk in the pond two years before was still providing fresh water to Enid's new residents, Charlie himself planned to stake his claim elsewhere. Just behind the lead group as it approached South Hill, Charlie and Neel—like Houston James, who was riding nearby—peeled off from the main group and headed across country. They went east, out into the open range.

They could pace themselves now, since they weren't fighting the first group for a piece of land in Enid and they were far ahead of the main body of settlers. The trick from here on was to ride smartly, but carefully, making sure one of the horses didn't break a leg in a gopher hole or stumble down a creek bank.

At some point, with quick words of encouragement, the two riders separated, with Charlie, on the faster horse, trotting towards the more distant plot.

The prairies' fires were at last behind him, so now Charlie rode under a bright blue sky filled with the classic fleecy clouds of a warm Oklahoma afternoon. He passed through meadows of prairie grasses as high as his knees, sending bobwhite quail, pheasants and songbirds fluttering into the air. He heard the gobble of wild turkeys and the endless buzzing of insects. Dragonflies darted about him. And he probably saw several herds of deer, perhaps even buffalo.

A farmer by upbringing, Charlie studied the soil as he rode. The ground was as he remembered it, a brilliant orange-red wherever it was exposed by a creek bank or a prairie dog town. The high ground, usually away from the creeks and rivers, was grassy and dry, the earth tiled with shards of broken shale. Good pasture land for cattle and horses. The lowlands, most often found on the inside curves of creeks, was rich with thick, dark sediment. That was where you planted your corn and vegetables and melons. Crops on the one side, cattle and wheat on the other—and along the creek, just outside the verge of the cottonwood trees, you could built your house and barn and plant fruit trees. That was the plan Charlie had formulated two years before, and that he now elaborated as he rode.

Did he find that exact spot he was looking for, the one he'd once seen from the railroad line? Charlie never said so precisely—only that he'd "seen the land he wanted and came back and claimed it." And the landscape is so similar for many miles around, with open range divided by numerous meandering creeks, all of it lined with trees that a single plot would have been hard to identify.

And yet, as a railroad worker, Charlie would have known the right distance marker, and the direction he needed to ride from it. Moreover, though the property at first glance seemed indistinguishable from those around it, with a closer look it proved quite distinctive and valuable.

The property straddles the creek, giving it a balance of both high land and low. Also, the cottonwood trees lining the creek are big and old and provide considerable cover. Further west, at the northwest corner of the property, the creek forks to create a small floodplain perhaps 200 yards across, that is home to the closest thing to woods for miles around. Even today, one can regularly hear turkeys out in this stand of trees, and for years bow-hunters set up blinds for what must be a considerable population of whitetail deer.

All of this argues for Charlie Hasbrook either finding exactly the property he was looking for—or being a very lucky young man.

He would have found that plot at about two o'clock in the afternoon. And when he did, Charlie probably would have kept moving, not letting the exhausted Old Prize stop to water and rest, but instead trotting him to each of the four corners of the property in search of the markers. Only after those markers had been found, the site number identified, and the ribbons tied, would Charlie have taken Old Prize, the foam-flecked racehorse now having completed its last and longest race, back to the creek for water.

But even then they couldn't tarry. Charlie didn't have to see what happened in Enid to Walter Cook to know that claim jumpers were the biggest threat he faced that day . . . and that the quicker he got to Enid and filed his claim, the safer he'd be.

Still, as Old Prize bent down and gulped the cool water, Charlie Hasbrook must have sat on the bank and taken stock. For an instant at least, before he began plotting where to dig the dugout cave, where to build the house, where to erect the barn, it must have hit him with a wave of disbelief and satisfaction that *he'd done it.* This beautiful plot of land was his. He could make a life here. Raise a family. Grow old. Right here.

AFTERMATH

Charlie grabbed the reins and pulled the resisting Old Prize from the water. He didn't want the horse to over-drink and bloat up. It was more than a dozen miles onward to Enid, and God only knew what was waiting out there in-between. The sooner he filed the claim and got back here and set up camp, the better.

Charlie climbed into the saddle, and with his heels urged Old Paint forward. Three murders had brought him to this point—the first of a boy he never met, the second of a man he loved more than any other, the third of a man he hated with equal singularity. Without them, Charlie's life would have taken a much different path. He might not have become the man he was. He most definitely would not have found himself, at the end of the Land Rush, standing on his own quarter section of land between Bison and Marshall, Oklahoma.

Immense tribulations lay ahead—the miserable years in the cave, the decades of hard work building and running a farm, the failure his beloved oldest son, the eventual loss of the land itself—but none would be greater than those he'd already survived, that had brought him to this beautiful, lonely place. This very moment was the turning point; henceforth it would always be *the* turning point in his life, dividing the unspoken *before* of Oregon and Kansas, from the celebrated *after* of Oklahoma, family and prosperity

And, as he rode slowly North towards the already growing lines at the Land Office in the teeming new city of Enid, it must have struck Charlie Hasbrook—if not as a fully-rounded thought, then as an emotion, an unconscious upwelling of happiness—that at long last he was free.

* * *

The path Charlie Hasbrook rode to that claim on Wolf Creek near Bison was far less circuitous and risky than the twenty-five year journey that had brought him to that Land Run starting line.

Looking back from his new life, he would come to realize that the direction of his childhood might well have been a straight line, like that of his forebears, had it not been intersected—twice—by dangerous men and sent reeling. Those two men had brought with them death and disorder . . . and this Charlie knew as well: both had been welcomed into his life by his own mother.

And now she was again begging him to come home.

BEN HASBROOK:
OREGON TERRITORY

In January 1931, the *Oregon Journal*, in an ongoing program to interview the last surviving pioneers of the state, sent a reporter named Fred Lockley to 975 Michigan Avenue in Portland to interview my great-great grandmother Emeline B. Woodley.

In one of those odd historical coincidences that populate the story of America, with its endlessly moving populations, it is quite possible that my great-grandfather Charles Short, my father's grandfather, who was an editor at the *Journal* at the time, gave Lockley the assignment.

Lockley's column, entitled "Impressions and Observations of the Journal Man" was of that happily extinct species of reportage that is essentially a cleaned-up transcription of reminiscence, targeted at an equally aged group of readers and designed to make them sigh with nostalgia. For anyone less than 75 years old, these articles must have been deadly dull—as they are to anyone who tries to read them today.

Inevitably, these nostalgia articles were sanitized of everything that offended the myth of a lost golden age—and Woodley's story was no exception. For example, she omitted the little fact that her first two husbands were murdered. Still, as a record for genealogists, it is quite useful.

"I was born," she begins, *"in Polk County [Oregon] on March 16, 1851. My father, Nathan Connor, was born in Virginia, July 16, 1821 . . ."*

A year later, in 1852, the Connors, with their ten children, moved to a farm in Ohio. I have a photograph of Nathan Connor, and his wife, Elizabeth Buell Connor, taken probably about 1868. It shows Elizabeth dressed in heavy dark cotton, with black velvet at the wrists, her hair pulled back severely, with the spindly hawk-like features that would grow even starker in later generations. For some reason it always comes as a surprise to be reminded that both her great-grandfather, and one of her great-great-uncles, fought in the Revolutionary War.

Nathan Connor, by comparison is big and robust, with thick hair and beard and wears a frown like a wide gash across his face. He wears his best suit, with a lapelled waistcoat. He has huge hands, one of which rests heavily on an equally heavy book on his knee. The overall impression is of a workingman who has found a measure of prosperity in his middle age. Sadly, Connor's very pale blue eyes also give him that zombie look not uncommon in the hot light and high contrast of 19th century black and white photography.

Fortunately, and guaranteeing that he wouldn't terrify generations of young descendents, there is a second, heavily retouched, portrait photograph of Nathan Connor that captures a much more handsome man with bright, friendly eyes.

"My mother and father had two children when they started across the plains in 1847. My mother's father and mother, Mr. and Mrs. Elias Buell, and her mother's brother and six of her sisters and an uncle were in the same wagon train."

This extended family would have been one of the earliest groups of pioneers to take the Oregon Trail. The tiny town of Buell, Oregon would be named for Emeline's father.

"My brother, Joseph Connor, was born at Vancouver (now just over the Columbia River in Washington) on March 5, 1848." In other words, he was conceived on the trail—meaning that frail looking Elizabeth Connor had walked across much of America pregnant.

The Connors wintered in Vancouver. In the spring they hired a guide and set off south—only to be abandoned by that guide once he had his hands on their money. So, led by Nathan's oldest brother William, the group took off cross-country, piling all of their belongings in a single floatable wagon box at each river they crossed. After considerable hardship, they finally reached their goal. Nathan staked a claim in Ballston, in Polk County, now a small county in west-central Oregon, but then covering a sizable portion of the coast.

Within a few years, young Joseph was joined by Emeline, Caroline and Elias. All attended a schoolhouse 2 1/2 miles away, though Emeline, as the oldest daughter, managed to attend only one term per year from the age of seven until fifteen. *"I didn't go after that, because I got married and I had to take care of my house."*

The man she married at fifteen was thirty-two years old. His name was Benjamin Hasbrook, and little is known about him. For a long time there was a family legend that he had been orphaned on the trail west and been taken in by a family bearing the Hasbrook name. None of it true.

In fact, the real story is even more remarkable. The earliest known ancestor on that side of my family tree was an English boy surnamed White, first name unknown. He appears to have arrived in America in the early 18th century as a "bound boy", a form of indentured servant, under contract to a Dutch family named Hasbrouch in the Huguenot town of New Paltz, N.Y. Amazingly, the house that young White lived in still exists, as part of New Paltz's famed historical district of colonial homes. The house has even appeared on a U.S. commemorative stamp—due to the fact that George Washington and the Continental Army camped at the farm one winter.

The contract between the Hasbrouchs and the young man was standard for the era: Mr. Hasbrouch would pay for the young White's passage to America in exchange for the boy's labor at a predetermined pay rate. Once the debt was retired, typically after seven years, White would be free to live his own life in the New World.

It appears to have become a little more complicated than that. By the end of the contract, young White apparently had become so much a member of the family that the Hasbrouchs were willing to make the relationship formal. And thus, White became Hasbrouch, and in the years and generations that followed, the name Americanized to Hasbrook.

As for the family myth: Benjamin Hasbrook, who would come to Oregon 150 years later and marry Emeline Connor, was not only not an orphan, but his mother would outlive him by four years. He was also the sixth of nine children who reached adulthood, most of them girls, and most of whom married and settled in Ohio.

And that, basically, is all that we know about Benjamin Hasbrook.

From the little available data, we can probably assume that Benjamin (who was named after his father, and would give his own second born the same name), was a moderately successful man who had probably made some money in the gold fields or working, perhaps as a farm hand, in California. He had now come to Oregon to find a wife and farm and settle down. And apparently he presented a prosperous enough image to convince the Connors to give up their teenaged daughter.

Despite the time frame, there is no evidence that Ben Hasbrook fought in the Civil War. In fact, thanks to remarkable coincidences in age and geography, nobody in this story, even many of the families that had lived in this country for generations, seems to have had any involvement in the single most convulsive event in American history. Ben Hasbrook, who was just the right age, was out in California, the site of only a few inconsequential battles, and probably like many West Coasters felt little part of the fight.

Still, no one in the United States and its territories fully escaped the consequences of the war. It may explain why Ben Hasbrook doesn't seem to have arrived in Oregon until 1866: the territory was too isolated during the war years, opening up again to new settlers like Ben Hasbrook only in the decade after Appomattox. Many came to escape a war damaged world, to start over stalled lives, and sometimes just out of the classic American desire to light out for the territories in search of a new adventure. Of Ben Hasbrook's motives we have little insight.

MARITAL BLISS

So, what was this newlywed couple, with the blushing teenaged bride and the groom twice her age, really like?

It's hard to really know. We have but a single photograph of Benjamin and several of Emeline, the earliest taken nearly two decades after the wedding. Benjamin looks stiff and sober, but then so did almost every man and boy who took a picture in that era—resulting from the long camera exposure times and hidden neck braces, as well as the then-accepted view that only a frowning man was of consequence.

It has also come down—from Emeline to Charlie to his daughter to my mother—that Ben was an unhappy and cold man. Perhaps, but that raises the interesting question of where such a likeable and optimistic personality as Charlie Hasbrook's came from. We only have Emeline's word for it, and that memory may be colored by a teenager's perception of a merely serious older man. Or, more darkly, it may be an unconscious justification for what happened later.

Of Emeline we know quite a bit more, including eyewitness accounts by her still-living great-granddaughters. Their descriptions certainly match what appears in the photographs: a short, round, humorless, judgmental woman without much imagination but with no shortage of pronouncements and opinions (most of them negative) about her descendents. Her son was dutiful to her, but only from a distance, and his wife hated her, her grandchildren feared her, and her great-grandchildren, little more than babies, were terrified of her.

Perhaps she was only that way in her later years, with that imperiousness that sometimes comes with age and distance from one's own failures. Furthermore, it might be the well-deserved countenance of a thrice-widowed woman who had seen more than her share of life's horrors.

But was the teenaged Emeline that way as well? Certainly her letters in the years to come suggest a woman of little humor and even less introspection. And the available photographs, especially the second 'Four Generations' portrait, seem to support that image.

But that is only at first glance. It is easy to be fooled by 19th century photographs. The women, answering to a different standard of beauty, inevitably look stern and self-righteous in their black high-necked dresses, big pigeon breasts, severe hair buns and thin-lipped frowns. Emeline Hasbrook, fulfilling all of those expectations, looks like nothing more than the bulldog counterpart of her witch-like crone mother.

However, if you look at her image long enough, you begin to see something else: fear, and the weakness that comes with it. From the first photograph to the last one forty years later, there is in Emeline's eyes— and even in the corners of that harsh mouth—something frightened, passive and wounded. It is there in the photo taken at age 35, and still there at age 70. And it finds an echo in her narrative to the Oregon Journal reporter:

I married Ben Hasbrook [on November 7, 1867]. We had three children, two of whom are living. After Ben died I married Homer Adkins of Kansas. We had four children, two of whom are now living. I moved back to Kansas with him, where I lived for some years. I married my last husband, Thomas Woodley, in 1899. He was a widower, but his children were all grown and lived back East. With the exception of the few years I spent in Kansas I have lived all my life, so far, in Polk county, Yamhill County, and here in Portland.

Had Mr. Lockley, the reporter, been tougher with his questions, or a little more diligent in his research, he would have discovered that this bland little life history omitted not only the murdered husbands but that the Widow Woodley had, in fact, been married four times, not three. It might have made for more sensational reading for Oregon Journal subscribers.

So, knowing what little we do, let's try to imagine this first marriage. It is probably not a love match, not like Charlie and Mary, or Art and Theresa, or my parents, or probably even Emeline's own parents, Nathan and Elizabeth Connor. Rather, this is a *suitable* match, the wife healthy but a bit immature, the husband a little too old and hardened. Nathan Connor, seeing a mature man who can give his daughter a comfortable life—and counting too few other good candidates in that under populated region—probably with great relief gave the union his blessing.

The couple set up housekeeping in a comfortable farmhouse on the standard quarter section of farmland. Emeline was probably a good housekeeper, if neither particularly bright nor, as might be expected from a sixteen year old, very disciplined. Still, with her mother's advice and her husband's expectations, no doubt she grew in the job.

Ben was also probably a pretty good farmer, especially if that's what he did during his lost years in California. He was most certainly a good businessman, given his age and the money he'd saved to buy the farm.

It was a short honeymoon. Within three months of the wedding Emeline was pregnant. If there had been a chasm of age and experience between husband and wife, there wasn't much time to bridge it before the couple switched to their new role as parents.

The baby, Charles, was born on November 14th, 1868. That he was born in Sheridan and not the smaller village of Ballston (as the next two children were), suggests a difficult first pregnancy—perhaps some toxemia or a hard delivery—that required a higher level of care.

Perhaps it was also a difficult infancy. A winter child, Charlie, would grow up to be at least four inches shorter than his younger brother; though his robust health in later years also suggests a genetic source for his short stature. That second son, Benjamin Jr., would also not be born for another three years, suggesting a long nursing period for Charles.

Thus, by her nineteenth birthday, Emeline Blair Connor Hasbrook had already been married three years, and was tending to a farmhouse, a husband, and two small children.   Even for someone raised on the frontier, the sudden transition from childhood and the schoolyard to marriage and motherhood must have been shocking.   Chasing a toddler, while nursing a newborn, sweeping the house and washing diapers, rushing to get meals on for a tired, impatient and perhaps disapproving 34 year-old husband, did Emeline ever wonder if she had made a terrible mistake?   Did she ever pray for escape?

If she did, she got her wish.

ACCOMPLICE

Sometime in 1872, a new, and shadowy, figure entered into the daily lives of the young Hasbrook family.

His name was Joseph Coxon (or Coxen; even the newspapers couldn't decide) and we know nothing of his appearance or his background—except that he had come from England the year before, that he had a "quiet, unobtrusive manner," was industrious, "sober and respectful" and a man of "good behavior" and "unblemished repute."

Finally, we know that during that year, Coxon went to work for Benjamin Hasbrook.   Coxon would later claim to be a business partner of Hasbrook, but the details of the arrangement suggests something closer to his employment as a hired hand in exchange for the right to work a corner of the farm.

As for the details of this business arrangement, we can only speculate.   There is no record of a second house.   So did Coxon sleep in the main house, or in the barn?   Certainly, on such a small farm, he would have taken his meals with the family.   Being little more than a teenager himself, did he make friends with little Charlie—and did that endear him even more to Emeline?

Joseph Coxon was 22 years old, just a year older than the lady of the house.   He was young and strong, worldly and full of dreams; she was young and plump and weary.   What did Emeline think when she looked down the table, first at her middle-aged husband, and then at the young man?   Did she desire him, or were his longing looks unreciprocated? And if Benjamin Hasbrook glanced up from his supper and saw the looks passing back and forth between his wife and the hired man he'd invited into the bosom of his family, what thoughts went through his mind? Anger? Dismay? And did he finally decide to force the issue?

For my part, I want to believe that Emeline didn't know. She is, after all, my great-great grandmother. I tell myself that she was still little more than a girl, probably in awe of her husband, busy managing a house, a little boy and a baby. She probably thought it was nice to have a young man her own age around the house, someone she could talk to in those rare moments when they both weren't busy.

Maybe she noticed his growing attentions, and perhaps enjoyed the flattery. Maybe she even promoted those intentions. Or, having little experience in men besides her husband, perhaps she didn't recognize that the interest was getting out of hand; and that a very dangerous situation was developing.

What I don't want to believe is that she was a co-conspirator. That, in the autumn and winter of 1871-72, the flirtation had deepened into an outright affair, and the two young and illicit lovers concluded that the odd man out had to be removed before they could live happily ever after.

BUSHWHACKED

It was a long, wet and cold winter, as only an Oregon winter can be.

These days, Oregon natives and long-time residents, if they have any money, undertake a mass exodus out of the state every February heading towards Arizona, Southern California or Hawaii.

But that kind of escape wasn't an option in 1872. Rather, the three adults and two children could only hunker down in their cabin, rarely seeing visitors or going to town. They had to endure the endless rain and wind and cold fog. Who knows what complex relationships and antagonisms were cultivated during those long weeks?

Here's what we do know, as related by a page one story in the Portland *Oregonian*, dated Saturday, February 8, 1873:

"The McMinnville Reporter has the following account of a

horrible murder in Yamhill County. On the evening of the 4th last, about 7 1/2 o'clock, Mr. Ben Hasbrook, living up the Willamina, about nine miles from Sheridan, was shot and killed by a man who was found in his granary.

"The particulars as we learn them are about as follows: The hired man went to the granary where he found two men. They had filed off the staple by which the door was fastened and made an entrance. The hired man seized one of the rascals and raised the alarm, whereupon the other thief ran up and struck his partner's antagonist with a knife, aiming at his heart, but some books and papers in his breast pocket staid the blow and not much injury was done to his person.

"At this juncture, Mr. Hasbrook came to his man's assistance, when one of the villains seized Hasbrook's own shot-gun, which was in the granary, and fired the contents, fifteen buck shot, though his body and he fell on his face with a groan—dead.

"The murderers then departed in haste, and at last accounts, had not been captured—although they had been traced some distance. Suspicion rests on some parties in that section, we understand, and there will probably be arrests made, as the Sheriff has gone there.

"Mr. Hasbrook was a peaceable, industrious, energetic man. He leaves a wife and young family to mourn his loss."

It is a terrible story. From the facts as reported, you can imagine the men struggling in the cold near-darkness, or in the dim light of a lantern dropped from the hired hand's fist, the shadows reeling around the room, mist panting from their mouths, the grunts of men fighting for their lives. Then the ferocious, deafening blast of a black powder shotgun fired in a tight space. Then a moment of pregnant silence, before one of the men gasps and topples forward—joining the other man, who is kneeling in the straw clutching his chest. The dying man, his last breath emptying his lungs, emits a long, slow groan. "Let's get out of here," says one of the other men hoarsely, and the two figures race through the light out the door into the windswept night.

The family legend takes over from here: Emeline Hasbrook also hears the hired man's shout. She watches her husband leap to his feet and race out the door. Then, a few seconds later, she startles at the shot-gun's report. She hears the footsteps of the two men running off into the woods. Her heart filled with dread, she puts down the baby in her arms, tells her four year-old to stay still, rushes out to the porch, down the steps and across the yard to the granary. There, in the pools of shadow, she sees the dreadful sight.

Backing out of the granary in horror, she hurries back to the house Showing considerable presence for someone in a state of shock, Emeline bundles up the baby and wraps herself in a heavy shawl. Realizing that the distance to the nearest farmhouse is more than three miles, down muddy and icy roads through pitch darkness, she reluctantly tells her four year old, little Charlie, that he must stay in the house and wait for her.

Baby boy in her arms, terror and grief in her heart, Emeline Hasbrook takes to the road, every noise around her threatening to be the murderers lurking nearby. After what seems forever, she staggers into the neighbor's farmyard and cries out for help. The farm family helps her in, warms her and the baby by the fire and tries to make sense out of her blurted story. Once they understand what she is saying, the farmer (or perhaps an older son) saddles up a horse and gallops into town for the law. . .

Three days later, a small news item in the *Oregonian* announced:

> "The man arrested on a charge of the murder of Mr. Hasbrook at Willamina, Yamhill County, last week is named Cox."

FALSE WITNESS

None of the facts of this murder, as recounted up until now, is true. Even Coxon's name is misspelled.

On first glance, the original story does seem plausible: *A decent man, in the prime of life, enjoying the fruits of his hard work and surround-ed by his loving family, is suddenly taken from this world in a moment of meaningless savagery. His loyal hired hand is nearly killed trying to defend the family. And the young widow, shattered by the sight of her beloved hus-band lying dead in a pool of blood, somehow gathers enough presence of mind to brave the winter night, babe in arms, and go for help.*

This is how I heard the story, as did my mother before me, and her mother before her. This is undoubtedly the story told to Charlie himself—having been only a young child at the time, he probably only remembered the shotgun blast and the confusion of adults racing about and shouting.

But the more you scrutinize the chain of events as they were first reported—as the sheriff, defense attorneys, and magistrate did at the time—the stranger it all seems. Time, place and motive all raise questions.

The *Oregonian,* with its skepticism only barely concealed, asked the some of these questions on February 22nd:

> "The case is, in some respects, a very remarkable one, and if Coxon is not guilty, he is certainly the victim of a train of singularly unfortunate circumstances.
>
> "There are sundry considerations which oppose the theory that the murder was committed, as was first reported, by persons seeking to steal grain from the barn.
>
> "The early hour in the evening when they put in their appearance is difficult to be accounted for, since the most foolhardy thief seldom goes forth at 7 o'clock, and while the house of the intended victim is yet lighted up. And then Hasbrook was shot in the back, a circumstance that leads to the conviction that he must have been deliberately assassinated.
>
> "Something may transpire between now and the next term of the circuit court to lift the veil of mystery and uncertainty which now enshrouds the case."

One hears in the reporter's words the voice of the sheriff or some other law enforcement official. It is my father's voice too—a professional crime investigator sensing that something is wrong with the story as it is being presented; odd little circumstances that whisper that the real truth lies buried elsewhere.

Let's re-examine the facts of the case.

First, there is the obvious matter of the timing. As the *Oregonian* noted, why would thieves burglarize a farm at 7 p.m.? February 4th, of course, is in the thick of winter, so the sun would have long since set. But still there would be some residual light on the horizon. More important, the Hasbrook family would still have been awake and, as the newspaper noted, moving about nearby in a well-lit farmhouse. There would also have been a good chance that Hasbrook or Coxon would have gone out with a lantern one more time to check the animals. Or Coxon might even have slept in a room off the barn or the granary.

So, why didn't the robbers just lay low for a few hours, until the house lights were out and the family was definitely sound asleep?

Then there is the whole scenario surrounding the granary. This being mid-winter it is possible that the thieves were looking to steal hay to feed their horses (though there is no indication they were on horseback) or to feed their starving livestock. But the barn sure seems like a better target: why steal bulky grain when you can take more valuable implements, sell them, and buy all the grain you need?

The thieves also reportedly filed off the latch to the granary to gain entrance. They brought a file with them? They stood there exposed to the house lights in the open for however many minutes it took to file through an iron latch? All without making a sound? Why couldn't they have tripped the latch—was the granary locked? Finally, if indeed it was locked, wouldn't it have been quicker, easier and less noisy to simply pry the latch off with a length of bar?

The thieves were now in the granary, probably a very crude plank building, perhaps with a dirt floor but more likely wooden, about the size of a modern suburban garage, filled with sacks or bins of wheat, corn or silage. It would have been almost completely dark in that room.

And that brings us to the next paradox: the shotgun. The *Oregonian* distinctly states, no doubt on testimony from the hired hand, the survivor, that the gun was Ben Hasbrook's and that it was kept in the granary, not carried out by Hasbrook as he answered the call for help.

The first question is: What was it doing in the granary in the winter? To keep it close at hand? But the most likely place for that would be the barn. Even then, most farmers, including Charlie Hasbrook a half-century later, have kept their defensive weapons in the house behind the front door, over the mantle or in the entry hall closet. This would have been even more the case in the mid-nineteenth century, when barrels and hammers were more likely to rust, stocks to split and black powder in the chamber to go damp in the wet Oregon weather.

But let's say, for argument's sake, that Ben Hasbrook did keep his shotgun in the granary to, say, kill mice and rats and other pests that were eating on the grain. Maybe—and this also seems unlikely for the era, Hasbrook had two shotguns, and kept the older, single barrel scattergun in the granary to shoot varmints.

Then why was the gun loaded with the equivalent of modern Double-Ought buckshot? Such a load, designed for large mammals like deer—and human beings—would be absurd to use in a confined space on a rat: it would blow gaping holes in the walls of the building.

A shotgun loaded with OO buckshot was then, and still remains, the most devastating anti-personnel weapon available to the average person. The *Oregonian* reporter and his copy-editor, seeking to sensationalize the story, went to unusual lengths to describe this round—*fifteen buck shot*—a number that could only be so precisely measured by counting the individual bloody holes in Ben Hasbrook's stiffened back   In presenting such information, the Oregonian was imparting to its male readers an understanding that would be lost on most modern readers. Those readers would have known, being hunters (or war veterans) themselves, just what such a blast would do.

And those readers might well have asked the same question: *What was that scattergun doin' full o'buckshot?*

Once again, imagine the chain of events, as related by Coxon to the sheriff. The two thieves are in the granary, stealing whatever it is they've found. Coxon, perhaps heading to the barn after dinner, hears a noise and investigates. He notices the latch is filed through and, instead of getting reinforcement, he decides to investigate. Does he have a lantern? Or are the thieves at work in a darkened room, using perhaps the few slices of light from the farmhouse that pass through the planks of the granary door.

Coxon enters. He holds the lantern before him. He sees one, or perhaps both, of the figures. But almost before he can react, one of the men charges draws a knife and plunges it into Coxon's chest. Luckily it hits a sheaf of papers (letters from England?) and a book (a Bible?) in his breast pocket. The knife still punches through, cutting the young man's flesh and pectoral muscle, but not enough to penetrate his ribs or collapse a lung or pierce his heart.

Coxon slumps to the floor in shock. But before he loses consciousness, he shouts at the top of his lungs ("Murder!" appears to have been a common response by victims of the era). Why didn't the men just shoot him with the shotgun? Let's say they couldn't find it in the dark. But now, with the lantern lying there on the hay-strewn floor, they see it, leaning in a corner. The second thief grabs it—just as Ben Hasbrook bursts into the room.

Why is Hasbrook unarmed? Because his only weapon is in the granary. He sees Coxon, but only one of the men. He rushes right past the other thief, who has just grabbed the shotgun in the corner. That man quickly swings the gun to his hip and fires.

Ben Hasbrook, caught by a full blast of buckshot between the shoulder blades—close enough to punch right through his vest and shirt, shatter his back ribs and spinal column and penetrate his heart and lungs—staggers forward a step, his arms outstretched, with a look of confusion on his face. He drops to his knees, and then falls forward on his face. Paralyzed with shock, the air escapes from the weight on his chest in a low, protracted moan.

"Let's get out of here," says one of the men, and the pair runs off into the night . . .

BLOODY LOGIC

There are an awful lot of coincidences that need to take place for this scenario to work—not to mention quite a bit of unnecessary mayhem. Besides all of the problems of timing, motive and location, why did the thieves try to kill the hired hand in the first place? Even in 1873, murder carried a much steeper penalty than thievery.

Then, to kill Ben Hasbrook—let's say to get rid of any witnesses to the stabbing—you need that unlikely shotgun with the unlikely load. After that, don't you make sure that Coxon is dead? And how about those other potential witnesses in the house—like the lady who is about to run out of the farmhouse door? And why, now that you've erased the immediate threat, don't you steal something before you run off—say the shotgun?

The *Oregonian* didn't believe all of those coincidences. Neither did the local sheriff.

Having been called to the murder scene, the Sheriff, his deputies and neighboring farmers all conducted a careful search of the site. As the newspaper would note from the testimony at the subsequent trial, "They examined and compared tracks, in fact, scoured the whole country around, but found only two tracks, a small and larger one, the former exactly suiting the boot worn by [Coxon], the latter that of Hasbrook.

"In reference to the scuffle [Coxon] had with the robber at the granary door, everything there was thoroughly examined. Witnesses state that if he had lain in the mud, which was very soft and from one to three inches deep, his clothes must of necessity have been very much soiled, which they did not indicate."

The sheriff also investigated Coxon's claim of being wounded. He saw no blood. He then looked at Coxon's vest and the life-saving book and papers. They were later put on exhibit at the trial. As the newspaper reported, "[Coxon] says they were in an inside vest pock. They show two cuts, one of which indicates that it would have been dangerous to have been on the other side of it at the time the cutting was done, as the cut is of the same size on both sides of the book, leading one to the supposition that the knife went through to the hilt, as it is in a single thrust and the prisoner is unhurt."

The sheriff arrested Coxon on the spot and escorted him to the Yamhill jail. There, "awaiting the action of the Yamhill grand jury at the April term of the circuit court." He joined four other prisoners whose names and crimes, remarkably, we know: "John Wilson awaiting trial on a charge of assault with intent to kill in Tillamook County; Thos. Markham and J. M. Russell under arrest on a charge of arson, [and] W. P. Bruce for an attempt to poison."

Note that, contrary to our image of violent life on the frontier, there are only five men in a jail covering at least one county—far fewer, a cop friend tells me, than a typical Friday night today in Great Falls, Montana. Moreover, Coxon is the only man in that jail, apparently in the course of a calendar quarter, who is there for a capital crime (or at least a success-ful one).

In fact, *Coxon v. State of Oregon* was an even rarer case than that. Violent murders were so uncommon in the region during that era that the Hasbrook slaying and subsequent trial became a cause celebre throughout northwestern Oregon. Not only were the unfolding events covered by local newspapers, such as the *Yamhill Reporter* and the *McMinnville Reporter*, but even the *Oregonian*, off in distant Portland, sent a correspondent to cover the case and file extended stories almost on a daily basis.

Needless to say, the locals were also deeply interested in the case. As the *Yamhill Reporter* noted on February 13th:

> " . . .the trial of Joseph Coxon, on charge of the murder of Benjamin Hasbrook, rendered by this coroner's jury on their investigation of the case, has been occupying the attention of not only the Justice's Court, but everybody else in this place dur-ing the whole week so far—and up to the time of our going to press, only the witness for the complaint had been examined.
>
> Great interest is drawn to the proceedings, and the court room crowded continually."

The notoriety of the case also drew the best regional legal talent— apparently something of an Oregon Dream Team. Wrote the *Oregonian* on April 29th, 1873: "The Coxon-Hasbrook murder case was called yes-terday. The talent engaged consists of Humphrey, prosecuting attorney; Hurley, his assistant and Boyes, for the State; Sullivan of Polk, McCain of Lafayette and Handley of McMinnville, for the prisoner—talent enough to bring justice out of Nazareth."

We will meet several of these men again in another twenty years at another murder trial.

CONFLICTING EVIDENCE

And so the Benjamin Hasbrook murder trial began.

Although this was the mid-nineteenth century, and not the late twentieth, getting a celebrated trial underway still presented some logistical barriers. Wrote the *Oregonian*, "The prisoner's countenance indicates that he takes a great deal of interest in all that is going on." After the arraignment a plea of 'not guilty' was entered. "It was supposed by many that it would be difficult to obtain a jury, so notorious had this case become . . . " But, this being the 19th century after all, the paper then added "but by 2 p.m. a jury was impaneled and the trial went on."

The prosecution had subpoenaed more than seventy witnesses. By the end of that first day, half had already given their testimony. The next morning, wrote the paper, "the judge made short work of the latter half of the seventy . . . . The prosecution rested when a few witnesses were examined on the part of the defense." Editorialized the reporter, "Nothing new has been indicated for either side."

Continued the report: "In the afternoon, the testimony was closed and argument by counsel was opened by a lengthy and eloquent discourse by McCain for the defense, followed by Hurley for the state."

The afternoon of this incredibly busy day closed with a dramatic speech by Sullivan, apparently the most famous attorney in the room. The crowd had come expecting a stem-winder from the "Lion of Polk", and apparently got their wish: "Pending the lengthy remarks of the Lion of Polk for the prisoner, which lasted until a late hour, the court adjourned until this morning, when the case was opened by Mr. Sullivan resuming his speech. "

"Boise, on the part of the state, will close the argument, and sometime today the case will go to the jury."

In the same story, the reporter also noted the ever-growing crowd surrounding the courthouse, suggesting that the entire populations of distant towns had piled onto trains to attend the trial:

> "Cornelius and Hillsboro are here on a picnic excursion, to the number of five car loads with the engine and tender crowded. I am not certain, but that there were some on the cow catcher. The excursion is accompanied by a band of music, who came into town with a flourish of trumpets. They are having a pleasant time. There are some three hundred and fifty of the picnickers and all is going off 'merry as a Marriage bell.'"

After two days, seventy witnesses and full summations, the jury retired to deliberate.

Their task appeared a difficult one. As the *Oregonian* correspondent noted, "The evidence on trial was somewhat conflicting. Indeed, it was observed that out of some twenty-five or thirty witnesses nearly every one made mistakes in regarding to some one or more small particulars."

The correspondent then tried his own summary of the details of the case—only to make at least one mistake of his own:

> "The main facts established were that Coxen and Hasbrook were partners, were good friends and both stood high in the community. Coxen states that he heard a noise at the granary that evening; he went there and found two men; had a tussle with them; Hasbrook came to his assistance and the men ran off, he chased one of them and when at a distance of 84 yards, heard the gun, which was usually kept in the granary; he returned to the barnyard to find Hasbrook shot in the back with small shot and already dead; he went for the neighbors, and the next day the whole neighborhood with the exception of one or two were assembled on the ground . . .The evidence went on to show that there were tracks found, which had evidently been made in the night, and did not compare with any boots owned by either Coxen or Hasbrook, and that there were some suspicions pointing to other parties, though nothing very definite in any direction."

In fact, those other boot prints, a pivotal point in the case, were only noticed by a later arrival. The first neighbors to arrive, in fact, saw only two sets of prints, corresponding to the boots worn by Hasbrook and Coxon. The correspondent, convinced by the argument of the "Lion of Polk", accepted this as fact. Most of the rest of the courtroom did not . . . except for the jury.

HIDDEN TRUTHS

The truth of this case is just as furtive as the death of Benjamin Hasbrook. First, there is the initial newspaper account, appearing just days after the murder. This story appears to be contradicted in part by subsequent stories—and nearly in full by court testimony. Yet, even the trial—especially the verdict—doesn't seem to give the real story. Crucial details, most of which would have been easily found with modern forensics, remain tantalizingly hidden.

After one hundred and thirty years, the true story of Ben Hasbrook's murder can never be fully exhumed. However, we can try to navigate our way through the various testimonies to find commonalities and logical connections.

Here is the actual chain of events as best I can puzzle it out:

About 7:30 pm on February 4th, 1873, Joseph Coxon, the hired hand/business partner of Benjamin Hasbrook, came into the Hasbrook farmhouse, having been outside—or perhaps in town—and announced that he had heard a noise at the granary.

He then rushed out. Five minutes later the people in the house heard a scream. Emeline Hasbrook, upon hearing that scream, said to her husband, "Hurry up, he is in distress." Mr. Hasbrook, hurriedly pulling on his boots, said, 'I think he's caught a fellow' and rushed out.

A few seconds later, Emeline Hasbrook heard the report of a gun. Then she heard someone yelling. She went to the door to find Coxon coming onto the porch. "Who shot the gun?" she asked, "Are you hurt?"

"I'm not hurt," said Coxon, "But poor Ben is."

Mrs. Hasbrook then stayed in the house, while Coxon ran off to the nearest farmhouse, owned by a Mr. Sleppy. He told Sleppy that Hasbrook had been killed and asked him to return with him on horseback to the Hasbrook farm. The two men mounted the same horse and rode it back.

On the way, Coxon recounted to Sleppy what had happened. He said that two men had tried to break into the granary, that he had encountered them, and that they had knocked him down in front of the doorway to the building. Sleppy noticed that, despite the muddy ground from the long winter rains Coxon's clothes, apparently contradicting his claim to having lain in the open ground, were not particularly muddy.

Sleppy asked the Englishman to describe the villains, but he was unable to. Coxon could not even tell if they were white men or Indians.

When they arrived, Coxon showed Sleppy Hasbrook's body, and the farmer had the presence to cover the dead man with a horse blanket. Coxon then walked him through the events of the evening.

Hasbrook, he said, had been killed by his own gun, which was normally kept in the granary, but on this night had been stored in a deer blind about fifty feet away, just beyond the fence. The gun, based on the autopsy, was loaded with no. 2 shot, smaller than buckshot, and more suitable for geese or turkey.

According to Coxon, he encountered the two robbers, who stabbed at him and knocked him down. Luckily, saved by the book and papers in his vest pocket, he was unhurt. Coxon yelled for help, and Hasbrook ran out of the house. He apparently scuffled with one of the men. [One witness suggested that Hasbrook had an axe in his hand when he died, but there are no corroborating reports of that, so it was likely hearsay.] As Hasbrook fought, Coxon got to his feet and chased the other perpetrator, who had already bolted to the fence. But before he could reach him, the second robber grabbed the shotgun from the blind, knelt at the fence to steady his sight, and fired.

The blast caught Ben Hasbrook square in the back as he stood in the granary doorway. He pitched forward. Claiming to have been momentarily stunned by the blast, Coxon recovered and again took off after the shooter, who was now running off to the north into the woods. Coxon soon lost him.

Farmer Sleppy, already made suspicious by the lack of mud on Coxon's clothes, retraced the events with the young man. He noted the site where the shotgun was purportedly fired (he found the wadding about twenty feet away towards the granary), and the spot, about fifteen feet from it that Coxon claimed to have reached when the shotgun fired. Looking at these two sets of tracks, as well as the ones leading up to the fence, Sleppy was unable to detect any difference. He also walked from the fence to the north, in the direction to which Coxon claimed the perpetrator had run, but found no boot prints anywhere. Nor, apparently were there any boot prints from the second perpetrator leading from the granary off into the night.

Under cross-examination, Sleppy also remembered that he saw Coxon, as he passed the granary, make a gesture as if he was throwing something through the doorway.

A second farmer, Jeremiah Lamson arrived an hour later. He too noticed the similarity of the tracks, adding that what mud there was on Coxon looked different from that found in the barnyard.

By now, Coxon was claiming that he knew the identity of one of the murderers: a local thug named Higly.

Other neighbors, alerted by someone, began to appear. When George Stephens arrived, Coxon told him that the robbers had been trying to steal oats. He described the man who knocked him down as being dark and heavy.

Coxon told Eli Branson that he'd heard a noise at the granary, and had walked up just in time to see a man burst in through the door. "I grabbed him and he threw me", Coxon then announced. Suspicious, Branson grabbed Coxon by the shoulder and turned him around. There was no mud on his back. Must have washed off in the rain, said another farmer nearby.

To Branson, Coxon described the man who held him down as having a sandy complexion. Sounds like Osborn and Higly, Branson said. Coxon agreed. But Osborn and Higly aren't in town, Branson told him.

Lansom testified that, in their first conversation, Coxon did not know whether the robbers were Indians or white, but "that he afterwards described them particularly." Wilson Booth found the gun in some brush near the road.

Frank Young followed the track down the hill. There was only one set, he testified, and the man did not seem to be running.

William Walling and Eddie Fendall managed to find a track leading from the granary into the woods—the only possible evidence of the second perpetrator. But, Walling added, he was convinced those tracks were old and not made that night.

This being Oregon in February, it rained that night, obscuring most of the tracks. The sheriff arrived the next morning at 10 a.m., to find a yard and house filled with neighbors. Between the rain and the curious visitors, most of the tracks had been obliterated. Ben Hasbrook's body had finally been moved into the house. Now, Coxon was convinced it was Higly, and he asked the sheriff if there was enough evidence to convict the man. "I said it depended on what he would swear."

Inspecting the granary, the sheriff found that the staple (latch) had been filed, and inside the building found the file that had likely done the work. Whether it was lying on the floor, having just been tossed there, was not mentioned. . .

Upon receiving the judge's instructions *(". . .Some men jump at conclusions and are willing to convict on too slight testimony, while others are unreasonably skeptical and apparently, cannot be convicted at all. You should study to avoid these extremes and endeavor to occupy the proper reasonable ground between them . . .")* the jury retired.

They would deliberate for eight hours. We don't know what they discussed. Surely it was the matter of the tracks, the time of night, the object of the robbery and the inexplicably un-lethal wounds in Coxon's vest. One hopes they touched on the missing mud on Coxon's back, his changing story about the identities of the robbers, the presence of a black powder shotgun outdoors on a rainy night (how did the robber know it was there?), and that odd, furtive gesture by Coxon as he passed the granary (where was that file?)

We only know the conclusion. At ten p.m., the jury returned with its verdict.

Not guilty.

THE COURT OF PUBLIC OPINION

A few observers, notably the correspondent for the *Oregonian*, exulted at the news—though his comments suggest he was more interested in the triumph over capital punishment than Coxon's vindication (apparently Oregon life has changed little):

> "There was much speculation as to what kind of verdict would be rendered. Some supposed that he would be convicted; many said that the jury would hang, whilst a few, acknowledging the existence of a "higher law" said not guilty. It appears the jury were composed of the latter class . . .I wish I had their names, I would spread them before the world, hand in hand with the declaration that here are twelve men in Yamhill County, Oregon, who have refused to lend their hands to a cold-blooded murder of which Nero might have been proud . . . This may appear to be strong language to many. Yet these same persons arrogate to themselves a high degree

of enlightenment and Christian refinement. Let them pause and examine what difference there is between this species of murder, miscalled "Capital Punishment" and the custom of the savages or "Heathen Chinese" and they won't find a very large balance standing to their credit."

But that writer was in the absolute minority. In most of the surrounding communities the verdict was met with dismay, horror and anger. That anger only grew more heated when it was learned that the *Oregonian* "correspondent" had, in fact, been a member of the defense team. Wrote the *Lafayette Courier*, "About as unprofessional and stupid of an exploit as we have known a lawyer to be in engaged in was the writing of a communication to the *Oregonian* by an assistant counsel of defense in the Coxon case congratulating himself that a Judicial murder had not been perpetrated! *Lawyers* seldom vouch for the innocence of criminals they are employed to defend."

The *Courier* went on to note "Somebody writes again to the Oregonian to say that the acquittal of Coxon had rejoiced most people acquainted with the circumstances of Hasbrook's murder and Coxon's trial! The father of liars [i.e., Satan] is just nowhere compared to this scribbler."

The *Lafayette Courier* also asked its readers, ominously in that era of vigilante justice and lynching, "What are you going to do about it?"

In the meantime, Coxon, who had spent the night in jail after the verdict, having no place else to go, was taken to Portland by one of the defense attorneys, T.B. Handley. They registered together in a hotel room, and in the following days Handley took Coxon around the city to introduce the notorious new celebrity to Handley's lady acquaintances. This only deepened the anger back in Yamhill County.

On May 9th an "Indignation Meeting" was held in the town of Sheridan. All of the local papers covered the meeting, the *Courier* headlining it: "INDIGNATION MEETING—The People Incensed at the Acquittal of Coxon, T.B. Handley's Conduct Denounced—The Entire Community Unanimous."

According to one reporter, the meeting was attended "by one of the largest and most respectable audiences that has ever been assembled in Sheridan." Almost unanimously, and to "clear their skirts of one of the foulest crimes that has ever blackened the fair name of Yamhill County", the assembled (which included the doctor who conducted Hasbrook's autopsy, as well as a number of the neighboring farmers who'd visited the scene that night) passed a resolution that stated,

> "WHEREAS, Benjamin Hasbrook, a peaceable, honest and industrious citizen was, on the evening of the 4th of February last, shamefully assassinated; and
> WHEREAS, We believe it to be the duty of every citizen in the vicinity where the murder occurred, to aid in investigating the matter, and, if possible, bring the guilty to justice; and
> WHEREAS, [Judge] J. Lamson and others did, at great sacrifice investigate the matter; procure the arrest and aided in the prosecution of Joseph Coxon, the only one upon whom any trace of guilt could be found; and
> WHEREAS, The jurors to whom the case was submitted, have expressed their belief, since the trial, that he did the killing and yet rendered a verdict of "Not Guilty," therefore, . . . The jurors to whom the case of Joseph Coxon was submitted, either misunderstood the instructions of the judge or they did shamefully betray the confidence reposed in them, and have justly merited the censure of all good citizens, in thus giving loose reins to vice and crime by their verdict in the face of all evidence and their own avowed convictions."

But there would be no lynch mob, if only because the jail was empty and Coxon one hundred miles away. And when, despite being warned by the local newspaper that "it would not be entirely safe for Coxon to put in his appearance" there, after a few days he did return, to McMinnville, to gather his belongings. He tried to find a job, but no one would hire him. Then, unmolested, he left for a job "in other parts for a time" and departed Yamhill County forever.

PARIAH

And what of my great-great grandmother, Emeline Hasbrook, the grieving widow?

As I said, despite my father's skepticism, I was prepared to give her the benefit of the doubt—though I must admit the apparent fact that she reputedly left Charlie behind when she went to get help I had always found to be deeply suspicious. Truth be told, my first draft of this chapter reflected that ambivalence. I didn't want to denounce Emeline, if only because of the legacy such a claim represented. Besides, I reasoned, how could she have produced a man like Charlie Hasbrook?

But then, just as I was completing the draft, the newspaper and court documents from the case surfaced. I read them with growing revulsion towards Emeline Woodley. I remembered that both Mary Hasbrook, Charlie's wife, and her daughter Theresa, my grandmother, two women of enormous integrity, both despised that judgmental old woman. I should have followed their lead from the beginning.

There is a mysterious passage in a story in the *Lafayette Courier*. It says, simply: "For not grasping the thing in all of its scope and pressing into the case the accomplice of the murder of Hasbrook, the prosecution in the case may very appropriately be said to have been a sorry failure."

Accomplice? Who was the paper talking about? At first I thought it meant the second robber in the barnyard. But then I realized whom the writer meant.

Emeline Hasbrook.

Emeline, it could be argued, had saved Coxon. Whereas the eyewitness testimony after the event was both confused in details and confusing in sheer quantity—a debate between who saw boot prints and who didn't—there was only one other witness, besides the defendant, who could describe the events leading up to the murder. And Emeline's testimony, though limited, absolutely corroborated Coxon's own. And, as she was the first witness, her testimony also colored everything that followed.

But if she helped Coxon's case, Emeline didn't help her own. Making its innuendo clearer, the *Courier* minced no words in its postmortem of the trial:

> "The wife of the victim of the hideous crime for the commission of which Coxon was arraigned, was obviously enough, either with or without her knowledge, connivance or consent, the prize coveted or was in some way the subject and object of the atrocious and fiendish taking off of poor Hasbrook.

"It is possible she knew nothing of the intended murder or the manner of its commission or the motive prompting it. We say it is possible and where we say this much we think we give her the full benefit of all that is due her actions from the date of the tragedy down to the hour that the jury of his peers pronounced Joseph Coxon 'not guilty.'

"We hope that we would be incapable of uttering one word which might in the remotest degree lacerate the feelings or add poignancy to the grief of a woman stricken as one would ordinarily be whose husband had been so cruelly brained by an assassin; but if the conduct of a wife under such circumstances shall be as to encourage the suspicion that all is not right on her part and it should happen that such suspicion is without foundation, why, she is doubly to be commiserated for being the victim of a train of circumstances at once so untoward and cruel.

"We have her own testimony to the point that, after the firing of the fatal shot was heard by her, and upon Coxon's first visit to the house after the murder, she asked him if he (Coxon) was hurt, when he replied no, but 'poor Ben is,' she flew not to his side but remained in the house, and during that long memorable night, and until during the next day, Hasbrook's body laid in the corral with no covering save a horse blanket and she visited it not nor sought the alleviation of the cheerless aspect surrounding it.

"And it was obvious during the trial that her [support] was manifestly in the direction of the triumph of Coxon, or if they were not, then action and non-action were devoid of significance whatever."

For twelve hours after the gunshot, Emeline Hasbrook did not see the body of her husband of six years and the father of her children; not until his body was carried by neighbors into the house and placed on the kitchen table.

Of those twelve hours, surely the telling one was the first. Coxon had run off to the neighbors to get help (or an alibi) and Emeline was left alone. By her own account, she had never even asked if her husband was dead. Worse, she had never even checked.

Was Ben Hasbrook dead? Coxon obviously thought so. But Hasbrook might have only been unconscious from the shock and trauma. He was dying, and probably could not have been saved anyway, but there is the possibility that he revived for a few minutes . . .and without succor, without gentle comforting words to help him over, he slowly died, alone, betrayed, lying there in the darkness and the freezing mud.

Meanwhile, inside the house, his wife put his two young sons to bed. Did Charlie ask where Daddy was? And what did his mother answer?

Emeline Hasbrook had saved Joseph Coxon, but at the cost of her own reputation. Now he was gone; and she remained, a widow with two small children, on a farm she couldn't work alone, under the angry glare of her neighbors.

The *Lafayette Courier* ended the article with a wish:

> "A murderer stalks forth! Not to communion with things pleasant to reflect upon; not to mingle and commingle with and be trusted by his fellow men; not to joy and gladness unalloyed, but to the perpetual companionship of a conscience whose chief function in the future shall be to smite and smite continually the most monstrous of sinners. The spectre of poor murdered Hasbrook will haunt his pathway, his daydreams and his night dreams, through his life and after death, well—then comes the judgement!"

Did Emeline Hasbrook's conscience suffer over the next sixty years for the events that winter night in 1873? Not obviously so—though one could say that a kind of divine retribution was at that moment heading her way along the Oregon Trail. She made no deathbed confession nor fell into any pits of perdition during her long life. Rather, she grew merely harder, primmer and colder—perhaps a kind of punishment as well.

And there is one other clue that she was perhaps indeed wracked by guilt over the murder. It was what led her to assassinate Ben Hasbrook once more, this time in the memories of his children; what made her rewrite the events of that night so that she, trudging with her baby down that long dark road for help, became the heroine of the story.

HIDDEN EVIDENCE

There is one last fact to add to the story of Ben Hasbrook's murder, one unknown to investigators, attorneys or jurors at the time of the trial—but perhaps not to Joseph Coxon:

Emeline Hasbrook was pregnant.

I discovered this one day cross-referencing dates. We often complain about the slow wheels of justice in modern America, how crimes often aren't adjudicated for years after they occur. But one advantage of our glacial system is that sometimes crucial facts emerge in the interim. As it was, Mr. Coxon had already been exonerated and the case closed before Emeline even began to show in her bulky Victorian clothes.

Dora Hasbrook was born exactly eight months to the day after Ben Hasbrook was murdered. Millions of first-born children have been born "prematurely" to newlyweds in desperate need of an official recount. But this birth, of a third child, may have involved a different kind of accounting.

The nicest, though most poignant, scenario is that Ben and Emeline conceived Dora in early January, and the poor unfortunate girl never got to meet her natural father.

But there are two other, darker, possibilities. One is that the murder would have about coincided with the moment that Emeline first missed her period. As the mother of two, she might well have recognized even that early what was happening and told the real father. Coxon in turn, may have decided to get Hasbrook out of the way.

The second possibility is that Emeline realized she was pregnant and told Ben. Ben, already suspecting that something was going on between his wife and his hired hand, either provoked a fight with Coxon or ordered him off the farm. Coxon, in turn, decided to retaliate and keep Emeline for himself.

Which is correct? It probably doesn't matter. In either case, Coxon pulled the trigger, Ben Hasbrook died, and Emeline never even checked on the fate of her husband. Instead, she stayed in the house, perhaps helping Coxon punch the knife holes in his vest and books. Then he took his leave, both of them praying to get through what would come next.

Daughter Dora, who died comparatively young at 51, left neither letters nor a diary. And even if she had, it's doubtful she would have known the truth about her beginnings. Even her older brother Charlie never questioned Dora's paternity.

Still, I find myself looking again and again at family photograph taken fifteen years later. Emeline had remarried by then, to Homer Adkins, who will soon enter this story. He is there in the photograph, looking hard and deadly. So is Emeline, small, round and fearful. In between are the three girls and one boy, all blonde, of the second family—including Ben and Pearl, the latter the mother of the cousin who left my mother the photographs. And looming behind, more like visitors than family, are Ben Hasbrook's children: Charlie, small and pugnacious, Ben, a half-head taller, but more passive; and Dora.

I try to tell myself that it is my own bias talking, but the more I look at Dora the less I see a resemblance with her blood siblings. The two boys, despite the differences in height and age, look like brothers. Dora shares their noses, but in every other way seems an outsider. She has some of her mother in that nose, but not in the shape of her face, her mouth or her eyes.

In the years ahead, as the family sat around the dinner table, or filled a pew at church, did anyone else notice the same thing? Did the ladies of the town, the ones who whispered "murderess" at the sight of Emeline, ever remark on it? Did Dora ever look in the mirror and wonder?

Most likely, no one ever thought of it—as no one questions the children of questionable parentage we unknowingly encounter every day. Certainly Emeline would never have commented on her daughter's differences. And sitting before them on the couch, posing for this photograph, is a new, equally sinister, presence that has entered into the life of Dora and her brothers who will distract them from much introspection in the years to come.

HOPE

Benjamin Hasbrook was buried at Pleasant Hill Pioneer Cemetery. The marker, though worn, is there still. It is a tall and narrow headstone that may have once held a carved urn or other device at the top that is long gone. The stone reads:

BENJ. HASBROOK
Died
Feb. 4, 1873
Aged
37 Y's 10 M's 14 D's

Carved above these words is a bas-relief of the Bible, wrapped in a ribbon title that reads:

HOPE.

If Benjamin Hasbrook's hope had been for justice, he never got it.

THE LORD KNOWS WHAT IS BEST: KANSAS

As family legend had it, Emeline Hasbrook would twice see a husband murdered, and twice subsequently marry the hired hand.

This story would seem as self-evidently false as the others—at least the part about the marriages. After all, Joseph Coxon was long gone within days after the trial, and Emeline (whatever her desires before) certainly didn't marry him. The same, as we shall see, was true regarding the circumstances of yet another murder and remarriage.

And yet I suspect that this family legend needs only a single twist to become true. The twist is that Emeline Hasbrook didn't marry the hired hand at the time of the shooting, but a later hired hand on the farm. This fits well both with the record and with human nature. On an isolated farm, with the few available men merely passing through, the most likely catch is the one sitting at your breakfast table every morning.

Enter Homer Adkins, the villain of this Victorian melodrama. As much as I would like to think of his appearance in Emeline's life as a form of cosmic marital vengeance, I suspect that they were—at least initially—a pretty good match. For one thing, they were only a year apart in age. Thus they escaped the chronological incompatibility that had likely been at the heart of the problem between Ben Hasbrook and his young bride.

Just as important, to put it bluntly, they were both people of flawed, but complimentary, characters. She was immature, untrustworthy and, possibly an unindicted conspirator in murder. He was probably a coward, and, as the later record suggests, a bully with a dangerous temper. He wanted a wife and she needed a husband. He wanted to own her and hide her from the world. She desperately wanted to be hidden.

It would be a match made in Hell.

And what of little Charlie? He no doubt heard the shotgun blast that killed his father. As his mother never left the house that night, he probably did not see his father lying in the doorway of the granary. But Charlie no doubt did see his dead and muddy father laid out the next morning on the dining table—that is, on the same table where he'd eaten with his still living father the night before.

Had he been left face down all night, Ben Hasbrook's face would have been discolored and swollen. But if the neighbors had turned him during the night, the father Charlie saw on that table would have looked like he was sleeping.

What kind of scars was left on Charlie that night and the next morning? What did he think when men carried his father away forever? What did he think when he saw Coxon, hands tied, being led away? Did he speak to Coxon and ask what had happened? Did Coxon have the nerve to answer the boy whose father he had just murdered?

Then came the trial. Neither of the two boys, Charlie and Ben, is mentioned by the newspapers—which would have loved to play up the fatherless children angle—so we can assume they weren't there. They were probably left with a sympathetic neighbor during their mother's testimony.

What did their mother tell them when she left for the trial? And what did the neighbors say after she had gone? To those questions, there is probably no chance now of ever finding the answers.

But there are a pair of questions for which we do have answers: Who was Homer Adkins? And what had brought him to Oregon?

For this information, which otherwise would have been long lost, I can thank my distant cousin Ben Wilkerson for a remarkable letter written in 1869 by a woman to whom I'm not related, but nevertheless hold in awe and respect.

DEAR DAUGHTER

Though it was coming on to the longest day of the year, for Hannah Adkins these were the darkest of days.

She had already written to her in-laws and given them the terrible news.

And she knew they would tell their grandchild, Hannah's second daughter Jane, 18, who was living with them.

But now, the funeral behind them, the danger passed, the soldiers settled in garrison nearby, it was time to write Jane directly and tell her the whole story. Hannah used a fine tipped steel pen and large, lined sheets of paper of about modern legal size. She wrote in a very fine hand with few corrections over the course of four pages. Nothing, except perhaps the very neatness of the letter, betrayed the deep emotions that rolled over her as she wrote.

June   13, 1869
Lake Sibley
Cloud County, Kansas

My Dear Daughter.

Jane, I know you must be very anxious to hear the particulars of our Ezra's death. I will again try to give it in writing. I wrote about it to Father Adkins folks last week but it is a painful recital. But his release was so sudden from this world I think his suffering was short.

Thanks to the Wizard of Oz and other twentieth century fictions, we think of Kansas today as the ultimate fly-over state: a flat American gothic world of endless wheat farms and grain elevators; foursquare people on foursquare lots thinking foursquare thoughts.

But Kansas in the 1860s was a place of almost Biblical terrors. They came one after another, so relentlessly, that they threatened to depopulate the state—leaving those who stayed behind, like the Adkins, wondering if they'd already gone to Hell.

The nightmare began in the 1850s when Kansas Territory, struggling for statehood, found itself a cats-paw in the deadly debate over the future of slavery.

In 1854, Kansas was a largely unpopulated region, more a portal to the West than a destination in itself. Like Oklahoma, it might have remained a territory for another fifty years, but for the misfortune of geography. The North saw it as bulwark to the spread of the America's Original Sin. The South saw it as more votes in Congress in support of the Peculiar Institution.

The result was the Kansas-Nebraska Act, which not only opened the region for settlement, but also allowed the citizens of Kansas to determine their own fate as Slave or Free. It wasn't long before the Territory was infested with advocates for both sides—slavery advocates from Missouri, abolitionists from Massachusetts—trying to rig ballots, subsidize settlements, and control local governments. The first group was more ruthless, and thanks to voter intimidation and fraud, the first two elections in the state, in 1854 and 1855, went pro-slavery.

The result was "Bleeding Kansas", a fertile ground for violence and fanaticism. And it found both in the messianic figure of John Brown. After pro-slavery thugs known as the Border Ruffians raided the abolitionist town of Lawrence, Brown, who believed only an apocalypse would end slavery, led a small band of true believers to murder five pro-slavery advocates in the town of Pottawattamie.

Brown got his apocalypse, but not before, as if in a sign of God's anger, Kansas first experienced a devastating drought in 1860. The springs and wells dried up and the earth cracked. It didn't rain from June 1859 until November 1860—sixteen months—and, according to one official history "was nearly as disastrous to the emigration to Kansas as the Civil War." Pioneers, many of them newly arrived from Ireland, found themselves going from one famine to another. Thirty thousand settlers—one-third the state's population—left "God-forsaken Kansas." Thirty thousand more approached starvation, and were only saved by emergency food arriving from the East. Even those who managed to hang on until the spring of 1861 now found themselves with good weather but no seed to plant

Some counties, such as Cloud, which had only seen its first white settlers just two years before, were quickly depopulated. Those not driven away by the drought left because of a growing Indian scare.

It was little wonder that the newly elected President, Abraham Lincoln, while visiting Kansas said, "No other territory has ever had such a history."

That history was just beginning. Sweeping in just after the welcome rains that winter, after Kansas gained statehood in January, came the greatest storm of all: the Civil War. Kansas gave the Union Army 20,097 men, out of just 30,000 men of military age. Though there were only

300 black men of military age in the state, two thousand volunteered—most of them escaped slaves from Arkansas and Missouri. Before the war was over, Kansas would lose more men as a percentage of its population than any other Northern state.

Despite its contribution of men, Kansas was the scene of only one major battle. It was simply too far west even for the War in the West. Nor did it collapse into the anarchy of nearby Missouri, a war of all against all that wouldn't find its match until places like Bosnia and Rwanda in the late 20th century. Still, Kansas could not entirely escape the Missouri horror: in August 1863, Confederate guerillas under the homicidal William C. Quantrill crossed the border and attacked Lawrence.

Lawrence was not only a Union bastion, but had come to symbolize abolitionism. Moreover, several Confederate sympathizers, all women, had been incarcerated there—and were killed when the building in which they were housed collapsed. Calling for vengeance, Quantrill hit Lawrence at dawn and ordered his men to kill every man and boy of fighting age in town. The result was a daylong orgy of violence and pillage. Quantrill's and his guerillas left behind a burned and sacked downtown, $1.5 million in damage and 150 murdered civilians.

But even as the war raged, changes were already underway that would change the face of Kansas forever. In 1862, Congress passed the Homestead Act, which offered 160 acres to anyone willing to become a citizen and farm that land for seven months of the year for three years [it was the same law that gave Charlie Hasbrook his farm forty years later.] In Kansas, much of this land was Indian Territory bought cheaply by the railroads and now offered to settlers in hopes of creating a future market.

The Homestead Act would populate the Mid-West, but only after the Civil War ended and the transportation grid was again safe and open to pioneers. But even as the Act opened the door to millions of new immigrants from Germany, Sweden and Ireland, it also closed the door to thousands of Pawnee, Cheyenne, Kiowa and Comanche Indians. Pushed into reservations, knowing they'd been exploited, and seething with frustration, raiding parties took advantage of the civic chaos and began slipping off the reservation. The first of these raids took place in

1864. By 1868, General Phil Sheridan, now directing the U.S. Calvary on the frontier, estimated that an average of 150 Kansans was being killed each year in Indian raids.

BUILT WITH BLOOD

Depopulated by drought, war and Indian attacks, Cloud County began again in 1862.

"Cloud", by way, wasn't the county's original name. It is a measure of the area's earlier incarnation as a wild land of soldiers, Indians and cowboys, that it was originally called "Shirley County," named after a whore who plied her trade around Fort Laramie.

To find Cloud County on a map, you need to think of the state of Kansas as a checkerboard seven counties tall and fourteen counties across. Cloud County is two rows down from the top and two columns east of center.

The defining geographic feature of the county is two river valleys, the Republican in the north, and the Solomon in the southeast. Both are noted for their rich alluvial soil, some of it ten feet deep, that makes for some of the best farmland in the state. The rolling upland in-between, though today heavily cultivated by modern fertilizers and machinery, was put to its more appropriate use of cattle grazing during the nineteenth century. The Republican River also featured several ox-bow lakes, left behind by various prehistoric changes of course. The largest of these was Lake Sibley.

As for the local fauna, it was most lyrically described by an official state history published in 1883: "The prevailing woods are cottonwood, elm and box elder, although in places large groves of oak abound. Walnut, ash, honey locust, will, hackberry, coffee bean and mulberry are found. In the list of wild shrubbery may be mentioned hazel, black current, choke cherries, black raspberries and grapes."

Small wonder that Cloud County appealed to the arriving settlers. But the gap between potential and reality was never greater than in those first years. A telling story about the harshness of life there on the banks of the Republican is that of the death to fever of Mrs. M.A. Munzel and her child in 1861-62. It was only after visiting numerous sod homes in the area that the surviving family was able to cobble together enough lumber just to make two coffins.

The next spring, two brothers, Charles and Peter Conklin, arrived with their two sisters and an adopted orphan child, and set about building the first wooden home in the county. To the locals, the house, with its hewn logs and shake roof and siding, must have looked like a mansion. And that in turn began to raise suspicions about how the two young men amassed such wealth.

Those suspicions seemed confirmed when James Fox, founder of the town of Clifton in adjoining Washington County, and another man known today only as Rose, arrived in town claiming that the Conklins were part of a gang of horse thieves. They apparently had no trouble organizing a lynch mob of local citizens to attack the house and haul out the desperados.

But the brothers were warned, and as the "company" approached, they hid in the bushes nearby. The lynch mob, discovering the men gone, then proceeded to tear down the beautiful house. The two sisters and child, trapped inside, screamed in terror. The mob responded by voting to lynch anyone who went to their aid.

When it was over, the three victims were left standing in the debris of their home with no chance of finding help or shelter. Meanwhile, the mob roared around the area, searching for the two men—at least once coming so close to their hideaway that the two Conklins were ready to shoot.

During the night they made their escape—only to be captured by U.S. soldiers and transported to Leavenworth . . . where they escaped a second time. One brother died years later in Missouri; the other disappeared forever.

Meanwhile, back in Cloud County, the Conklin sisters and child managed to salvage some sheets and a little food from the debris. Stretching the sheets over poles they managed to create a minimum of shelter against the cold and rain. And there they stayed for two weeks, with no way to leave and no hope of aid from their neighbors.

They would have died had not one neighbor finally summoned the courage to help them. His name should be remembered: J.M.Hagaman. Mr. Hagaman yoked up his ox team, drove over to the miserable remains of the Conklin House and rescued the group. He then drove them down to the river to the last place they had friends who would take them in. Then, with amazing bravery, Hagaman publicly denounced the would-be lynchers.

No one raised a hand against him.

Were the Conklins horse thieves? We will never know. But what we do know is that the instigator of the mob, James Fox, turned out to be one himself, and a desperado to boot. He eventually joined a group of bushwhackers . . . and was soon found dead from numerous gunshot wounds.

THE RAID

This was the world the Adkins family entered as they arrived at Lake Sisley from Illinois at the close of the Civil War.

The patriarch, Homer, was forty-seven in 1869. His wife, Hannah, was six years younger—and, if her letter writing is any indication, a woman of intelligence, education and considerable literary talent. Both had been raised in Connecticut, educated there, and no doubt it was there they met and married.

They arrived on the banks of the Republican River with eight children in tow. The oldest, daughter Hannah A., age 24 in 1869, was married to Jasper Scribner, five years her junior. They appear to have lived nearby. Next came Homer Jr. 21, the future stepfather of Charlie Hasbrook; Jane 18, the recipient of the letter; Lucy 16; Ann, probably 12; Ezra, 10; Ashael 8; and baby Paul, age 2.

They were part of a wave of pioneers who hit the roads and trails in search of a new life almost from the instant hostilities ceased. While the popular image is of them heading West to Colorado or California, continuing the pre-War first emigrant wave, most of these settlers in fact merely moved—like the Ingalls family of "Little House on the Prairie" fame—a few hundred miles to the nearest available cultivable land.

For thousands, that meant the band of prairie stretching from North Dakota to central Texas. Cloud County, for example, grew from a few hundred hardy souls in 1867 to more than 15,000 by 1880—creating in the process the booming city (pop. 2000) of Concordia, six miles from the Adkins farm.

The Adkins were at the very leading edge of this wave, and as such, they found themselves in a world largely unchanged for a thousand years. Even the basic infrastructure of farming was largely absent: the nearest post office was sixty miles away, the nearest mill 150 miles, and the nearest railhead even further.

Still, they managed to build a sod house and a corral, and get seed into the ground. And, like all pioneer families, they established a cordial, and mutually dependent, relationship with their neighbors, the Nelsons and the Duttons, each of whom lived about a mile away.

These were hard, desperate times. And life as a prairie sodbuster was especially harsh and dangerous. Spring and autumn brought floods; summer carried malaria, drought and tornadoes, and winter was crueler yet. A few years later and a few miles away, the Collins family, my paternal great-great-grandparents, would try to survive a horrifically cold night in a soddie by putting the whole family, including my great-grandfather and half-dozen of his sisters and brothers, in a single bed under every available blanket. They lived . . .but in the morning discovered to their horror that they had suffocated the baby.

There were also wolves, rabid rodents and venomous snakes, and, as we have already seen, dangerous white men. But in their own minds, the biggest threat to families like the Adkins as they clung to the red earth of Kansas and tried to survive, came from Indians.

To make up for past bigotry we today often cast Native-Americans, especially the Plains Indians, in a romantic glow. But the reality on the ground in 1868 and 1869—eight years before the Little Big Horn, twenty-one years before Wounded Knee—was far different. These were desperate times. The nation was still binding the wounds of the Civil War and the loss of 800,000 men. The crippled South was now occupied by armed troops. Angry, desperate rebels, such as the James and Younger brothers, had taken skills learned with Quantrill and other guerrillas and turned them to crime.

Thousands of military weapons—revolvers, lever action rifles, knives and swords—had made their way to civilians and, with the support of the government, into the hands of Native Americans on reservations. Meanwhile, thanks to the occupied South and the traditional

American practice of sweeping post-war demobilization, a skeleton U.S. Calvary, under the command of General Sheridan in the field and General Sherman in Washington, represented the only law and order on the frontier.

Mobility, anonymity, firepower and a lack of law enforcement were a volatile mix. in Frontier towns—such as Abilene at the northern terminus the newly created Chisholm Trail that ran from Texas to Kansas—became wildly violent places . . . enough to create popular myths about cowboys, gunslingers and desperados that endure to this day.

Indians trapped in inhospitable reservations and forced to abandon their traditional ways of life, saw their opportunity. Soon, young Comanche, Kiowa, Cheyenne and Arapahoe braves, looking for adventure and prizes, were forming raiding parties and slipping off the reservations.

Make no mistake: these raiding parties were less Sitting Bull and Chief Joseph and more like the Crips and Bloods. They were looking to rape women, steal horses and property and kill white people whenever they got the chance.

They did just that in August 1868. A neighbor of the Adkins, Hannah White, was alone on the farm with her sixteen year old daughter and three smaller children when they were attacked by six Indian braves bearing revolvers, lances, bows and quivers of arrows. The Indians came, three from each side, whooping war cries, and surrounded the house. Presumably, they had been stalking the house and, after determining that Mr. White was away, charged.

As Mrs. White and her children cowered in the house, the braves, in war paint, peered into the various windows. Assured that only women and children were inside, they burst through the door, and proceeded to tear apart the house in search of booty.

Hoping to escape, the oldest daughter, Sarah, made a break for the door—only to be grabbed by two braves. Mrs. White, holding a baby in her arms, fought to save Sarah, but was beaten down. She watched helplessly as her screaming daughter was carried away—in the language of the era: "The powerful savages bore the girl away into captivity, her pitiful, agonizing screams wafted on the breezes to the half-crazed, suffering mother, growing ever fainter until they disappeared in the distance, leaving the desolate woman haunted by the worst fears—fears that her fate might be even worse than death."

As the two Indian braves carried the girl away, the remaining four redoubled their efforts to strip the White home of all valuables. When they became distracted while dragging the family sheets, blankets, shawls and other linen out and hanging them over a nearby fence, the next oldest daughter, Annie, whispered to her mother that this might be the time to take off after Sarah.

They started their escape . . . but after no more than a few steps they were caught and rudely dragged back to the cabin and flung inside.

The Indians went back to work, now packing the horses, and once more forgot the women and children inside. Again, Mrs. White gathered up her children and attempted to escape. This time they were already in the woods and heading down towards a nearby creek when their disappearance was discovered. Mrs. White heard the angry shouts of alarm, war whoops and clattering of hoofs—and quickly secreted her family away under a nearby cottonwood log surrounded by thick underbrush. The tiny group ducked just in time as the braves, crashing through branches and dried leaves, rode past.

The braves only searched for a few terrifying minutes. Then, no doubt assuming that the woman and children were at that moment racing towards the group of farmers the Indians had seen working on the river bottom, the braves roared off towards that camp, trying to reach there before any alarm sounded.

Because of yet another drought, most of the farmers along the Republican had abandoned the high ground and planted hay below on the flood plain. In fact, the entire Republican basin in Cloud County was dotted with scores of hay camps.

Benjamin White and his three sons were in just such a camp. This being harvest time, Mr. White was atop a haystack keeping things organized while the boys pitched hay up to him. Six horses were hitched or lariated nearby. Unlike most of his neighbors working nearby on both banks of the river, Mr. White and the boys had guns. But they kept them in a tent a good distance away.

The Indians charged. In terror, the three boys leapt onto two of the horses and took off for the river, with the braves in furious pursuit. One of the braves caught up to the single rider, John, and knocked him off his horse with the butt of his lance. Now almost overtaken, the other two boys leapt off their horse, stumbled to the river and waded across.

Meanwhile, the third Indian rode to the remaining picketed horses and began to untie them. Mr. White "who was a brave and fearless man, bordering onto recklessness, descended from the stack and walked toward the Indian..." Ben White appears, like a man witnessing a crime, to have passed rapidly through a series of emotions: anger, then second thoughts, then sober appraisal, then outright fear. He marched towards the Indian, then slowed, then stopped . . . then he too turned and took off in a dead run for the river.

By now, at least two neighboring farmers had heard the commotion. As Mr. Brown and Mr. Eaves watched in horror, they saw Ben White approach the Indian brave, then turn and run, with the Indian in hot pursuit. Just as the two figures passed out of sight behind some intervening timber, Brown and Eaves heard a gunshot—and soon after the Indian rode off with the White horses.

Mr. Brown and a second neighbor, a Mr. English, arrived at the White camp to find young John White injured but not dead. He had crawled off into the high grass and hid until his pursuer had given up. But his father, shot through the chest, was dying. As his fellow farmers tended to him, Ben White had just enough time to ask about the safety of his boys, then died.

Two hours and two miles away, three other farmers, including the Adkins's neighbor Chester Dutton, were talking about the terrible news when one of them noticed tiny figures in the distance moving along the high ground. One of them rode out to see.

It was Hannah White and her three young daughters, barefoot, bleeding and exhausted. Having escaped the Indians they had gone to high ground, then had taken a wide swing around to get to the camp and their men. Every step of those five miles had been taken in sheer terror, convinced that any moment the braves would appear again to ride them down and murder them. Now, at last safe, Mrs. White was desperate to tell her husband about what had happened to them, and to their beloved daughter.

"White told her story and then inquired for her husband and sons. Not for several moments could any of those stout, big-hearted frontiersmen reveal to this woman, whose cup of bitterness was already full to overflowing, the sad fate of her husband—the words that would convey his tragic and cruel death were frozen upon their lips as she looked from one to another for her answer. At length Lieutenant Johnson broke the painful, melancholy silence. These were his words, 'The boys, Mrs. White, are safe, but the old man is killed.' A wagon and team was placed at the disposal of the brave but heart-broken woman, and she with trembling little ones were taken to a place of safety."

PURSUIT

The Indian attack wasn't wholly unexpected. Tension had been rising for months. Just days before the assault on the White farm, Kansas State Adjutant General McAfee had visited Lake Sibley and suggested that the settlers form their own militia. He announced that he would formally commission any officers this militia would elect—and promised that he would soon send Maynard carbines. [The Maynard carbines never arrived; they were only substituted months later by lesser Starr carbines.]

A general meeting was quickly called among the local farmers, including Homer Adkins. Officers were quickly elected and on Wednesday, August 12, 1868, they received their commissions.

The very next day, Ben White was murdered and his daughter Sarah kidnapped. Peter Johnson, newly commissioned lieutenant, was one of the four farmers who found and tended to Mrs. White and her three daughters. As they were consoling her, Captain Sanders, just twenty-four hours in command of the militia, rode up and began to ask Mrs. White questions.

Did she know what tribe the braves belonged to? Pawnee, thought Mrs. White. This was welcome news, as the Pawnees would be a small group far from home. On the other hand, were they Cheyenne or Arapahoe—currently in a large encampment on the nearby Solomon River, and sending out numerous raiding parties—any direct confrontation would have been impossible.

In fact, the raiders were Arapahoe. But the newly sanctioned, inexperienced and poorly armed militia rode out of Lake Sibley convinced it was on a brief mission of mercy and vengeance. Captain Sanders had deemed the mission so urgent that the militiamen, once mustered, weren't even allowed to return home to gather food or blankets.

Company C of the 1st Battalion of the 19th Kansas Volunteer Militia, composed of seven men and three officers, rode off along the west bank of the Republican. At Oak Creek they were joined by two others, George Dutton and, entering this narrative in his earliest public appearance, twenty year old Homer Adkins Jr. After sending Lt. Johnson off to reconnoiter the White farm, look for tracks, and enlist additional volunteers, the company rode off towards its first destination, the nearby town of Salt Creek.

They were still riding when night fell and a violent storm erupted. What had no doubt begun as an exciting excursion that mixed rage, fear and adventure into a heady brew, now took on a nightmarish tone. The company rode along in single file, almost blind, the officers picking out landmarks during lightning flashes. They knew that at any moment they might be ambushed and scalped.

It was worst of all for George Dutton, taking up the rear. He barely knew how to ride a horse, and was often lost in the pitch darkness for minutes at a time. "The others were all soldierly fellows and fine marksmen," says the official state history, "but perhaps none were more valiant than he."

The night grew more ominous by the hour. After midnight, the company came upon a group of fellow hay farmers. They were hiding behind a hastily built stockade. These farmers too had been attacked the day before, and one of their fellows, a young farmer from Illinois, had been murdered. That's when the militiamen learned for the first time the real identity of the Indian raiders.

That discovery, and the fact that Lieutenant Johnson hadn't returned, seemed to take the fight out of the new soldiers. They pressed on a few more miles, but their hearts were no longer in it, and in the early hours of the morning they turned back to Lake Sibley feeling they'd done their duty.

They arrived at Lake Sibley to find a message from Kansas Governor

Crawford that is a classic of political bombast: "Tell the settlers of Lake Sibley to stick together—By the eternals, I'll see that they are protected."

The settlers didn't believe it—and their assessment proved accurate: help didn't come for weeks. In the meantime, the militia set up protected and guarded sites along the Republican where threatened settlers could seek sanctuary. They also placed Mrs. White and her children in a vacant log house in a comparatively populated region near the new mill.

BEECHER ISLAND

The Indian attacks continued through the rest of the 1868. In mid-September, just weeks after the White attack, Cheyenne braves attacked an Army supply train in the western end of the state near what is now the town of Winona.

The Army quickly responded by ordering a company of scouts, under a Major Forsyth, in pursuit. Second in command was Lieutenant Fredrick H. Beecher, nephew of the noted clergyman and cousin to the novelist.

On the evening of September 16th, the troop, having spotted a Cheyenne camp nearby, pitched camp at the fork of the Arikee and Republican River just into Colorado Territory. At dawn, just as the scouts were rising, they were attacked by a band of Cheyenne led by a war chief named Roman Nose. Under heavy fire, the scouts held off the attack with their Spencer repeaters, and retreated to the only defensible position, a wooded sandbar in the middle of the river.

There they remained for nine days, slowly being picked off. Half the troop was either killed or wounded. Among the dead was Lt. Beecher, after whom the island and the battle would be named.

The scouts did manage to sneak two messengers out under the cover of darkness and the river. After several days of forced marches, these messengers finally reached the 7th Cavalry garrison at Fort Wallace. Upon hearing the news, the commanding officer, Col. Carpenter, saddled up with a command of 17 colored troops, an ambulance and a wagon of supplies. Scouting for the column was eighteen year-old James J. Peate, who would live until 1932 and supply many of the details for future historians.

The column moved out at five miles per hour and maintained it for entire day and night, a devastating pace. They arrived just as the battle was nearing its conclusion: Roman Nose had been mortally wounded the night before, and then lingered until morning to die. The leaderless, dispirited Cheyenne braves shot the scouts' remaining horses and then retreated. The exhausted, arriving solders chose to break off pursuit and tend the wounded.

The news of the Battle of Beecher Island, following the White murder and kidnapping—and before that, a series of raids in June along the Solomon and Saline rivers that had led to the murder of fifteen men and the rape of five women—was the last straw for General Sheridan. Earlier that summer he had toured Kansas to whip up local morale—and found himself cornered by furious Kansans at every stop demanding a solution to the Indian problem.

The creation of the scouts had been Sheridan's immediate answer . . . and now half of them were dead or wounded. In response, as was his character, Sheridan took the war to the next level: all Indians in the territory were to surrender to the Indian Agency. Those that didn't would be deemed renegades.

As he wrote on September 19th, even as the bullets were still ricocheting through the trees on Beecher Island: "I now regard the Cheyenne and Arapahos at war, and that it will be impossible for our troops to discriminate between the well-disposed and the warlike parts of those bands, unless an absolute separation be made."

Surrender or die. That was Sheridan's message. As he had shown in the Shenandoah Campaign and on the road to Appomattox, Sheridan was a ruthless warrior. But the Napoleon of the Saddle was also no fool. Though history would make his name synonymous with the cold-blooded remark that the only good Indian was a dead Indian, his understanding of the situation was far subtler. As he would write in 1870:

> "We cannot avoid being abused by one side or the other. If we allow the defenseless people on the frontier to be scalped and ravished, we are burnt in effigy and execrated as soulless monsters, insensible to the sufferings of humanity. If the Indian is punished to give security to these people, we are the same soulless monsters from the other side."

To Sheridan there was only one solution. Hit the Cheyenne and Arapahoe hard. Do it during the upcoming winter, when the diverse parts of the tribes would gather in large encampments. And hit them so savagely that those who survived would beg to return to the reservation forever.

Sheridan had just the man for the job: a fearless, sometimes foolhardy young man Sheridan had favored (and often protected) since Gettysburg . . . George Armstrong Custer.

But getting Custer wouldn't be easy. He had, in December, been court-mailed and suspended from the Army without pay for a year. Sheridan had been fighting to get him reinstated ever since—an effort that had failed largely because President Grant couldn't afford to mix with the negative publicity that had attached itself to the trial.

But now, with ten months passed, Sheridan thought he had a chance. He first obtained approval from General Sherman, a warrior at least as ruthless and even more brilliant than Sheridan. Wrote Sherman, "These Indians require to be soundly whipped and the ringleaders in the present trouble hung, their ponies killed, and such destruction of their property as will make them very poor."

Sherman knew exactly what the appointment of Custer would mean out there on the prairie. So, no doubt did Grant, who quietly made his approval through the auspices of the War Department. On September 24th, Sheridan wired Custer in Monroe, Michigan.

Six days later, the most dangerous man in the Army stepped off the train at Fort Leavenworth.

Custer spend the next two months training his troops, including the growing number of new recruits who'd signed up on news of his arrival. He then moved them south into Oklahoma Territory to Fort Supply. There the troops trained for battle. In his spare hours Custer indulged in his favorite activity, hunting. His hunts, mostly for buffalo, took him out into what would be called, a quarter-century later, the Cherokee Strip. He may very well have passed along Wolf Creek near the future site of Charlie Hasbrook's homestead.

As the first winter storms arrived, Custer decided the time had come. The troops were trained and the Cheyenne were no doubt in their winter encampment. In the pre-dawn hours of November 23rd, nine hundred soldiers of the Seventh Calvary, led by a dozen Osage Indian guides, and to the tune of "The Girl I Left Behind Me" rode out of Fort Supply into a blizzard.

They weren't the only soldiers preparing to wage war on the Indians. On October 9th, Sheridan had received permission to organize a regiment of Kansas Calvary for six month's duration.   There probably wouldn't have been a shortage of volunteers anyway, but four days later Indians attacked settlers in Ottawa County, killing four men, raping two women and kidnapping one other woman. Enlistment numbers leaped, quickly filling out the quota. Among the names on the rolls was young Homer Adkins. James Peate, the scout, signed up too, and became orderly sergeant. Even Governor Crawford, a former Civil War general, finally lived up to his rhetoric: he resigned his position and joined the militia as its commander.

By late November, this "19th Kansas Militia" was still training and an impatient Custer was unwilling to wait. He no doubt assumed they'd be an impediment anyway. So he rode out of Fort Supply without them.

Even as Custer was on the move, his target, Black Kettle's band of Cheyenne, was suing for peace. Through the autumn, sensing that the situation was becoming dangerously hostile, various Indian bands had been streaming into Ft. Cobb, south of Supply on the Washita, seeking peace and protection. The Army gave that protection to the Kiowa and Comanche bands, but refused it to the Cheyenne and Arapahoe because of their predations in Kansas. These latter were told they could only surrender directly to Sheridan at Fort Supply.

For the next four days, though ever-improving weather, the Seventh Calvary raced across Southwestern Oklahoma, one day covering thirty-five miles. The march, of just less than one hundred miles, to a bend of the Washita River, took just four days. The next morning, Custer led the 7th Cavalry in attack on the encampment of 150 Cheyenne braves and their families.

It was Black Kettle's band. Black Kettle himself had just returned from Fort Cobb the day before, and, in a council of elders, decided to send emissaries to Sheridan and to move the camp downriver closer to some neighboring tribes.

It was too late. The Seventh Cavalry came roaring in from three sides, with sharpshooters firing from the fourth. The main force, under

Custer, charged from the North into the center of the village. All, for the first time, to the tune of "Garry Owen."

It was a slaughter, and its images, thanks to cinema, still haunt the American imagination even if the battle itself is nearly forgotten: blue uniformed cavalrymen galloping through an Indian camp, crashing through teepees, riding down or shooting men and women, red blood staining the white snow; the survivors retreating to the river where, huddled, they are shot down.

The whole engagement lasted no more than ten minutes, and was probably as violent—if not quite as vicious—as the movies portray it. The attack did catch the Indians by surprise, but it was uncoordinated. With only three sides fully covered, the braves were given an exit through which many fought their way out into nearby ravines. Black Kettle didn't make it—he died in the river.

Nor was there indiscriminate slaughter of the women and children—most in fact were rounded up and herded into one of the largest teepees. Ironically, it was only then that they risked annihilation . . . from the Osage scouts, who were preparing to kill them all when Custer rode up and stopped them.

What Custer didn't know was that just downriver, hundreds more Cheyenne, as well as Arapaho and Kiowa, were encamped. When they heard the gunfire, the braves in those encampments jumped on their horses and raced towards the battle. Before they got there, these Indians ran smack into a twenty-man company of the Seventh galloping down the river in pursuit of the last of Black Kettle's braves. The soldiers were quickly pinned down and killed to the man.

Before long, the braves were pouring into the high ground around Black Kettle's camp and the Seventh was formed into a defensive perimeter to repel them. When the soldiers began slaughtering the Cheyenne's 900 ponies, the enraged Indians attacked . . .to be repelled by Captain Benteen's troops. Then, in a remarkable display of bravado, Custer formed up his troops and, to music from the band, began to march downstream towards the other Indian encampments. The braves, suddenly on the defensive, retreated to protect their families— and as they did, Custer turned and marched the 7th Calvary smartly out of the Valley of the Washita.

He returned to Camp Supply trailing clouds of glory. He reported only one trooper dead, fourteen wounded and nineteen missing. By comparison, he claimed 103 Indians killed (a number that included an uncounted number of women and children). His reputation, in eclipse since Appomattox, was now again on the rise, and it would continue to rise for the rest of the century, even after the fateful day in the Valley of Greasy Grass eight years in the future.

In fact, much of the Battle of the Washita seems like a rehearsal for the Little Bighorn: the surprise attack, the dangerous division of forces, the uncoordinated assault, the failure to reconnoiter the size of the enemy's forces, the vainglorious frontal charge—even the odd little details like the playing of the "Garry Owen" and the presence of Custer's nemesis, Captain Benteen.

On the Washita, Custer had won, defeating the Cheyenne and Black Kettle. But in the process he had learned all the wrong lessons; he had been validated in his command errors. At the Last Stand, against Sitting Bull, Crazy Horse and the Lakota Sioux, those wrong lessons would catch up with him.

But for now there was fame—and scandal. If Custer was cheered by Kansans, he and Sheridan were censored by progressive voices in the East as "savages." Sheridan replied that "the victory was complete, and the punishment just." Custer answered his critics by setting off again on a march—this time with Sheridan (in an observer role), the Seventh Calvary, and all 1,900 men of the Nineteenth Kansas Militia.

The first destination of this march was the Washita battleground. They arrived on December 10th to find the frozen and mutilated bodies of their lost command. Sheridan, who had seen what canister could do to human flesh, nevertheless described the sight as "animalistic behavior of devilish savages." Young Homer Adkins no doubt saw the bodies too; including those of Clara Blum and her two year-old son Willie, captured by the Cheyenne two months before. In their retreat, the Indians had shot Mrs. Blum in the head and smashed the little boy's skull.

With the exception of Mr. White, these may have been the first murder victims that Adkins and his neighbors in the Militia had ever seen. They would have been grisly and unforgettable sights—and no doubt raised in the minds of the Lake Sibley boys horrible thoughts about the fate of Sarah White.

The presence of the murdered mother and child enraged the troops, especially Sheridan, even more than their dead comrades. They angrily vowed vengeance. Three Indian trails left the battlefield; Custer chose the one heading east, towards Fort Cobb. It took them five miserable days in a snowstorm across rough country to reach the Fort.

All evidence pointed towards the Cheyenne; but one of the women captured at Washita—Black Kettle's sister Mah-wis-sa—convinced Sheridan that it was the Kiowa who had committed the deed. Sheridan bought the lie and ordered Custer and his troops to pursue and engage the Kiowa chiefs Lone Wolf and Santana.

But the Kiowa were already waiting, and sent forward a call for parley.

Custer, two senior officers, several interpreters, fifty Indian scouts and a newspaper reporter rode forward into a valley to meet the Kiowa. All but the reporter were armed and wary.

The parley was tense. The Kiowa had reason to be nervous—they had planned an ambush. As Santana, the mighty Kiowa chief, spoke to Custer about peace, his braves were preparing to massacre Custer's party and quickly break camp. But, just as the signal was about to be given, Sheridan suddenly appeared with the main column. The Kiowa chiefs surrendered . . . and when the rest of the village tarried coming into the fort, Sheridan hurried them along by threatening to hang their leaders.

With these victories behind him, and various tribes now turning themselves in all over Kansas, Sheridan was able to declare, on New Year's Day 1869, that he "considered the campaign ended."

But Custer wasn't done. The first weeks of 1869, in the thick of winter, found him marching around the state, with a small company of picked men, hunting down tribal parties and ordering them into the government forts. He established a new fort, a base for the 7th's and 19th's operations, and called it Fort Sill after a West Point friend lost in the Civil War. In late January, with his handpicked team, he rode four hundred miles in two weeks, living on his extra horses and parched corn when they ran out of food.

He returned to Fort Sill to find his men and the Kansans—Homer Adkins among them—dispirited and starving, living on quarter rations.

But that still didn't stop Custer—especially after Sheridan offered to push his promotion in Washington—and by March 2nd he and his command were back in the field again. Now the march, heading into the Texas Panhandle, slogged through rain and mud. Because the Cheyenne had scattered at the Army's approach, sometimes Custer was reduced to following a single track.

But on March 13th, they found them: 260 Cheyenne lodges on Sweetwater Creek. With one lieutenant and several scouts, Custer rode into the camp and to the tent of Chief Medicine Arrows.

CAPTIVE

Despite the despair of the Kansans, Sarah White was in fact still alive—and had spent the last six months as a captive of Medicine Arrows' tribe.

On the day she was taken at Lake Sibley, Sarah was carried by horse five miles across Buffalo Creek, where she was met by fifteen Cheyenne warriors. Then as the braves raced off to what, unknown to her, would be the murder of her father, Sarah was left on a hillside with two guards. She expected death or rape at any moment. She assumed her mother and sisters were either dead or wounded, but took consolation in the mistaken belief that her father and brothers were safe.

But she was left unassaulted, and after several days ride they reached the headwaters of the Republican River and Sarah saw the Cheyenne camp, her new home, for the first time.

Though some accounts put her age, probably for propaganda purposes, at just twelve, she was in fact about sixteen, though apparently young enough looking that she caught the attentions more of the maternal squaws than of the young braves. The women caressed her and called her poor child and set about instructing her on the ways of the tribe.

The same could not be said for Anna Morgan, another captive, brought into the camp three weeks later. Mrs. Morgan, in her early twenties, was the victim of a raid on Ottawa County, just south of Cloud. She had been married just four weeks, and she had seen her new husband, James, apparently murdered by the attackers.

If Sarah was docile, Anna was brash. Their first meeting captured the personalities of the two: Sarah, overcome with emotion and speechless, burst into tears; Anna merely announced, "Sister, how do you like this life?" and gave the girl a hug.

Their treatment by the Cheyenne was equally different. Where Sarah was given a dress taken on a raid to wear, Anna was ordered to wear native dress. And where Sarah helped the women with the chores, the Cheyenne squaws planned a different role for Anna. Ordered to help drive ponies by one of the women, Anna refused, and was struck to the ground. She immediately jumped to her feet, chased the woman down and beat the hell out of her—all to the cheers of the other squaws and even the braves.

In the months that followed, the two women were traded from one chief to another. They tried once to escape, only to be captured two days later.

Six months had passed by the time Custer rode into the Cheyenne camp and was escorted into Medicine Arrows' teepee. There, with the tribal leaders, Custer smoked the ceremonial clay peace pipe. He knew the Cheyenne were tired from a hard winter. When the negotiations lagged, Custer decided to continue it the next day. The Indians told him of a good place nearby to camp. As he left, a tribal holy man tamped the ashes from the pipe on Custer's boots, warning him that if he were treacherous, he and all of his men would die.

Custer returned to his column, waiting about a mile away, to find an angry, murderous mob. In the words of historian Jeffrey D. Wert:

> "For months, the Kansans had been away from home, enduring miserable rations and worse weather, searching for these Indians, whom they believed had killed, raped and burned in Kansas. At last, the murderers had been found, and the volunteers wanted vengeance. 'It looked, at one time, like they could not be restrained,' recalled a Kansan about his comrades. 'The line officers argued, begged and cursed. The accidental discharge of a carbine, or the shout of a reckless soldier, would have precipitated a killing that could not have been stopped.' But Custer sent [Lt.] Cooke with orders against firing. He had learned that the Indians held two captive white women. To a Kansan, however, Custer was 'a coward and traitor to our regiment.'"

The negotiations took three days. Finally, after the Indians tried to sneak off, Custer arrested three chiefs and, ordering ropes thrown over a nearby branch, threatened to hang them unless the two women were released immediately. The Cheyenne chiefs finally relented. The women were turned over—though the chiefs were retained as hostages (and would die months later in a riot in the Army stockade).

Stepping up to meet Anna Morgan was her brother-in-law, Daniel Brewster. He'd been hired by Custer as a scout to help search for her. At first he didn't recognize the woman, so changed was her appearance, but he quickly regained himself and delivered to Anna remarkable news: her husband had survived his wounds and was waiting for her on the Ottawa farm.

For Sarah White the news, delivered by the Lake Sibley boys, was both happy and tragic: her father's death, her mother's and sisters' survival. She was taken to Junction City and, once there, her militiamen neighbors chartered a carriage to take her home.

Three months after returning home to Ottawa, Anna Morgan gave birth to a half-Indian boy. The child lived only three months. Despite the child's beginnings, Mrs. Morgan appears to have loved the boy and deeply mourned his death. She and James Morgan would have several more children, but, despite her strong character, Anna seems to have never fully recovered from the trauma of her captivity. In the words of the official history, she became "dissatisfied, morose and unhappy." After a few years, she left her husband and children. Thereafter, she slowly lost her mind, and eventually was committed to an insane asylum. She died in 1902, at age 52. She had found the fate worse than death.

By comparison, Sarah White apparently emerged from her captivity unscathed. In time, she married and raised a healthy family in Cloud County. She also taught school, and likely counted among her pupils the youngest Adkins children.

As for her mother, Mrs. White lived well into old age. She stayed on the farm, running it with her two younger sons. Interviewed at the turn of the 20th century, she would say that when "she hears people complaining of hardships and hard times, she often thinks their knowledge along these lines is very limited."

EZRA

After the encounter with Medicine Arrows, Custer would announce to the press "the end of the Indian War." He and wife Libby would go on to enjoy one of the happiest summers of their lives, a hiatus on the way to the Little Big Horn. Meanwhile, the summer of 1869 would in fact prove to be one of the least murderous for Kansas in several years.

But that was not so in Cloud County. If the major tribal encampments had been dispersed, destroyed or forced to surrender, the smaller raiding parties were still on the loose. The 19th Militia, its men beat but happy, enjoyed a welcome homecoming in late June. The militiamen, mustered out, returned to their farms—except for a few on sentry duty—to get in some late planting and await their official discharge on June 15th.

Among the returning heroes was Homer Adkins. One can imagine him, emaciated and sunburned, sitting at the kitchen table, eating his favorite meal, telling his mother and father, but most of all his baby brother Ezra, now an excited twelve year-old, all about the march to Washita, the suffering at Fort Sill, and the rescue of Sarah White. He would have told them about how Indians lived, and of their ruthlessness, and of the legendary generals, Sheridan and Custer, he'd seen. The family would have swelled with pride at the young hero in the family. Homer Adkins Sr. would have looked at his son in a new way. And the children would have held their big brother in awe.

But there would have been little time for celebration. Farm life was hard life and soon the family would have been back to work.

As a dream during the long cold marches, the thought of standing behind a plow under a sweltering sun may have been appealing. But in reality it must have been a disappointment. Another young man might have made the best of the situation, parlaying his military experiences into something larger in his personality and his career. But in learning about the life of Homer Adkins Jr., though admittedly most of the material comes from his middle age, one gets the sense that he was a taciturn—even sour—and humorless man. Was he already that way at 21? Probably: a man's personality is usually fixed by that age. And even in his mother's sad letter, young Homer's presence is like a shadow compared to that of his brothers and sisters. Had the misery and gore of the previous months darkened his view of the world? No doubt; and what was about to happen could only have made things worse.

From Hannah Adkins's letter:

Jasper [the Adkins' son-in-law, married to Hannah A.] *got a horse of Mr. Himes the second day of June and came to see how we were getting along; about half-past four he said he guessed he would start home. I was then making up the last of the flour so I proposed to Jasper to let Ezra take his horse and go to Mr. Nelson's and borrow some flour. He spoke of taking a spur, but Jasper said that he did not need any as he was going on a strange horse.*

Why send twelve year old Ezra? After all, these were dangerous times. Indian raids were still taking place throughout the region. Soldiers were patrolling a few miles away. One answer is that ever-present dangers are often forgotten in everyday life. The raid on the White farm was now almost a year past. The home guards had just passed through an hour before and assured everyone that the area was safe, never seeing the Indians hiding nearby in the high grass,

Besides, young Ezra, thrilled at the prospect of riding a spirited new horse, no doubt pleaded with his mother to go.

Why not send the older and wiser Homer Jr.? It is only well into the letter, as if suddenly realizing that her oldest daughter will want an explanation too, that Mrs. Adkins abruptly writes: *Homer was sick in bed all that day and the night before.*

How sick was he? That, of course, is impossible to know. We do know that his sister, Anne, was also ill, in her case with scarlet fever. Whether Homer was seriously ill, worn out from the preceding months or just suffering from a case of discharge blues, Mrs. Adkins obviously deemed him incapable of travel and handed the task to her next oldest son. Giving Ezra such responsibility was apparently something new.

Aschel, Paul and I went to see him cross the river. Before he crossed the river I saw four objects northwest on Mr. Nelson's. I told [Ezra] *I thought it was the cows. I told him to leave the sack at Mr. Nelson's for them to fill while he went and started up the cows, and when he got them started to get the flour and drive the cows home.*

Ezra, thrilled to be invested with such responsibility, did as he was told.

He went to Mr. Nelson's as directed and then on after the cows among the sand hills . . .

Nels Nelson Jr., who would describe the scene thirty years later, was out with his teenaged brothers James and Christian breaking and plowing the prairie, when Ezra rode by. Asked where he was going, Ezra replied that he'd dropped off a bag at their parents' house and now was rounding up the cattle and driving them across the river before he went back to pick up the flour.

. . . I suppose that he was not aware of any danger until he was surrounded by some forty or sixty Indians, mostly on horseback.

The Cheyenne braves were watching from the other side of the river when they saw the boy riding towards them. According to Nels Nelson's account, the Indians came swooping down between Ezra and the Nelson boys. Says the 1903 official history, "There were about twenty of the yelping, howling savages mounted and about ten or a dozen more hanging on to the tails of the ponies." It adds, in a bitter editorial aside, "They were all armed with guns and weapons of warfare they had received from the government, seemingly to aid the blood-thirsty Cheyenne in their fatal attacks on the settlers."

Seeing the Indians bearing down upon him, a terrified young Ezra Adkins, spurless and on a strange horse, wheeled and kicked it into a gallop. The Nelson boys scattered for cover. And, a quarter mile away, their father, Danish immigrant Nels Nelson Sr., looked on in horror.

The Indians chased him a half mile on horseback, then Ezra jumped from his horse and ran a quarter-mile. Based upon shell casings found later, during this pursuit the Cheyenne probably shot at Ezra at least four times.

Says the history: " As they came across the country shooting and making the hills back from the beautiful valley resound with their fierce war whoops, the terror-stricken boy dismounted from his horse thinking his chances would be better for gaining the tall grass and bushes along the river where he might elude them by hiding."

He didn't make it. As the lead brave on horseback caught up with the horse and grabbed its reins, a second brave, who had been hanging on to the Indian horse's tail, raced ahead and ran down the boy. He caught Ezra by the wrist, gripping it so hard that it later turned black.

As the Indian dragged him along, Ezra struggled with all of his strength to pull free. Hiding in a nearby sand knoll, Nels Nelson watched, powerless to help his young neighbor. As he looked on, the rest of the Indians rode up. One of them, apparently the leader, ordered the boy released. The instant Ezra was unhanded; the leader raised a revolver and fired twice.

Conditioned by movies and Remington paintings, we think of Indians with rifles, not revolvers. But the bullets were the same—large caliber, slow-moving slugs—and the effect equally devastating. From Hannah's letter:

An Indian rode up on horseback within two yards of Ezra's face and shot him in the face with a revolver; one shot followed the other as quick as possible. Mr. Nelson said he dropped backwards dead at the first shot. One shot pierced his left eye and came out at the back of his head, the other bullet passed in two inches and a half above that, tearing open the skull so that there was room enough to lay in a man's thumb. Oh, it was a fearful looking wound. The imagery, written by a woman described by others as "frenzied with grief, refusing to be comforted for many months" is astonishing.

From his distant vantage point, Mr. Nelson watched the Indians gather and kneel around the prostrate figure. He assumed they were scalping the boy; but in fact they were tearing off and stealing Ezra's clothes. *The Indians robbed him of his little black coat and cap you made for him. His shirt and pants were ragged, I suppose was the reason he was not entirely stripped, and he was barefooted.*

Watching this monstrousness, Rev. Nelson froze. But now the danger of the situation asserted itself. He quickly gathered up his family and retreated into the house. While one group of braves murdered and stripped Ezra, the rest took off towards a nearby plowed field, where John Nelson, 17, his brother already escaped behind the sand knoll, was trying to unhitch and save his team of a horse and two mules. The Indians quickly caught up with the team and, as John backed away, set about cutting the animals from the plow. One brave turned his horse and headed towards John, lance at the ready to impale him.

Then, incredibly, John pulled out a gun and aimed it at the Indian. Stunned, the brave reared the horse, turned it and, as it galloped off, slung himself over the far side of the pony for cover. Thanks to the pistol, in the words of the official history, "the young man made his escape to live and become a prominent farmer and stock man of Republic County and the father of Dr. Nelson of Concordia."

The raiding party, equipped with Ezra's horse and the Nelson team, now regrouped and held a brief council. While they were doing so, Nels Jr. bolted from the sand bar to the house and convinced his father that the family—his aged father, his two newly arrived two younger brothers, his wife and their baby—had to escape, quickly. Nels then grabbed the family rifle and returned to the sand bar, from which he could watch the Indians' movements and offer covering fire if needed.

While the Indian's attention was taken with killing Ezra and capturing his horse and Mr. Nelson's team, Mr. Nelson's family were making good their escape, keeping the sandhills between themselves and the Indians, till they came to the woods. They then came under the cover of the woods until they got opposite our house, then waded across. The boys came first, then Nels' wife and baby, struggling through the waist-deep water, and finally Nels and his enfeebled father.

They were met by an anxious Hannah Adkins, who begged for any news about her boy. When they told her what had happened, she nearly collapsed in grief.

As the two families watched, the raiding party wheeled and rode to the Nelson farmhouse. There, apparently believing people were still inside, the Cheyenne braves dismounted at a good distance, crawled through the grass to within striking distance, then opened fire into the windows. *Then from our house, [the Nelsons] could watch the Indians rob them of all their worldly goods (Oh I had so much rather that they had taken our all in this world, than the life of our faithful boy. He died in the faithful discharge of his duty.)*

Says the official history: ". . . finding the inmates had vacated, the marauders entered and stripped the home of its contents, taking what they could, including a line full of clothes that had just been laundered by Mrs. Nelson, and destroyed what they did not want. A feather bed was carried to a nearby hill, where it was ripped open and emptied of its contents. [They] carried the ticking away, while the feathers were left to swirl in the air." They took all of the food provisions from the house, except for a side of bacon, which, for some unknown reason, they merely speared a few times.

The Indians stayed at their house an hour and a half or two hours and then went off at their leisure with none to molest or make them afraid.

Now the devastated, diminished Adkins family faced two terrible tasks: bury poor little Ezra, and tell their father the news. In the worst imaginable irony, while his son was being murdered, Homer Adkins Sr. was in Junction City on behalf of the neighboring farmers trying to convince the local authorities to send more militia to protect them from Indian raids.

HELP US WHAT THEY COULD

Now it was time to retrieve the body of Ezra Adkins. Nels Nelson Jr. and the Adkins son-in-law Jasper Scribner waited until darkness fell, and then set out across the river. Homer, the Indian fighter, did not go. Instead, accompanying them was a big Newfoundland dog, probably Scribner's, a playmate of the murdered boy. Says the official history, "The canine readily found the remains of his little master." The dog sniffing and whining, the two men carried the body home, navigating by a fire built for them next to the Adkins's house.

Hannah: *I was in hopes Mr. Nelson was mistaken about his being killed, but alas it was too true. He was brought home a mangled corpse, bespattered with blood and brains.*

Ezra's body was likely placed on the dining table. It would have been a horrifying sight. Ezra probably never knew what hit him—the image of the pistol firing wouldn't have registered in his brain before the bullet did, having smashed through the same eye. The second shot hit him in the forehead, the heavy slug burrowing into his skull and splintering off a long patch of bone. Lying there on the grass for hours, his face was covered with dried blood and oozing brain tissue. Who can doubt that it was Ezra's mother who cleaned his face for the last time?

The horror was now settling in, not only in the Adkins house, but also throughout Lake Sibley. Hannah: *Mr. Dutton's family fled the settle-*

ment that night. Mr. Nelson went the next day. Men came from the settlement the next day with horses and wagons and armed men on horseback to take us below or help us what they could. The Adkins decided to stay.

As it happened, Rev. Nelson had hidden an envelope containing $200 in greenbacks in an extra pair of pants. The Cheyenne, while tearing the house apart, had taken the trousers, but in the excitement never noticed the envelope falling to the ground. Nels Jr. found the envelope in the debris—and the money enabled his father and the other two sons to quit the County and head for safe country. But Nels Jr. refused to leave. With his wife and child, he returned to the house, though it offered only four walls, and tried to survive as best they could while suffering "many sleepless nights and days of fear and uncertainty."

At the Adkins house the immediate task was to bury its lost child.

Hannah: *The grief of the family was terrible to behold and a scene never to be forgotten by the little group of settlers gathered there, where a few hours before the family had rejoiced in dreams of a future happy home."*

Only now does Homer Adkins re-enter the story. It fell to him and Jasper Scribner to build Ezra's coffin. It wasn't easy, as there was little lumber nearby. Finally, they managed to secure some rough boards from the mill and constructed a crude box.

Hannah: *They wanted to know where to build the grave. They thought that the funeral should be at three o'clock as the weather was warm. Some of them went back to dig the grave on Mr. Taylor's place six miles off and said they would come back . . . They said they did not consider it safe to bring any of their women folks on account of the Indians.*

At three o'clock they returned with two wagons and an escort of armed men on horseback to pay the last tribute to the dead.

Homer, Lucy, Aschel and myself were all of our family that could follow his remains to the last resting place. Homer was hardly able to go. Jasper stayed with Ann and Paul. [As she does not appear a year later in the census records, it is possible that this would prove to be Ann's last illness—yet another family loss.] *Paul was asleep when we started away.*

There were twenty-four I believe at the grave in all, including two women, Mrs. Lois and Mrs. Hull. When the grave was almost filled, I asked Mr. Berry if there could be a prayer made. He said there should be. But he looked over the crowd and said to me, "There is no one here who makes any

profession of religion but yourself." And I said, "We have lost so much con-
fidence and others have too, that it will be useless to try."

I then asked whether we might have a hymn. He thought that would
not be any more possible than the prayer. Poor man, he felt as badly as
myself.

This isn't John Ford, or even Willa Cather. These are shattered people who no longer believe in God because they have concluded that He
no longer believes in them. Looking down at Ezra's grave, and beside it
those of Mr. White, Miss Platt and Miss Taylor—all victims of Indian
attack—and that of *Mrs. Sander's little boy that was drowned and buried*
the day before Ezra was—it easy to understand why these forlorn people
now doubt the existence of a just and merciful God.

Among the two dozen men and women standing around Ezra
Adkins' grave, many have already begun packing to leave. Others,
including Homer Adkins, are making plans. Remarkably, heroically,
among those assembled only the mother of the murdered boy, Hannah
Adkins still believes in God and her little plot of earth.

I asked him then if he would please return our thanks to the friends for
their kindness and assistance in burying our Ezra, which he did. Then we
had to turn again to our sorrowful home.

But, oh Jane, I do believe he is with our Saviour, and all the redeemed
of the Lord praising and glorifying Him. That takes away the sting and
makes it easier to bear. We shall soon go to him, the time will soon roll
around, and he has got through a little sooner than the rest of us. I feel now
that I have two children in Heaven, happy feeling. But Oh, it is hard to part
with him, we miss him at every turn. Oh I pity your father, he misses him
so much. I can't see God's Providence in it yet, but the Lord knows what is
best . . .

HOMER

After the mourning came the guilt and blame.

Their arrival was delayed by another. Hannah Adkins doesn't end
the letter to her daughter with the statement of faith. She then adds, perhaps a day or two later, the fact that as many as forty soldiers, led by both

the Adjutant General and a Captain Wintzel, have made the Adkins home their temporary headquarters. A General Graham, and yet another captain soon joined them.

This must have been almost unbearable to a mother who was awaiting the return of her husband, had just buried one child, had three more sick in bed (she finished the letter after administering an emetic to Lucy, who had just come down with typhoid), and now another, Aeshel, refusing to eat in his grief.

But at least the presence of so many soldiers offered an unprecedented degree of security to the family. Benjamin Adkins finally arrived home the day after the funeral—though one can imagine, with such a crowd, that husband and wife had little private time together to share their grief. Two days later he left again, this time for the day to help scout a location west of the farm, near where Ezra was murdered, for the troopers to bivouac.

Now Hannah and her children were alone with their thoughts and their misery. As on all such occasions, they must have silently asked hard questions of themselves and others. For Benjamin Adkins there was the question he must have asked himself the rest of his life: What if I had been there? What if I hadn't deserted my family in their greatest crisis? He would have wished it had been him who had met the savages and not his little boy.

For a woman of Hannah Adkins intelligence and imagination, the ghosts would have been overwhelming—it's not surprising that the official history says she was inconsolable for many months. Was her boy's life worth the loaf of bread she wanted to bake? Why had she sent him out at a time when Indians were raiding in the area? And why hadn't she given him a gun—a pistol like the one that saved John Nelson? No doubt friends and family would tell her in the days and years to come that it wasn't her fault, that there was no indication of the horror that was coming, that the militia guard had declared the area safe . . . but it is hard to believe any of those words, though filled with truth, would have given much consolation.

And what of Homer? In the silences of his family and the looks of his neighbors, what was left unsaid? A strapping twenty-one year old, a veteran soldier who had spent the last year chasing Indians—was illness a sufficient excuse not to save, or at least avenge, his brother? Why wasn't he a hero like his neighbor Nels, or his brother-in-law Jasper?

For the first time, we begin to get a sense of the character of Homer Adkins. There is, as noted, the little aside in Hannah's letter about Homer's illness, as if she feels the need to justify his actions. Homer is also too ill to go search for his brother's body, but not too weak to help build the casket. And finally, there is the fact that, despite still being officially on active duty for two weeks after Ezra's death, Homer chooses not to join the soldiers quartered at his own house. He doesn't put on the uniform one more time, or even just ride along as a volunteer scout (as Mrs. Morgan's brother-in-law had) to help kill the men who murdered his own flesh and blood.

It would be an easy mistake, especially in light of later events, to read too much into the subtle clues given during this period. Nevertheless, one can't help but sense a strangeness, even coldness, about this young man. Where did it come from? His mother appears a woman of high intelligence and warmth, his father a man of deep responsibility. Was Homer just one of those contrary and dark personalities that randomly appear in even the warmest families? Or did something happen to him when he saw those corpses at Washita, or while he was trapped and starving during the miserable winter at Fort Sill?

Even for a bright, outgoing personality, it wouldn't have been easy to live at Lake Sibley after that. For Homer it must have been a special kind of hell. His mother lost to grief, his sister dying, every ride around the farm a reminder that it should have been him and not his brother, each encounter with Nelson and Scribner a reminder of his own weakness, the knowing looks of the men and women he met at the mill. And just a week before he'd been a hero. . .

In the face of this, Homer Adkins might have made a clean break and started over somewhere else. Or, conversely, he might have redoubled his efforts to prove his worth. Homer might have joined the other pioneers heading west or, on the same path as George Custer, north to the Dakota gold fields. Or, he might have re-enlisted with the Kansas Militia and gone to wreak a personal revenge on the Indians.

Instead, just two days after his mother penned the dreadful letter to his sister, Homer Adkins left the service. The Census, taken a year later, found him at age 22 still living on the farm at Lake Sibley; his parents having carved off some acreage to let him earn his own living. Homer was still there three years later.

What kept Homer in Lake Sibley, given all of the reasons for him to leave? Probably not duty to his parents: his younger brothers and sisters were old enough to help with the farm. Certainly not opportunity—not with a corner piece of farmland and a damaged reputation.

The only clue to what kept Homer Adkins in Kansas can be found in an affidavit by his sister Lucy, five years his junior. It was filed in November 1927 in support of Emeline Woodley's application for a military widow's pension. By then, Lucy Pollett, as she was known, was a 75 year old widow and self-described "inmate" of the Union Soldiers Home in Oklahoma City. She had already outlived her brother by 35 years.

According to her affidavit, in 1873 Homer married a woman named Martha L. Wright. As her name does not appear in the 1870 census, it is likely that she was a newcomer to town who, within a brief period of time, met, then married Homer Adkins.

Was she a farmer's teenaged daughter, thrilled by the attentions of this brooding older man? Or an eldest daughter, fearing spinsterhood, who saw an opportunity in a hard-working young farmer? Or perhaps a rare young woman on her own—a schoolteacher perhaps—who saw something special in the most eligible local boy? Was it love, or pragmatism, or both?

There is no way to know. The only apparent record of Miss Wright appears in her sister-in-law's affidavit a half-century later. And that document adds only one other devastating bit of information: "...of her own personal knowledge that said Martha L. Wright died in the year 1874."

Men and women died from any number of causes in 19th century America, including disease, crime, epidemic, fire, and the accidents of everyday life. But most young women died on the Prairie (and in Eastern cities and Western towns) in their first year of marriage from only one cause: childbirth. So many things can go wrong giving birth, and most of the ways to deal with them wouldn't be available for another century. If that was indeed the cause, Martha and the baby probably died in Ben's and Hannah's farmhouse, perhaps on their bed. Their bodies may have been laid out on the same table as young Ezra had six years before—adding a devastating resonance to the tableau for all in attendance. Then mother and nameless child would have been buried— near Ezra? In her own parents' plot?— and then would have fallen out of history but for the far distant financial need of her replacement as Mrs. Homer Adkins.

If there had been any reason before for Homer to stay in Lake Sibley, it was now buried in the earth. Within months, perhaps days, like a man running from a nightmare, he packed up and headed for the furthest inhabited place he could reach by horse and still remain a citizen: the Pacific Northwest.

WESTWARD

One of the interesting features of the westward expansion of the United States is that it didn't occur like a tide of humanity sweeping across the continent, inhabiting each degree of longitude in turn. Rather, the pioneers treated the mid-West largely as air travelers do today, as "fly-over" states. In the case of the gold miners and farmers and cattle ranchers heading for Washington, Oregon and California, the mid-West could be more accurately described as "roll, ride and walk-over" territory. The men and women in the wagon trains, and later on the transcontinental railroads, only asked from the Great Plains that it didn't kill them in some particularly awful way.

Robert Louis Stevenson, passing through on his ardent pursuit of Fanny Osbourne, would pen some of the most famous lines about the prairie (*"We were at sea—there is no other adequate expression—on the plains . . . a world almost without feature; an empty sky, an empty earth . . . the green plain ran till it touched the skirts of heaven . . ."*). But, awestruck as he was, even he didn't linger for long, racing off instead for Monterey and Northern California.

By the time Homer Adkins left Kansas, American settlers had been moving, in large numbers, to the Pacific Coast for nearly thirty years, a Diaspora only briefly halted by the Civil War. Despite the hardships of passage along the Santa Fe, California and Oregon trails, their numbers had been far greater than those taking the much shorter path to, say, Kansas or Nebraska. For example, the Murphy-Townsend Party, founders of what is now Silicon Valley, came over in 1846. They sold the land (in whose farmhouse I write this book), to William Wright, a Baltimore shop clerk who had made good in the gold fields, in 1851.

This helps explain some of the weird historical and geographic juxtapositions that occur in the United States in the second half of the 19th century. Thus, San Francisco, Seattle and even Denver were great cities with their own opera houses and cathedrals, while Cloud County was still trying to build a flour mill. Colis P. Huntington built a mansion atop San Francisco's Nob Hill even as Dwight Eisenhower is being born in a Kansas sod house. And General Custer, leading the 7th Calvary, was annihilated by Neolithic Sioux warriors on a barren hilltop while a few hundred miles away in St. Louis the Democratic National Convention was waiting to nominate him President of the United States.

So, Homer Adkins, in abandoning Kansas and heading out West to Oregon, was in fact not getting away from it all, but moving uptown to a more civilized setting. And because of that, in particular because Oregon had a much more developed newspaper industry than Kansas at this point in history, we also have a much better record of what came next.

DARK APPARITION

Homer Adkins, now a widower and leaving behind in Kansas a life composed largely of failure and death, arrived in Oregon probably in autumn 1874 or spring 1875.

The trail led him to Sheridan, where, if the family legend is true, he found work as the new hired hand for the Widow Hasbrook and her three young children.

What Homer Adkins would have found was a farm in disarray and in dire need, depending on the time of year, of immediate planting or harvesting; a young widow desperate for a strong male presence to run the place . . . and probably no shortage of whispers in town about what had really happened on the farm two years before.

The little family was definitely in need of rescue. Years later, Charlie would recall to his sons how bears took to invading the undefended farm looking for food—forcing little Charlie to hang any freshly killed meat out of their reach high in a tree near the house.

Homer Adkins—dark, angry and suspicious—might not have been the best job candidate around. So he may have found the Widow Hasbrook to be his best opportunity in the region. The same may have been true in the other direction.

What did Charlie, now six, think when he first saw the dark figure coming up the road? He must have been curious. But was that curiosity mixed with foreboding? Did he see danger in the man's face? Or was he just curious, wondering if this man, unlike all the others in recent months, would be the one who would stay? And if he did stay, would he be like the first hired hand?

Homer Adkins did stay—and before long, there would be for Charlie a different kind of strangeness in the house. Did Homer begin staying in the house longer after dinner each night? Did he begin to sit in Charlie's father's chair? And did Charlie ever hear odd sounds emanating late at night from his mother's room?

Certainly there would have come that moment, found in every such relationship, when his mother made a gesture towards this new man that told Charlie that something fundamentally had changed. Perhaps it was an unexpectedly intimate conversation between his mother and Homer, or maybe even just a look. Or perhaps Homer had casually touched his mother in the way only a mate does. Or maybe it was more blatant: perhaps one night Homer just took his place at the head of the table for dinner—and Charlie's mom said nothing.

Then would have come the Announcement. There were many things parents never discussed with their children in the 19th century, but this wasn't one of them. Did Emeline have the courage to quietly sit down with little Charlie and tell him the news? Her age and character suggest not. More likely it was simply presented to the boy by Emeline, with Homer standing behind her, as a fait accompli: "Charlie, Mr. Adkins and I are going to be married soon. He will be your new father now."

I like to think that at some point Emeline would have told her son about her loneliness, and about the desperate need for a man to run the farm. But frankly, I doubt that conversation ever took place. Charlie would just have to deal with it.

The couple was married on March 12th, 1876. Emeline had been widowed for just over three years, Homer was a widower of 17 months.

Emeline had gained a defender; Homer had gained a family and a farm. The wedding, such as it was, was likely conducted in the farmhouse. We know the Justice of the Peace was named Thomas Blair. Eight year-old Charlie, six year-old Ben and two-year-old toddler Dora would have been in attendance.

There would have been no honeymoon. Rather it would have been back to the farm that night—the only change, if it hadn't already occurred, being Homer's move into Emeline's bed. In the morning, Homer, Emeline and Charlie would have arisen to their chores, just like every other day on the farm.

Did the children feel the change? Ben and Dora, having no real memory of their real father, would probably have found the new situation disconcerting. But it is also easy to imagine Charlie feeling great relief at a void at last being filled. He had a complete family again. Once more he would call a man "father."

That relationship would be formalized two years later when Homer Adkins filed for legal custodianship of the three children in Tillamook County, and again two years after that with a similar filing in Polk County.

CENTENNIAL

Eighteen seventy-six, the Centennial year, was a time of great change not just for the fledgling Hasbrook-Adkins family, but for all of America. The Republican Grant administration, with its secretly dying President-war hero, was ending eight years marked by both the opulence of the Gilded Age and incompetence, scandal and corruption in high places.

In the South, Reconstruction, with its occupying Army, was creating great bitterness—an attitude deftly exploited by a resurgent Democratic party. The result, in November, would be the most disputed presidential election in American history. The Ku Klux Klan was on the rise, and early attempts at economic independence by ex-slaves were systematically crushed.

In the mid-West, settlers and prospectors rushing to the Black Hills of South Dakota incensed the local Lakota Sioux and Cheyenne tribes—which responded by unifying under the charismatic religious chief

Sitting Bull and warrior leaders Crazy Horse and Gall. Their increasing belligerence began to inflame other tribes throughout the states and territories of the Great Plains—and prompted the uncompromising old generals William T. Sherman and Phil Sheridan of the War Dept. to order the overburdened and undermanned U.S. Calvary into the field. As winter 1876 turned to spring, the region braced for conflict.

In the Northeast, these events were a sideshow to the accelerating pace of change. Teeming with ambitious new immigrants and entrepreneurs made rich by the war, its factories employing the latest tools, processes and organizations of the Second Industrial Age, the great cities were impatient to enter the new epoch . . . and weren't going let any savages or unrepentant Secessionists slow them down. The North would celebrate its success with a world's fair that summer, the Philadelphia Centennial Exposition, which, in retrospect would herald the arrival of the modern world. There, visitors (including a young Henry Ford) would see the first fruits of mass production, the telephone, the beginnings of professional baseball, and, thanks to a protest at the opening ceremony by Elizabeth Cady Stanton, the birth of the Women's Movement.

Only in the Far West was the year less than earthshaking. There, after a quarter-century of extraordinary change, the pioneers and their progeny seemed to pause and catch their breath.

So it might have been on the Hasbrook-Adkins farm in Polk County, Oregon. The three children would have time to get to know their new father, to put the terrible three previous years to rest, and re-learn how to be a family. After all, Homer Adkins brought much to the family. He didn't have much money, but he knew how to farm. And the family, after being so vulnerable so long, must have felt secure at last with a veteran soldier watching over them.

I can imagine Homer sitting in Ben's old chair after dinner that Spring, after a hard day of planting, winning his way into little Charlie's heart by telling him stories about Indians and the U.S. Calvary. Did he tell Charlie about his brother's violent death, or was that deemed too shocking after the boy's own experiences with murder? Surely he told Charlie about riding with the great General Custer, chasing Comanche across Kansas, of the deprivations that winter at Fort Sill, and the glorious rescue of Miss Sarah White.

On July 4th, the great Centennial of the Republic, Homer would have built a bonfire and the three children would have danced around it. And then, in the days that followed, as the first reports came out of the Little Bighorn valley, Homer would have read in shock about the death of his old commander. Perhaps he would have gone into town to get the Oregonian early, even waiting to hear the early reports as they were read off the telegraph.

Taciturn Homer would have been a celebrity in Sheridan and its environs, the local man who had once fought shoulder to shoulder with the martyred American hero. As the local children and their mothers listened intently, the men would have asked Homer to recount again and again his exploits with the 7th Calvary. And perhaps, when more sensitive ears were gone, he would have told the men about Ezra, as the listeners spit and muttered oaths against 'those bloodthirsty savages.'

All might have turned out well, if there had only been enough time. But there wasn't. By Independence Day, Emeline was already again pregnant. The baby girl, Martha, was born in early 1877. A second daughter, Mildred arrived in January 1879.

Now the family dynamic would change. Now there would be Ben's kids and Homer's kids, and Ben would not be there to defend his own. Dora, the youngest of the first generation, and the odd child out, would fit best with the new brood. In the years to come, and as the girls drifted away from their mother, Dora would increasingly serve as their surrogate mother. Of the Hasbrook kids, only she would enter adulthood as a member of the Adkins family. For the boys—Charlie, small and quick witted, and Ben, big and gentle—the brief and happy respite was already over.

In 1880, for reasons that remain unexplained, Homer Adkins, suddenly sold the farm, packed up the family and moved back to Kansas. One possibility is that his parents, now in their fifties, asked him to come home and take over some, or all, of the 1,500 acre family farm. But then, Homer already had his own working farm in Oregon.

Another possibility is that the Oregon farm was failing and Homer decided to cut his losses and head for home. But the Oregon economy during this period was strong, and unless Homer was an incompetent farmer—and there is no evidence of that at any time in his career—it seems unlikely that the Sheridan farm was anything but a moderate success.

A third possible reason is that Homer would have been receiving letters from his eloquent mother telling him that, now that the Indian problem had been resolved, Kansas was undergoing a boom of historic proportions. Homer might have decided that, knowing the country well, a return to Kansas offered him the best shot at striking it rich.

The fourth and last possibility is a darker one. It is that, after four years, the unsociable Homer Adkins had at last made enough acquaintances in Oregon that he finally heard the rumors about his wife. Or conversely, it may have been Emeline, anxious to put half a continent between herself and her past, who actively reinforced Homer's homesickness.

But life, not least the relations between husband and wife, is never simple. So, ultimately, perhaps the reason for the move was a combination of some or all of these possibilities. Kansas may have been merely the easiest choice for two unsociable people short on imagination and fearful of ever again taking a risk.

Two things are for certain. First, the Adkins family, by heading east, was going against the current of the society around them. And second, Emeline Adkins was pregnant during the journey, delivering daughter Pearl (sometimes listed as Pearle) that September. Avery, the couple's first son, would arrive three years later—making him fifteen years younger than Charlie.

SCHISM

The Kansas that Homer Adkins returned to with his growing family was stunningly different from the one he'd left less than a decade before. That earlier Kansas was a place of growing lawlessness. The era of Indian raids had peaked in the year Ezra Adkins was murdered, but continued intermittently throughout the 1870s, ending finally in 1878. The most tragic of these encounters occurred during that final year when a band of Northern Cheyenne, starving on a reservation in Oklahoma, broke out and made a run for their homelands in Yellowstone. Their pursuit ended in a bloody shootout at Beaver Creek.

Meanwhile, thanks to the Chisholm Trail, Kansas had become the main highway for Texas cattle—several million during the decade—in one of the most mythical epochs in American history. The cows brought the cowboys, and they in turn brought near chaos to wide-open cities along the trail like Wichita and Abilene. [At the latter, my paternal great-grandfather, the man who would send a reporter to interview Emeline fifty years hence, was preparing to apprentice as a newspaperman.] Lawmen, like Wild Bill Hickok, Wyatt Earp and Bat Masterson (elected county sheriff at just 22), were brought in to help quell the growing violence. Often criminals themselves, these violent men were of only marginal effectiveness. Meanwhile a whole new generation of thugs, like the Doolins and Daltons in Coffeyville, was just coming of age and would bedevil the state throughout the 1890s.

Despite all of this, emigration to Kansas continued to pick up speed throughout the decade. Easily the most famous of these pioneers were the Ingalls, the family of the "Little House on the Prairie"; but there were tens of thousands of others: Ohio farmers, laying over in Topeka before heading out onto the high prairie; Italian miners heading for the coal fields in the southeast corner of the state; Mennonites arriving from Russia carrying red wheat seed; and, enjoying an 1876 state law removing all color barriers, ex-slaves arriving from the Old South.

That most bucolic of American anthems, "Home on the Range", was written in 1872 by Kansan Dr. Brewster M. Higley, M.D. But the world it described was already slipping away. By 1878, the last of the buffalo were gone, and though the deer would remain, most of the antelope would soon disappear as well. In 1874, a locust plague ("pestiferous insects" writes the official history) hit the state—and one can assume it led to a few discouraging words from the locals. So did the tornado that hit Cloud County the year before, darkening those cloudless skies.

When Homer Adkins left Cloud County, Lake Sibley, with its population of several hundred, had been the dominant town in the region. By comparison, Concordia to the south, which had been voted the county seat in 1869, was something of a joke: at the time of the election there were literally no buildings within the city limits, and just two houses. It didn't help that in 1872 the fledgling town all-but burned to the ground.

Nevertheless, the fates of the two towns went in opposite directions

throughout the 1870s. Both were objects of land speculation, competing to attract the waves of new arrivals. Sibley Township would more
than double its population—to 758—just between 1876 and 1880. But
Concordia won the race: by the end of the decade, the population of the
city alone had passed 1,800 and was growing fast. Lake Sibley would
fade away, while Concordia would become a crucial entry point from the
Northern Plains into Kansas.

Thus it was that when the Adkins family finally arrived after their
long journey from Oregon, it made its address not at the farm, but in
Concordia. The city they encountered must have been undergoing phenomenal change. There exists a photograph of Concordia, taken along
Broadway in the mid-1870s, showing a wide, muddy road flanked by a
handful of humble, false fronted wooden buildings. By comparison, a
collection of photos taken fifteen years later presents a classic Main
Street of brick and stone buildings, with sidewalks and elaborate cor-
nices and bright awnings. Concordia seems to have leaped from the O.K
Corral to the Music Man in the course of a single decade.

In the grandiloquent phrasing of the official history:

> "The Concordia of 1882 was the largest and most flourish-
> ing town of the county, nearly at its center, on the south bank of
> the Republican River. The site is an admirable one, being suffi-
> ciently above the river to be free of the overflows and to afford a
> good system of drainage. From the more elevated portions a
> commanding view of the surrounding county can be obtained.
> The great river meandering down the valley, fringed here and
> there with groves and massive trees, and the far off bordering
> hills and bluffs that seem to be guarding the valley, during cer-
> tain portions of the year, compose a picture at once interesting
> and beautiful."

We have almost no record of the life of the Adkins family during the
ten years it spent in Concordia. Homer Adkins appears to have never
having written a letter, and he may in fact, having grown up on the frontier, been largely unlettered. On the other hand, his extraordinarily eloquent mother must have given him some schooling. With the exception
of her comments made to the *Oregonian* well into the next century, we

have only one letter written by Emeline, and it only covers events in Oregon. In later years, she seemed to treat her decade in Kansas as little more than a diversion from a lifetime spent in the Pacific Northwest.

So, we have to extrapolate from bits and pieces of information. First, we can assume that Homer again took up farming in Kansas, since that was his profession in every recorded part of his adult life. He may have bought land with the proceeds from the Oregon farm, or, more prudently, banked that money and worked all or part of his parents' farm (the Concordia address may have been just a convenience).

The three Hasbrook children would have attended school in Concordia, the town having built a large public school building. They might even have attended one of the town's many churches each Sunday. Concordia also boasted three newspapers, which may or may not have been read by the Adkins, though in all probability either Charlie or Ben worked as a paperboy. Homer would have taken his wheat to a new gristmill, the Concordia Mills, run by five French immigrants, on a new dam across the Republican River. And in autumn, the family would no doubt have attended the County Fair, located east of town. There, standing at the rail of the half-mile racetrack, teenaged Charlie Hasbrook might have first learned his love of horse racing.

He may also have first seen the love of his life. Mary Annis Ellis, four years his junior, had been born in Clay Center. When her mother died in 1884, Mary was sent to live with her adult cousins, the Browns, on a farm just outside of Concordia. As a quiet, heartbroken twelve year-old, she might well have looked on in wonder at the clever, compact and handsome sixteen year-old as he passed her in the schoolyard.

Now the track gets a little obscure, and record contradictory. According to the Hasbrook family history, Emeline and daughter Dora returned to Oregon just four years later. But according to Pearl Adkins, in an interview with her son Ben Wilkerson in 1945, the family stayed in Kansas for ten years, returning to Oregon in 1890. This latter story also is confirmed by later newspaper accounts.

Even accounting for the second-handedness of Charlie's account, and Pearl's age at the time of the interview (65), it is hard not to believe in the truthfulness of both stories. So, how do we reconcile them?

I think the answer is that Emeline and Homer separated in 1884.

The presence of poor Dora is the clue. The Hasbrook record says that Emeline and Dora went back to Oregon after just four years. There is no mention of Homer or the other children. Where did Emeline and Dora go? Probably home to the bosom of the Connor and Buell families, most likely to that harsh-faced Mother Connor whom subsequent generations have misjudged on looks alone.

Why did Emeline leave? That's easy: Because every time in her life she found herself unhappy, she looked for a way out. The last time had been Coxon. This time it was a run for home, taking along the thirteen year old daughter who could attend to her, and abandoning all the rest.

That's *how* she left. *Why* did she leave? That answer is easy too. Nothing in the story of Homer Adkins, from the time we first meet him at Lake Sibley until the very minute of his death, contradicts a single overwhelming impression of the man. It is that he was first-class son of a bitch. One of those petty tyrants; a mean little nobody, friendless, terrorizing his family and anyone else weaker than him, feuding with his neighbors, nursing grudges against unseen enemies, endlessly scheming to get ahead—and bitter that none of those schemes ever work out.

And what of Charlie? He was now sixteen years old, and his actions suggest that of a young man who understands his parents all too well—and is thoroughly sick of both of them. He makes a decision that will change all of their lives: Charlie refuses to leave Kansas. He lets his mother and sister go alone on their arduous and dangerous journey - probably the beginning of his guilt towards Emeline.

But Charlie also refuses to stay with his stepfather. Knowing what we know about Homer Adkins, this comes as no surprise. But add to that one more piece of evidence: For the rest of his life, Homer regularly carried a .32 caliber pistol that, court records say, had once belonged to Charlie. That a teenager would have a pistol (and not just the standard varmint rifle), especially a young man with the friendly temperament of Charlie Hasbrook, says something about family life at the Adkins. One can imagine the confrontation between father and stepson that put the gun in Homer's pocket forever. At some point—and this fact has survived in both family legend and court record—Charlie looked up the barrel of his own gun.

And so, when the split came, Charlie had no desire to spend another second in his stepfather's house. And we can assume the feeling was mutual.

Charlie quickly found a new place to live, with a family in town. Did he take his brother Ben with him? Probably not; the boy was just fourteen. And one shudders to think of the genial young man left to the cruelties of Homer Adkins. My mother remembers her Uncle Ben as a tall, very gentle man who was wonderful to his nieces—perhaps an echo of his childhood survival skills.

Living in the same town, Charlie would have seen his brother often—and, when needed, protected him. That may be another explanation for the pistol.

Emeline would eventually return to Concordia, her children and Homer. But not Charlie. By the time she arrived he was gone; his schooling done, Charlie was off to make his way in the world.

ALONE IN THE WORLD

Charlie found his first job in Eastern Colorado, working on an irrigation project. It would have been backbreaking work, but to a young man out on his own for the first time, it was probably glorious. Responsible, tough for his size, and a person who made friends easily, Charlie probably fit in well with his fellow canal diggers and the local cowboys.

The next year, probably thanks to contacts he'd made in Colorado, found Charlie in Deadwood, South Dakota working for a construction contractor. Deadwood had faded from its wide-open days of a decade before. But, for a nineteen year-old, footloose and with money in his pocket, the faro games, saloons and whorehouses that remained must have been both exotic and magnetic.

It was probably a good thing he didn't linger. The contractor had sealed a deal with the Rock Island Railroad to lay down the grade for a new track to run from Deadwood 900 miles south to Concho, in the middle of the Oklahoma Territory. It would one day be the railroad that opened up Oklahoma to pioneers.

For the next two years, with few vacations or breaks, Charlie's life would vary only with the scenery. A few hundred yards each day, every day, he would drive a team of mules pulling a "slip" machine to lay down a level bed of dirt and gravel to support the rails.

It was solid, reliable work, and one of the best paying around: wages were $20 per month, plus a dollar per day for board. The land was nice and flat, though the weather could sometimes get rough. The job also had other eccentricities—for example, every half-mile or mile, the team came under the jurisdiction of a new contractor boss. Some were good men, others were bastards, and still others were jerks. To keep his job, and get paid, Charlie learned to deal with them all.

Some time early in the second year, the crew passed through Concordia. Emeline had returned to her husband, so Charlie no doubt stopped at the farm. Even Homer couldn't have interfered with that. It would be the last time Charlie and Homer would ever meet—and it was probably not a pleasant encounter.

Much more bittersweet would have been Charlie's reunion with his mother, sister and brother. They would have brought him up-to-date on all of the news from Sheridan and Concordia. He would have told them about all he'd seen in Colorado and along the railroad line. The girls, Martha, Mildred and Pearl, now almost in their teens, would have thrilled at the sight of their grown-up step-brother; little Avery, just three, would have looked on in awe. Charlie wouldn't see any of them again for a dozen years, until after the dawn of the new century.

It was probably on this visit that Charlie also rekindled his relationship with Mary Brown, now grown into a charming young woman of sixteen.

Charlie celebrated his 21st birthday, November 14, 1888, still on the railroad line, on yet one more day of laying down slip. One can sense the boy growing into a man, taking on ever more responsibility—and for the first time, thinking about his future.

In early 1889, the crew crossed the southern Kansas border and entered Indian Territory. From here on it would be wilder country. No more settlements, no more meals and soft beds at friendly farmhouses. Now the food they ate they'd either have to carry with them or shoot. And, of course, there were the Indians—ostensibly peaceful, but there was no telling how they'd react to this latest, and most permanent, intrusion by the White Man.

As it turned out, the Indians were unthreatening. And as the crew worked its way South, Charlie found himself more and more enchanted by the countryside around him. It struck him that someday, if it was ever made possible, he could imagine living here and raising a family.

One day, a hundred miles into the Territory, the crew found itself at a watering hole—a small, very shallow lake, to be precise—used by generations of Indian tribes, stagecoaches, and, more recently, by passing cattle drives on the Chisholm Trail. It was a natural springs, shallow and perpetually murky from stirred up silt. Charlie, showing his new maturity, organized a team of men and together they waded out into the pond and sunk a barrel into the muck to act as a filter.

The result was the first perpetual, and copious, source of clean water in the area. It wasn't long before the word got out and travelers made it a part of their itinerary to stop at Government Springs, as the pond came to be called. Eventually, the new train stopped there as well, to water up and rest weary travelers. And when the territory finally opened up to settlers and the railroad planners needed to decide on sites for depots, the pond was an obvious choice.

The new town, adjoining Government Springs, was named Enid. The standard joke was that someone had nailed a sign to a tree at the pond reading "DINE", which had flipped over in the wind to read "ENID". In fact, the new town had been named, like most others along the railroad line, by Mr. M.A. Low, vice president and general counsel of Rock Island Railroad. Riding the train south just a couple months after Charlie and his crew had passed through, Low inquired about the name of spot. Upon being told that it was called "Skeleton" after the old Skeleton Stage Coach line that had once passed through, Low reportedly replied, "We will not have that name. Nobody would want to live in a town with such a name. We will name it Enid." His source was a poem he'd been reading, Tennyson's "Idylls of the King," in which Enid is the beautiful wife of the knight, Geraint.

Only a few people in American history can lay claim to having founded a city. With his small, pragmatic, but pivotal act, Charlie Hasbrook became one of them.

A few days after leaving the springs, the crew found itself working its way across a slowly rolling, red earth countryside crossed by meandering creeks, all of them tributaries of the Cimarron River a few miles to the west.

On the banks of these creeks stood cottonwood trees, some one hundred feet tall. And where the creeks joined at forks, these trees clustered in groves several hundreds of yards across. The high ground was loose shale, well suited for pastureland; the lowlands by the creeks were thick with rich sediment, ideal for crops.

Charlie and his new friend, fellow slip grader Will Neel, would often spend their free time at the end of each day riding through this territory, exploring. The landscape stirred something in Charlie's soul. Born a farm boy, he'd spent his teenaged years on similar land in Kansas. But this was better—not least because nobody owned it yet. He told Neal and his other companions on the work team: 'Someday, if they ever open this land up, I'm going to own a farm right here.' Then he filed the memory in the back of his mind and went back to laying slip and working his way south.

Sometime in the spring or summer of 1891, the crew reached the town of Concho, almost at the geographic center of the current state of Oklahoma, 22 miles from Oklahoma City, and the spiritual heart of the Cheyenne nation. Concho was also to be the southern terminus of the Rock Island Railroad—and thus, the end of the line for Charlie Hasbrook's job as well.

As family tradition has it, he then took his pay, rode north, and caught the train heading to Chicago. After two years of continuous work, it was time to have some fun.

VICTIM AND SURVIVOR: OREGON AND BEYOND

About the time Charlie crossed the Cimarron River, his family was again pulling up stakes. Once again, as if trapped in some closed loop from which they couldn't escape, Homer and Emeline again decided to sell everything, pack up . . . and head back to Oregon.

We can assume that this was a mutual decision. Emeline certainly wanted to go—she'd proven that when she'd left for Oregon the first time. Homer hadn't chased her then, so we can assume that now, after a decade in his hometown, he was ready to go.

Why? One reason may have been the economy—the United States was sliding into one of the worst depressions in its history. The Great Plains had also experienced, in recent years, one of the worst winters in recorded history. Homer, a man with little talent for success, may have just found it just too hard to make a living in Kansas.

There may have been one more reason: Nathan Connor, Emeline's father, died in July 1888. Allowing for delays in the mail, selling off the Kansas farm, packing up and moving, the dates seem to jibe. In other words, it is possible that Homer Adkins and his family ricocheted back and forth between Kansas and Oregon chasing the legacies of dead and dying parents.

Whatever the reasons, by the end of 1890, the family was living on a farm, just up the Wilson River from the port city of Tillamook. They were now 20 miles from the Hasbrook farm they'd left years before.

Homer and Emeline were both approaching forty, though the stress of the years, according to contemporary reports, had made Homer appear ten years older. If the couple was hoping for a comfortable middle age on the coast of Oregon, they were gravely mistaken.

Trouble began almost from the beginning. In the summer of 1891, the ever-truculent Homer began feuding with a neighbor named Frank Harris over a boom Harris had constructed over the river. We don't

know the precise nature of the complaint—Homer apparently also feuded with another neighbor, again over a river boom—but we do know the
situation deteriorated to the point that Homer began regularly carrying
Charlie's old pistol every time he went out. At least a half-dozen people
saw that gun, and a newly bought second pistol, so Homer must have
either ostentatiously worn them on his hips or showed them to various
acquaintances while threatening to take violent action.

This was not what you would call a good start in the neighborhood.
It got worse.

During this period, Homer signed on 18 year-old Ed Illingworth as
the hired hand. Illingworth, a local orphan, was such a pathetic character that his hiring suggests either that Adkins was so disliked in the community that no one else would work for him, or, bully that he was,
Adkins hired someone he could easily exploit.

According to a reporter for the *Tillamook Headlight*, Illingworth had
"always been regarded as a good boy, although somewhat given to fanci-
ful and imaginative story-telling in relating his experiences. He is unobtrusive, apparently honest, and appears to be absolutely inoffensive,
although he does not seem very bright mentally."

A doctor's report is more devastating:

> "His hearing was impaired, so he was liable to be deluded as
> to what was said to him. He had been affected with catarrh, and
> his right ear was filled with pus, which injured the auditory
> nerves. He was in a staggering or unstable condition, [and]
> couldn't keep his balance. He was troubled with sleeplessness.
> His disease was probably the result of injurious practices which
> he had probably indulged in, and perhaps other causes . . .Such
> practices are liable to produce epilepsy, makes the patient nerv-
> ous, backward and also blunts the moral sense. It causes the
> patient to rely on impulse without reason . . .
>
> "The boy at times complained of hallucinations, that is,
> strange sounds from some unknown source. Such patients are
> easily alarmed. I find on recent examinations that he has been
> troubled with nocturnal convulsions lately, and he has a contin-
> ual headache . . .He has a convulsive twitching of the muscles of
> his face . . ."

A lot of this, of course, is Victorian medical gobbledygook. For example, "injurious practices" might just mean obsessive masturbation. But, given all of the other symptoms it more likely suggests the drinking of bad alcohol—or, and this seems the best fit, an advanced case of syphilis.

Probably retarded, possibly demented, and certainly sick, young Ed Illingworth now found himself at the mercy of a man who preyed upon human weakness.

INTERREGNUM

Family tradition has it that Charlie Hasbrook spent the next two years in Chicago. Other than that, the records of that period are lost.

However, with little lost to the narrative, we can speculate on those missing months. For example, Charlie certainly would have stopped in Concordia on the way north. His family was gone, but there would have been others he would have wanted to see, including the family that had taken him in, schoolmates, and, if the relationship had already bloomed, Mary Ellis, now nineteen. Charlie, now worldly, lean and strong, dark brown from the sun, and with a pocket full of money, would have cast an impressive figure . . . and it's hard to imagine him missing the chance to do so.

How long would he have stayed? Probably a month. Then he would have gone off to see the big city lights.

Why Chicago? Several reasons, I think. First, it was the mightiest city in the mid-West, and thus a magnet to every Prairie farm kid with dreams of adventure. Second, there was Charlie's friendship with Will Neel, whose skills as a carpenter and lack of them as a farmer suggests a city boy, perhaps a native Chicagoan. I suspect that he and Charlie traveled together after the railroad work was done—two young bachelors on the loose in the Big City.

The third reason I believe the Chicago story is "Old Prize", the racehorse that Charlie rode in the Land Rush. I envision Charlie and Will, after stopping in Concordia, using their free railroad passes to ride the Rock Island north to Illinois. There, as the money began to run out, they took work in something they knew well—say, grading local roads and railroad lines—all while enjoying the various vices of a great metropolis.

One vice in particular, I suspect, caught Charlie's fancy: horse racing. After all, in his old age Charlie spent long afternoons listening to broadcasts from horse tracks all around the country. That habit probably began in those lost two years. As for Old Prize—the name a clue in itself—Charlie may have picked him up in a claiming race, or used his winnings and his track contacts to purchase the horse. How else to explain a Kansas farm kid with a thoroughbred racehorse?

With his railroad connections (or his continued employment by Rock Island), Charlie wouldn't have likely stayed in the city. I can see him travelling back and forth to Concordia, devoting ever-more attention to Mary . . . until at some point the two reach a mutual understanding about their common future. And with that understanding would have come an abiding desire in Charlie to find land and build a farm for his bride-to-be.

The answer to his prayers came in the form of the official announcement, published in newspapers throughout the United States, of the opening the following summer—via a Land Run—of the Cherokee Strip in the Indian Territory of Oklahoma.

About the same time, Charlie also received a desperate note from his mother, describing the worst imaginable family tragedy and begging for him to come home.

For the decision he finally made between the two, Charlie would feel guilty the rest of his life. But he never regretted his choice.

AN ANGRY END

On July 2, 1893, at 9 a.m., Homer Adkins made his way out of the farmhouse and started up the path along the river towards Tillamook.

A few moments later, a man's hoarse voice screamed, "Murder!" An instant later, a rifle shot echoed up and down the river.

Then came that terrible moment of silence that follows as a crime turns into its consequence.

Three mornings later, Emeline Conner Hasbrook Adkins, as her mother-in-law did twenty-five years earlier, sat down to compose a letter about a murder. I quote it in full, adding some punctuation and proper spelling for coherence:

Tillamook, Oregon
July 5, 1892

Dear Father & all the friends,

It is with a sad heart that I take my pen to write you the sad news that Homer was shot and killed instantly on the morning of second of July at 9 A.M.

I will try and tell you as near as I know how the trouble came about. Homer had a boy at work for him & he lived in the family for about six months, he was about 18 years old, his name was Ed Illingworth. There had been no serious trouble between them until the evening of the 1st when supper was through with. Ed asked H to go and milk the cow (it was Ed's chore to milk). Homer replied: No, there had to be some wood cut and he would cut the wood and then cut down some weeds that were growing in the yard.

Then Ed replied: I will cut the wood that is needed while you milk. H replied: I have you hired and expect you to milk. Ed replied: You have done nothing today & you can do as you like about milking her. If you [would] have her milked you can milk her yourself.

Then Homer got quite angry and advanced a step or two toward Ed who was sitting by the woodbox. Homer said: Ed that is a lie and I think you are an ungrateful scoundrel. Homer talked on that strain for a very short time when Ed caught up a stick of stove wood about two foot long and struck Homer three heavy blows across the left temple. Ed was strong and struck as hard as he could.

The blows staggered Homer. Martha and I rushed in between them and separated them. Homer was grasping for the stick and Martha jerked the stick out of Ed's hands. He continued to scratch and strike at Homer over our heads.

The tussle lasted only a very short time. I can't calculate on the length of time but it was short. During this time Martha and I kept begging him to desist. Ed swore when he reached for the stick he would kill him. Then

Homer turned from him and started for the bedroom door and said: *If you don't get of here I will kill you.* I told Ed to get out, which he did immediately without hat or coat.

Martha and I succeeded in getting Homer in the rocking chair and applied hot cloths to his head. It was the work of a moment and we talked about it for about an hour—when it was bedtime.

Next morning, Homer's eye was badly blacked and swollen and his hand was quite sore. Meantime, this boy went to a neighbor about one mile from the house. They were two young men living there, 'baching'. He stayed all night with them and told his story of the trouble.

Next morning, he borrowed the gun and they asked where he was going. He replied: *I am going back to [the] Adkinses.* The two men went out to milk about twelve cows when they say Ed started [out] with the gun.

On the morning of the 2nd, Homer got up feeling quite bad. He was not able to work. He sent Millie on ahead to a pasture to get the horses up and harness them. Millie and Avery passed over the road for about one quarter of a mile. They saw nothing of the boy.

When the horses were harnessed Homer started to go where they were. When he had gone about one hundred yards from the house, Martha and I heard the cry of "Murder!" and the next instant we heard the report of a gun.

Martha and I started as fast as we could run—and when about half way we met Ed as white as a sheet with gun in hand. He told us he had killed Homer in self-defense. We hurried on until we came to his body. Martha kept ahead of me several feet when she called out: *Oh! Here he is.*

When I got to him he was struggling. His eyes were shut and his mouth was filling with blood. His head was lower than his body. I raised his head up level with his body, but I think he was unconscious.

Ed followed up and begged us not to cry. He said he was sorry he had done it and wanted to know if wanted him to go after anybody. I said: *Yes. In a hurry. And tell them you did it.*

Oh! Imagine if possible our feelings at that moment there by the road side. The children and me with Homer dead at our feet. His hat fell back off his head and filled half-full of clotted blood.

I held his head up and his warm blood run through my fingers and down on the ground.

Assistance came in about five minutes—but left to call the neighbors. Millie and Avery went to [the] Harrises, about one mile. Martha and Pearl stayed with me until more assistance came. I think we were alone about one-half hour. Time passed slowly.

The Coroner came and removed the body in about three hours. The murderer went immediately and gave himself up. The Coroner held the inquest over the body. Neighbors and friends came and done all they could to assist and comfort us & telegraphed immediately to Ben—and he and Dora came sixty miles on horseback inside of twelve hours.

There is more I could tell you on the subject but my strength is exhausted. I will try and write and get assistance to let you know all I can.

Good Bye all, all
E.B. Adkins

I first read this letter, which was part of the original Wilkerson packet, years before I saw the newspaper coverage about Ben Hasbrook's murder and came to my own conclusions about Emeline's culpability in that murder. Yet even in that first reading, I was struck by my great-great grandmother's detachment, almost clinically objective, in the letter. Even as a trained reporter, I don't think I could witness the murder of my spouse, then write about it to my mother—even in that epistolary age—and describe my murdered mate as "the body", as Emeline does in the next-to-last paragraph.

Not that the letter lacks passion. The section describing how Emeline cradled the dying Homer's head, as his blood poured through her fingers—and the blood from a still-living man with a large caliber head wound would have been copious—is particularly shocking.

But when you compare Emeline's letter with that of her mother-in-law a quarter-century earlier, you can see what is missing. Emeline's letter has the horror, but not the devastation. In Hannah Adkins letter you can hear the howl of grief to God; you can feel that the death of her son has torn Hannah's heart right out of her chest. Her description of her boy's mutilated body—as precise as Emeline's, but never clinical—is haunting and almost unbearable to read. You are not surprised to learn that, soon after the letter was written, Hannah Adkins sunk into depression.

By comparison, Emeline's letter to her father, beyond the formal announcement of tragedy at the beginning, reads like a police affidavit. It may have been: Emeline may have just given such a testimony to the local constabulary and, in writing the letter, may have fallen back into the same rhythms.

But that still doesn't seem an adequate explanation for the tone of the letter. Even the ejaculated "Oh!" seems less aimed at Homer's death than at the memory of Homer's convulsions and the gushing blood and the look on the faces of her children as they watched their father die.

One may argue that there is a difference between a mother, with limited experience with murder, seeing her dead child, and a widow, who has already been through the murder of her first husband, coming upon the death of her second. Perhaps, but that still doesn't explain to me why the "Homer" of the first third of the letter, becomes the pronoun "he" in the second third, and "the body" in the final section.

There is one other thing. I remember, when my father died, helping my mother home from the hospital. My wife, my sister and I stayed with her as much as we could for several days afterwards. During those days, she often talked about my father, about their marriage, about how he was a good man, a good husband and a good provider. Most newly widowed women I know are the same way. They feel an understandable need to eulogize and honor the man with whom they've spent their lives.

There is none of that in Emeline's letter to her father. Perhaps, to be charitable, this objectivity was the only way Emeline could deal with the horror and loss. Still, she doesn't even write, "He was a good man, father," or just, "He didn't deserve to die like this." Emeline didn't even come out of the house to attend to Ben Hasbrook. She at least did that, after almost twenty years of marriage, for Homer Adkins. But now, just three days later, he has already been objectified him into a corpse.

BLACK WIDOW

It is interesting to speculate on what went through Emeline's mind as she waited for the Coroner to arrive. Certainly there would have been the sense of loss, of a sudden cavity in her daily existence. Like any mother, she must have been deeply concerned about the effect of the morning's events on her children, not just short term, but for the rest of their lives.

And, if only for a moment, it must have flickered through her monochromatic mind that she was in the rare, and unlikely, position of being twice widowed by murder. Surely there were still many people, if not in Tillamook, then in Yamhill and Sheridan, who would receive the news with raised eyebrows. The one consolation was that no one could possibly accuse her of complicity in this second murder. At worst they would think of her as uniquely cursed—and at best, especially among the newcomers to the area who were the majority of the population, they would see her as a tragic figure, someone chosen by God to shoulder an extra heavy set of burdens.

Among the citizens who raced to the murder scene from town was a reporter from the *Tillamook Headlight*. The news of the murder had reached the town just minutes before Illingworth himself appeared, announced his guilt and surrendered to a Deputy Sheriff Steinhilber. The young man was quickly locked into the county jail. Meanwhile, the reporter grabbed a horse and buggy and drove up-river to the scene.

His report, which ran in the July 7th issue of the paper, tells what he saw:

> "[I] found the body of the murdered man lying on the roadside, a few hundred yards this side of the Tillamook River bridge, on the road to Netarts. The wife and three little girls were standing over the remains of the dead man, wailing most piteously, and a few of the neighbors were doing what they could to comfort her and the little ones and were watching the body until the coroner came . . .

> "Where the dead man lay the road runs very close to the river bank, and his head was almost on the brink. He had apparently turned back from the direction in which he was going just before he was shot. He fell on his back, and the people who came say they did not change his position, but covered the body with a sheet and a few shading boughs, waiting for the jury of inquest. He was dressed in his working clothing and had not coat or vest on . . ."

As it happens, in her letter Emeline was confused: there was no Coroner available. Rather, a group of leading local citizens—including a doctor, a justice of the peace, and seven businesspeople—were empanelled as a jury of inquest. They made their way upriver, and, in an image at odds to our modern world of forensic science, ambulances and emergency rooms, convened on the riverbank literally in a circle around Homer Adkins' body. The doctor, Dr. Petrie, was sworn in as the "scientific expert", and an A.W. Severance was empowered to conduct the examination of witnesses.

There were two immediate tasks at hand: establish what happened and determine, if possible, the proximate cause of Adkins' death.

The first was easy. Illingworth had already confessed everything to everyone he'd met, and none of the witnesses suggested anything to the contrary. It was agreed, in the words of the reporter, "that the deceased came to his death from a gunshot wound inflicted by Ed Illingworth."

But the actual cause of that death was more complicated. It was a nasty wound, inflicted by a .44 caliber Winchester rifle—that is, by a ball the size of chickpea fired from less than fifty feet away.

As described by the reporter, the preliminary observations were not conclusive:

> "The ball entered his face at the base of his nose, about two inches below his right eye and came out of his right ear, crushing and shattering the upper jaw bone, and knocking out several teeth. It is thought that the brain was not penetrated, and that the shock, not necessarily fatal, stunned him until he died of strangulation, the flow of blood into his throat being copious . . ."

But others were not sure:

> " . . . Some think that the shot came from the other direction, and others are of the opinion that the hole near his nose was made by a splinter of bone and that the bone ranged backward into his brain. No thorough post-mortem examination was made, and it was difficult to locate the course of the ball on account of the shattered condition of the upper jaw."

Only days later would an official autopsy take place. The coroner would determine that the bullet had entered beneath Homer's nose, bounced off the base of his cranium—fracturing it—then exited through the upper jaw and out his ear. Given the medicine of the era (and even today), Homer would likely have died after a few days from the swelling of his traumatized brain. But it is also likely that in a terrible irony, Emeline, by lifting Homer's head, may have hastened her second husband's death.

The inquest completed, Homer's body was taken to the house, washed, and prepared for burial.

Wrote the reporter: "Adkins has generally borne a good reputation though he was frequently mixed up in law suits and is said by some to have been quarrelsome, and even dangerous."

The reporter also had a chance to speak to Illingworth, who had been brought back up to the scene of the crime to answer questions of the inquest. He report: "The boy talks very freely regarding his deed and said he did it in self-defense. He said he started after his clothing Saturday morning and met Atkins in the road and asked him if he could get his clothing. He says Adkins refused . . . and made a motion as if pulling a pistol from his pocket."

VERDICT

The trial had to wait until September and the autumn term of the circuit court.

And indeed, it was eagerly awaited. It seems that the murder and the upcoming trial were the single most common conversational topic in the region that summer—enough to seriously taint the jury pool. The *Tillamook Headlight* reporter would report that during the trial "The streets have been very quiet . . . Most people are anxious to know the minute details . . ."

Illingworth's jail time seemed to suit him well. Wrote the reporter, "He looked thin when first incarcerated, but seemingly has been thriving on prison fare, as he has gained a great deal of flesh."

The legal teams on the case included some familiar names. Twenty years before, James McCain and T.B. Handley had been the winning lawyers for the defense of Joseph Coxon. Now they were on opposite sides of the aisle. Handley was on hand to help represent Illingworth; but McCain, after a long and distinguished career as a defense attorney, found himself in the unusual role of prosecutor. It would be interesting to know their thoughts when they first learned that the wife of the victim was the former Emeline Hasbrook.

As might be expected from a case that had two months to ferment in the crucible of a small town, jury selection proved a nightmare. It began on a Friday morning and "the regular jury list was soon exhausted." That night a second attempt was made using a new list of candidates. "Few were accepted". Another venire (a formal call for jurors) was issued Saturday, and selection continued that day and night.

It wasn't until late Monday morning, after one hundred local men had been examined—"most all of them seeming to have their minds made up in advance"—that twelve comparatively objective jurors were selected and empanelled.

After preliminary testimony confirming the site of the crime scene, the first witness was called: Emeline Adkins.

As she sat there, once again on the stand in a trial of her husband's murderer, looking out at the faces of Ben and Dora, and Handley and McCain, did Emeline for an instant feel the sickening crush of déjà vu? Did she momentarily feel trapped in a cruel cycle of history? Or was this just one more unhappy moment in a lifetime of unhappy moments?

Her testimony was identical to the narrative of her letter, with a few wrinkles. In particular, Emeline added that as she and the two girls rushed towards the bridge they encountered Illingworth walking towards them, carrying the rifle. He told them he had killed Adkins. That it had been in self-defense. Furious, Emeline told Illingworth that if that were true, he would hang for it. He replied that he didn't care. She also added that she found a cartridge between Homer's body and the bridge.

Next came the Adkins daughters. "The testimony of the three girls was substantially the same and was given in a remarkably clear and straight forward manner. They used excellent language and were not at all disconcerted by the cross-examination. Even the little eleven year-old daughter appeared better on the witness stand than many lawyers would."

Then came the neighbors, who confirmed the cry of "Murder!", the shot, and the disposition of the body. G.W. Phelps also testified that the grass and weeds were trampled down behind a stump at the roadside near where the spent cartridge had been found—but "could not tell whether it had been done by a man or by cattle running at large."

Next up, and a critical part of the prosecution's case, were the Lyster brothers, the two shady bachelors to whose house Illingworth had repaired after the fight with Adkins.

T.W. Lyster testified that "Illingworth came to his house on the evening of July 1st, and came in without hat or coat, saying that he had left them outside because they were wet. He stayed all night. While there he said he a little trouble with Adkins that evening. He left between 8 and 9 o'clock next morning, taking Lyster's gun, a .44 Winchester rifle. Illingworth asked him for the loan of the gun. Lyster said, 'There it is.'" R.D Lyster, next on the stand, confirmed everything brother T.W. had said.

As they described themselves, the Lysters were just friendly neighbors putting a friend up for the night, then graciously loaning him their rifle—no questions asked—in the morning. No culpability there. It probably surprised no one in the courtroom when, later that day, Tom and Dee Tomlinson, another neighboring pair, testified that T.W. had remarked to them that "Illingworth went hunting and got his game."

As the prosecution's case continued, the reporter for the Headlight noticed something interesting:

> "Some of the witnesses seemed very reluctant to tell what they knew about the case, were very forgetful, and would tell nothing but what was forced out of them. Some of them talked very freely on the outside, and related to a representative of this paper much more than they were willing to disclose on the witness stand. The sympathy and partiality thus shown for the defense made it very hard for the prosecuting attorney to make a thorough presentation of the case for the State."

On the first day, the courtroom was crowded; but now, on day two, as the defense made its case, the room was positively jammed. Handley and his team immediately began an assault on Homer Adkins' character. One neighbor after another took the stand to describe feuds with Adkins or to confirm that the man regularly went out packing a pistol.

Shopkeepers testified that he had purchased bullets from them. Most also said they had contributed to Illingworth's defense fund.

Devastating, but not conclusive. However, Handley had saved his best for last.

He set the stage by calling Curtiss Johnson, an acquaintance of Homer, to the stand. Johnson testified that on the day before the murder—that is, the day of the fight, Homer had told him "in a joking way" that "he could run his hired hand away at any time he chose."

Then defense called the young man everyone had been waiting for: Illingworth. He took the stand. During the first day he had sat stolidly, exhibiting little interest in either the jury selection or the proceedings— except when the girls took the stand and gave what appeared to be damaging testimony against him.

Now he told his version of the story: He had been forced to plow a field from dawn until 7:30 p.m. Exhausted he had finally sat down in the kitchen and was feeding wood to the stove. Homer took that moment to demand that he go milk the cow:

> "Adkins came at me and asked why I couldn't milk. He called me a liar and commenced kicking me. I struck at him. Then I dropped the stick." At this point, according to Illingworth, Emeline and the girls intervened—which only gave Homer the opportunity to pick up the stick and go after him. "He struck at me over the heads of the children in the doorway. Then he dropped his club and went after his gun.
>
> "They told me to run. I did. I ran down the hill across the bridge and secreted myself in the brush for ten minutes.
>
> "When the girls came to milk I called to them and asked if the old man was quiet. I went with the girls about perhaps half a mile. I asked them if Adkins would have shot me. They said, 'Yes, *that he drew a gun on young Hasbrook.*'
>
> "I asked the girls if they could hide my things out where I could get them. They said no.
>
> "The girls said their mother put Adkins in [the rocking] chair and bathed his head where I struck him. I said, 'What shall I do?' They began to cry and said not to say anything. I cried too. I told them I was going over to Tom's [Lyster]. They begged me not to tell it to Tom.

"I went to Tom's and went in without any coat or hat. I stayed all night. The next morning I got his gun and went back. I took the gun because I was afraid. I can't say what time it was.

"When I got nearly there I saw Millie, the little girl, across the road with the team. I then met Adkins.

"I said 'Good Morning', but he did not speak. I went to the side of the road, twenty feet away. I said, 'You were going to shoot me last night.' He said, 'Yes, I will shoot you yet.'

"I shot him."

On cross-examination, Illingworth admitted that during the fight that night he never really believed that Adkins would shoot him, but only left because Emeline and the girls wanted him to. He also said that during the fatal confrontation he never saw a gun on Adkins, and that he had quickly fired without taking aim.

On re-examination, Illingworth said that he assumed that Adkins was carrying Charlie Hasbrook's .32 caliber pistol, because he usually did when he went out.

The final major testimony was given by Dr. Stanley. He first noted that he had seen individuals with wounds like Homer Adkins survive, and that most likely Homer had not died from his wounds but from strangulation induced by shock and drowning on his own blood.

He then presented the scary list of Illingworth's symptoms. They had their intended effect, and the *Headlight* reporter captured a memorable instance of human nature at work:

"On Tuesday the crowd in the Court room was very large. More women than usual were present, eagerly listening to the details. Dr. Stanley was on the stand giving expert testimony as to Illingworth's mental and physical condition. Yr scribe was standing on one foot jotting down the testimony as well as he could. At his side a gentleman vacated his seat, but the ladies spread themselves a little, filling up the vacancy, and this weary quill pusher saw all chance of his getting a place to sit down disappear beneath rustling petticoats.

"All at once Dr. Stanley's testimony took an interesting turn. The ladies all seemed to get smaller. There was room for the

Oregon Pioneers
Nathan Conner and
Elizabeth Buell
Conner, c. 1860.

The only known image of
Benjamin Hasbrook, c. 1865.

Benjamin Hasbrook grave, Pleasant
Hill Pioneer Cemetery, near
Ballston, Oregon.

The Homer Adkins family, 1886, Concordia, Kansas. The stepchildren—Charles, Ben and Dora—are in the back row. Front row: Avery. Middle row: Homer, Martha, Mildred, Pearl, Emeline.S

"Four Generations" No. 1, 1900: Elizabeth Buell Conner, Emeline Woodley, John Focht, Dora Hasbrook Focht.

The Adkins family, c. 1890, about the time Homer drew a gun on Charlie.

Government Springs, c. 1900: Where Charlie Hasbrook sank a barrel and helped to found Enid, Oklahoma.

The Hasbrook Homestead, near Marshall, Oklahoma Territory, c. 1903. "Old Prize," the aged racehorse who ran the Land Rush, is at right.

Emeline Blair Conner Hasbrook-Adkins-Newton-Woodley, c. 1910.

The Hasbrook Farm, with barn, silo and windmill, c. 1915.

Charlie and Mary Hasbrook, with 'Old Shep' in front of the farmhouse, c. 1925.

Theresa Madora Hasbrook, with younger sisters, Audrey and Hazel, atop roof of dugout, c. 1910.

The Charles Hasbrook family, c. 1915. Front: Hazel, Mary Hasbrook, Charlie Hasbrook, Audrey. Back: Merrill, Nate, Theresa.

Alliene and Nadiene Collins on the Hasbrook farm, 1922.

"Four Generations", No. 2, 1919: Clockwise from top: Theresa Hasbrook Collins, Charlie Hasbrook, baby (Mary) Alliene Collins, Emeline Woodley.

Theresa Madora (Hasbrook)
Collins.

(Lela) Nadiene Malone left, age four, with
sisters Alliene, Loriene and Wanda, 1924.

(Lela) Nadiene Malone

Age 18, about the time the
Hasbrook homestead was lost.

Newlywed, age 28.

Mother, age 45.

Grandmother, age 75.

Matriarch, age 85.

The Hasbrook barn, 2005.

The Hasbrook farm house, 2005, abandoned for thirty years.

Restoration of the Hasbrook farm house begins.

The author, with son Tim, before the doorway of the dugout, 1999.

The nearly finished restored barn, 2009.

The restoration/construction of the Hasbrook barn,
photographs taken a century apart.

The Dugout.

Oklahoma Land Rush, noon, September 16, 1893: That may be Charlie
Hasbrook on Old Prize at the center of the famous photograph.

scribe most anywhere. In fact, the audience had shrunk into such small space that perhaps one hundred more persons could have found comfortable seats. The scribe sat down."

Testimony closed Tuesday evening, followed by closing arguments by the prosecution and, for the defense, "an able and eloquent speech" by T.B. Handley. Wednesday morning, the order was reversed, giving James McCain the last word. The bizarreness of the situation—a famed defense attorney giving impassioned argument for the prosecution— was lost on few present. Noted the reporter: "His resources were all utilized just the same and his alert and keen faculty of grasping and making good use of a point, never appeared to better advantage. He presented the case for the prosecution in a masterly manner, and made a terrible arraignment of the public for the rampant tendency to condone crime and bestow sympathy on criminals . . ."

Ironic indeed.

The jury deliberated for three hours. It returned with a verdict of Guilty of Manslaughter. Illingworth was sentenced to seven years in the state prison and fined $2.

We can probably assume that Ed Illingworth emerged from prison at the turn of the century happier and healthier than when he went in.

FULFILLMENT

Homer Adkins was buried within days after the murder, as soon as the autopsy was completed.

Every death carries with it finality. But in Homer Adkins' miserable murder there is also a sense of inevitability. It is as if there was a rail running straight from that bloody spot on the Kansas prairie to that equally gory murder scene on the Tillamook riverbank. Homer could have stepped off that track at any time, and at any place, in those intervening years—but he never did.

He didn't because on that earlier day Homer made a fateful—and ultimately fatal—choice.

That choice wasn't predestined. Homer came from a good family of considerable gifts. As a young man, a teenager, he had made a brave decision to join the militia and fight in the Indian wars.

But then the day came, as it does in every life, when Homer's character was fully tested . . . and he failed. Because of his selfishness, he made a terrible mistake that cost his brother's life.

At that moment, Homer Adkins made his choice. He could have later redeemed himself—and in doing so regained his soul. But he didn't. And because of that he became a bitter, angry, paranoid man; a man who restlessly moved back and forth from failure to failure, unhappiness to unhappiness; who abused those weaker than him; endlessly feuded and fought with his neighbors; and acted in every way like a man who believed the entire universe was arrayed against him.

In a way, it was. Homer Adkins's death seems ordained from the moment he let Ezra ride away. It just took a quarter-century for Homer to find his murderer.

The brief funeral took place the following Sunday afternoon at the IOOF (Odd Fellows) cemetery on the outskirts of Tillamook. In the years to come if any of Homer's children or stepchildren wished to visit the gravesite (and it appears none did), they would have found it impossible to locate.

Emeline, even after seventeen years of marriage and four children, never bought Homer a headstone. Thus, with chilly appropriateness, Homer Adkins now lies forever in an unmarked grave.

FAMILY CIRCLE

Following Homer's death, Emeline drew her children around her. With Homer gone, even Ben and Dora could now safely return—and they did.

They never really left again. Only the youngest, Avery, would live as an adult outside Oregon, in Cincinnati. Ben would marry, divorce, marry again and have a son, always staying in Oregon.

Dora never left either. She and Pearl grew very close, and within a few years after Homer's death, Pearl went to live with her until she finished school. Dora married, had two sons, John and Orville Focht, and died long before her mother, in 1924. John would grow up to buy his grandmother's house. Orville, gassed in the First World War, became an invalid, subject to uncontrollable emotional swings, for the rest of his life.

Pearl became a schoolteacher in Tillamook and married a future judge, J.B. Wilkerson, in 1903. Her two sons, Burford and Ben, would grow up to become military officers and, in their later years gather the genealogical materials that would become the basis for this book. One of Burford's children would found a major winery in Oregon.

The two oldest Adkins girls, Martha and Mildred (Millie) would both marry and have children. Martha's boy Paul would die in battle in World War I. At the end, the two sisters would choose to be buried in the same grave at Riverside Cemetery in Portland.

Emeline Conner Hasbrook Adkins would soon add, briefly, a new name to the growing list of surnames—that of Benton Newton, once again probably the hired hand, and whom she divorced within a matter of months. Then she sold the Tillamook farm and with its proceeds moved to a home a few miles away in Ballston. There she met Thomas Woodley and added the final surname by which she is still known. She stayed in the house after Woodley died in 1910, remaining until the feebleness of age forced her to move to the Patton Home in Portland. That's where the *Oregonian* reporter found her, eight years before her death, and somehow saw in her the last living embodiment of the strong virtues, courage and dignity of Oregon Pioneers.

She had reeled them all in . . . except for the one I suspect she wanted most. Her oldest. The one who remembered the shot ringing out on the Hasbrook farm. Her favorite.

Charlie.

HOMESTEADER:
OKLAHOMA TERRITORY

For Charlie Hasbrook, like the thousands of other "Boomer" pioneers now scattered across the seven million acres of prairie on their new farm claims, the pressing task now was to build some kind of shelter in preparation for the winter just a few months ahead.

According to the terms set by the federal government, the pioneers were only required to stay on their claims seven months out of the year during the three years they needed to qualify for ownership of the land. But the reality was that the kind of people who were willing to risk everything on a free Land Rush were not likely to also be folks who could afford to winter over somewhere else. Train tickets were expensive, and it was weeks by wagon to any real city—and then you had to pay rent wherever you went.

So, for most of the "Boomers", with the realization that they had successfully staked their claim, was the recognition that they weren't going anywhere for a long time . . .and that they'd better build a place to sleep and figure out a way to eat if they were going to survive until the next Spring.

Charlie, by comparison, was content in the belief that he had an unbeatable strategy—and that, at least here on the first day, it was unfolding exactly as he'd planned. He would get as much building done on the claim this fall, until the weather turned, then head north on Old Prize to Concordia, where he'd stay with friends and court Mary . . . to return in the spring for planting and building, and then head north again right after harvest.

After that, once he and Mary were married—knock on wood—he would leave her with her parents during the summer while he traveled down to the farm, then stay with her at the Brown house during the winter. Once the house was built, the young couple would finally head down to Bison to stay, and then start thinking about a family.

That plan must have comforted Charlie as he took stock of his new farm and realized just how much work awaited him. It could take years. He'd never built a house before, nor a corral, or a barn, and now he'd have to figure out how to build them all on his own.

Well, not entirely on his own. Will Neel was, in fact, a very good carpenter. Being a city boy, he also knew nothing about farming, something Charlie had spent his entire life doing. So we can assume that when the pair teamed up for the Run they already had a tacit agreement to trade one skill for another.

There's no record, but it is likely that once he had the claimed staked out Charlie rode over to Neel's claim a mile South (or vice versa) and the two rode in to Enid to register. They might have chanced upon Miss Lilly, whose claim was to the West of Charlie's. Whatever the combination, Charlie would have gotten to Enid by late afternoon and joined the long line to the Land Office in what would eventually become the town square.

Enid itself would have been sheer chaos, a far cry from the quiet little pond Charlie had last seen three years before. Now it would have looked like a military encampment—though the thousands of Boomer tents would hardly have exhibited army discipline or consistency. The instant city would have been filled with celebrants showing off their deeds and getting drunk one last time before heading back out onto the prairie, disconsolate riders who had lost out, men arguing and fighting over disputed claims, families packing up to begin their new lives, and a small army of confidence men, whores and salesmen all conspiring to lighten the settlers of their claims and their money.

Charlie had ridden light for maximum speed, so now he would have had to stock up on equipment for what promised to be a two month encampment. He might have purchased some of those goods that afternoon, or the next morning. But given the high prices demanded by sutlers, it's more likely that he brought as much gear and foodstuffs with him from Chicago as the railroad would have allowed—and he probably tipped a porter or other rail employee to watch the items for him while he was gone.

Having all of those items now in hand would have made Charlie a ready target in a tent city that was both lawless and boiling over with unhappiness and frustration. And, after his time in Deadwood and Chicago, Charlie was shrewd enough to know it. So, by all odds, he and

Will would have taken advantage of the still-long daylight hours and ridden back the fifteen miles to the claim.

On the other hand, that still would have brought them home long after sunset—a difficult journey back to sites they'd only visited once. Perilous too, given that there would have been a lot of nervous settlers between them and their goal, all of them fearful of a strange countryside, wild animals and claim jumpers, and fingering the triggers of rifles.

So, perhaps the two men made their way out of town to a safer location—probably about where Vance Air Force Base now stands—and camped for the night; then finished the rest of the ride the next morning.

Once they returned to their respective claims, their horses burdened with a canvas tent, pots and pans, an ax and rifle, a bedroll and flour, beans and coffee, their most immediate and pressing task was to build some kind of permanent shelter. Living solely in a tent during the mild months of late summer and early autumn was endurable, though the days could get very hot and the nights, especially in October, increasingly frosty. And a sudden storm on the prairie could easily blow down tents, expose the settler to the threat of lightning, and, at the very least, leave everything a sodden, muddy mess. Moreover, once winter came, with its freezing rains and snow, a thin wall of canvas and a couple blankets, even with a stove, would be almost unbearable to any Boomer (and there were many) trying to winter over on an undeveloped claim.

Even for someone like Charlie Hasbrook, who now probably thanked his lucky stars for the chance to get to a town for the winter, the prospect of several months in a tent—and not the well-stocked tent of his railroad days—was probably not too appealing. Moreover, like everyone else, next Spring would be a time for plowing and planting, fence building and driving in cattle and horses—there would be few moments then for building a shelter.

So, as he unlimbered the goods and saddle from Old Prize, Charlie would have known that his very first task on his new 160 acre farm, would be to dig a very big hole—and then climb into it.

DUGOUT

In April, 1889, four years before the great Cherokee Strip run,

Harper's Magazine, still America's premiere news magazine, sent one of its artists (a 'W.V. Harencourt') to cover events surrounding one of the earlier and smaller Land Runs, this one near Purcell on the Kansas border. He returned with the expected images, rendered into an engraving by the magazine, of a vast tent city, a lonely train station, and a canoeist on the nearby Arkansas River. But on the bottom of the published page are two particularly arresting and rare images, each showing how Boomers actually lived during those pioneering days.

The left image shows a small encampment near the starting line. Its residents apparently arrived several months ahead of the run, and have settled in. There are a few plank structures, but mostly the families live in tents with wooden doors and stove chimney projecting through the roof. But what is particularly telling is that every one of these structures is half-buried *in the ground*. The tents are essentially just roofs, the dug out earth (hence the name 'dugout') serving as walls, security and temperature modulator. There are also other structures with wooden doors dug directly into low mounds of earth, probably root cellars for the cool storage of vegetables, milk and other perishables.

Because this encampment appears to be part of a larger one, there is also a prominent privy both for modesty and sanitation, a clothes-drying rack made from saplings, and a number of barrels and worktables.

Primitive as this image is, it is positively sophisticated compared to the image on the right, which is captioned "A Boomer's 'Dug-Out', on the Banks of the Canadian River."

In this latter image we get an unequalled glimpse of one of the most common solutions to the challenge of living on the prairie. Though the sod house or "soddie" is a more famous design, that kind of construction was more common further north, where the tall grass prairie was more dominant and woods much rarer. In much of Oklahoma, including the Cherokee Strip, tributary streams wandered through the countryside, typically lined with cottonwood trees. Charlie's claim was almost unique for the sheer size of its woods—but it was a rare (and often doomed) claim that didn't bear at least some source of water and a small stand of trees.

That combination offered two important advantages: logs for beams and a creek bank for walls. Hence, the 'dugout'. The construction is quite evident in the engraving: a deep trench is dug into the bank and then roofed crossways with several logs. If a large log is available (perhaps from one of the fallen ancient cottonwoods on the property) it is set perpendicular to and centered with the roof logs so that a second set of logs or planks can be rested upon it to create a roof peak for runoff. And then, for insulation, this roof is in turn topped with sod. Finally a hole is created in the roof near the back for the stove chimney. Cut logs, rocks and dirt create the front wall, and a plank door is mounted at its center. The result may be cramped, musty and dark, but it is sturdy, warm in the winter and cool in the summer, and it is out of the wind, rain and snow. It would probably even survive a tornado better than any above-ground structure of the era.

The *Harper's* engraving shows just such a dugout, with a mother and son standing out front, the boy pulling a toy wagon. Nearby can be seen a couple of barrels, a pair of tents still being used after the family has moved into the dugout, a wash basin and a large butchering block just outside the dugout's door. The scale of the structure, thanks to a miscommunication between artist and engraver, is a bit confusing, but the dugout seems to enclose a space about the size of a modern camper van or minibus. That's home for the months, or even years, it will take to build a proper house while still plowing, planting and harvesting, milking, calving and slaughtering, and building fences, paddocks and corrals.

Interestingly, the dugout on the Hasbrook homestead is different from the illustration in a number of important ways. Despite the presence of nearby woods, Charlie used almost no lumber other than the front door. Rather, his dugout, which is about twelve feet deep, eight feet wide and seven feet at its peak, is designed in a barrel vault, like a Quonset hut, with sun-dried mud bricks lining the inside to create a sturdy arch.

Why the difference? Perhaps there had been a small revolution in shelter design in the intervening years—though I suspect not. A more likely possibility is that chopping, sawing, adzing and placing a number of large logs was a daunting task for one man, even with the assistance of a horse and ropes. But, in looking at the site itself, it appears that Charlie was once again lucky: the creek bank just behind where he planned to build his house had a natural shelf, probably an old flood line, and a small hump. That hump itself might even have been torn open by the root ball of a fallen tree—so that it would have been easy to excavate.

The creek bottom, exposed by the end of summer, feature nice thick clay mud which would have been perfect for forming into bricks, and the eroded areas of the lower bank had exposed blocks of sedimentary rock shale—almost bricks themselves—that were ideal for constructing the front wall of the structure . . . and later as a nice, level (and more than a century later, still intact) foundation for the house.

Finally, and I think most important, Charlie's dugout expressed an attitude. He was a precise, careful man—that's what had made him a good surveyor—and, unlike many of the increasingly desperate families on other surrounding claims, he wasn't in any particular hurry. He would do it right—which is one reason why the structure still stands. It must have taken him weeks to excavate the cave, form and sun dry a couple hundred bricks, and carefully stack them in an arch.

It's hard to believe he could have done all of that by himself, so Charlie and Will Neel likely took turns helping each other. However, there is no record of that teamwork, nor does anything survive of whatever structure Neel built for himself.

By the time the rains began to fall, Charlie had stacked and mud-mortared the front wall to the front wall, attached a door to a simple wooden frame, and in an unlikely touch, lined the entire vault with muslin to break the fall of any dripping water, mud . . . or falling brick.

As he rode north the 200 miles to Concordia that winter along the muddy, sodden Chisholm Trail, Charlie must have felt very pleased with himself. All of his dreams were coming true: he had a farm, a humble but sturdy home—luxurious by Land Rush standards—and he was on his way to court the girl of his dreams. At last, he held his own fate in his hands.

Change of Plans

When he returned the next Spring, Charlie was a man with a purpose. He was engaged—Mary had accepted his proposal that winter—and now he set to work with a vengeance preparing the farm for her arrival. He drove a wagon this time, apparently loaded with a plow, bags of seed, a bureau, cot and a small stove. He'd earned the money for those items during the winter in Concordia by shucking corn and doing odd jobs.

Back on the farm that spring Charlie planted feed, both corn and wheat, and when it sprouted he stayed up through the nights guarding it from the deer that traveled up and down the creek bed searching for food. On the few occasions when he could, Charlie rode into Enid— now a whirlwind of construction and newly arrived shopkeepers displaying their wares—for tools and supplies.

After bringing in the harvest that autumn, Charlie saddled up Old Prize and again rode north. Now he had a working farm . . . and better yet, money in his pocket. It was time to make another major change in his life.

On January 15, 1896, in Concordia, he married Mary Annis Ellis Brown. And though they would remain happily married (and if family stories are true, ardently in love) until the end of their lives, almost from that day Charlie's carefully constructed plans began to unravel. For the next decade, it would take everything he and Mary had just to respond to the next twist that fate had in store for them.

First, as with many newlyweds, biology trumped strategy. Mary never got to Oklahoma that summer, because on October 20, 1896, ten months to the week after the wedding, Theresa Madora Hasbrook was born on the Brown farm. There is no record that Charlie was there for the delivery. Rather, he would most likely have been bringing in the harvest . . . and probably would not have heard the news for several days afterwards.

Now Charlie had a problem. In theory he could have convinced Mary to stay with the baby in Concordia for another year or two until some kind of structure could be built on the farm. But this was real life, and one can imagine a myriad of forces working against such a sensible plan. For one thing, despite (or perhaps because) of their long separations, the couple was deeply in love.

Now with a newborn daughter, Mary no doubt wanted to be with her husband—and Charlie with them—and no amount of argument about the miserable conditions awaiting them over the horizon in Indian Territory was going to dissuade her.

There may have been other factors as well. Lost to history are the attitudes of Mary's stepparents to the perpetual boarding of their adult daughter and grandchild. Finally, we can assume that Charlie's financial situation was tenuous enough that he couldn't afford endless trips back and forth to Kansas, or support a long-distance family.

Whatever the reasons, that April, after the spring rains ended and the roads dried under the bright sun, Charlie, Mary and baby 'Tressa' left the train station in Enid, climbed aboard Charlie's wagon and rode the long, jolting miles to the farm. What awaited them, whatever had been Charlie's efforts to slick up the place, was literally a hole in the ground. And because Charlie hadn't expected a family so soon, he likely hadn't even started on the house . . . which meant they would be living in the dugout, with few chances to escape to Kansas even in the winter, for several years. The little family was now, in a very real sense, stuck in the middle of nowhere.

It's hard to imagine what it was like for the three of them during those years: the crushingly hot summer days, the spring storms that seeped through the walls bringing with it worms and bugs, the flooded creek after downpours, the ice storms and blizzards of winter that froze the walls and cracked limbs overhead that penetrated every corner of the little cave and the hungry predators lurking just outside, smelling the food and dirty diapers.

What was it like for Mary to try to keep a baby clean and healthy in a dirt cave, when she had to climb down to the creek for water, sometimes even breaking through the ice to get it? Did she leave baby Theresa in the dugout when she went, alone with the hot stove and the butchering knives and the roaming coyotes and wolves? Or did she bundle her in blankets and take her down to the frozen creek with her?

Charlie and Mary had a few sticks of furniture. All the family clothes were hung in a wooden closet, built by Charlie, which stood behind the door. On the east side of the dugout, the couple set up the stove and a table. On the other side, three feet away, was a small bed on which the couple slept. My grandmother slept in a box that was shoved back under the bed during the day.

And it only got more difficult. Two years later they were still in the dugout when a second child was born, on March 20, 1899. His name was Nathan Benjamin Hasbrook—my charming great-uncle Nate—his middle name taken from Charlie's murdered father.

As a simple statistic, taken from the cursive writing of the 1900 Census for Garfield County, Oklahoma Territory, Nate's birth seems unremarkable. But standing in that dugout, imagining what it must have been like, gives you chills. Picture January, the snow howling outside, Mary seven months pregnant, little Theresa a curious two year old. Charlie still had to work the farm, and as much help as he would have tried to give, it still would have fallen on Mary to prepare the meals, change Theresa's diapers, sweep out the dugout and probably hike down to the creek. Now picture March: freezing mornings, frosty days, Charlie tending the animals, and Mary going into the labor as little Theresa stares.

Did they fetch a mid-wife? Did Charlie leap on a stiff and cold Old Prize, and gallop across the countryside to get help? Did Miss Lillie attend to the birth? Or did Mary go it alone, moaning and effacing as Charlie tried to help and Theresa cried? Did they take the little girl outside into the cold during the delivery?

There is no record or even a family legend about this period. All we can be sure of is that this was a moment of enormous danger and risk for the little family out there in the wild. And it may begin to explain why my grandmother, whose beauty stands out in the old photographs like a prairie rose, was also a person who rarely laughed or smiled and who treated life as if it was one long, unforgiving task to be endured.

Having survived this birth, life could only get better for the family. Charlie was a hard-working, ambitious man, so at some point he must have dug a well to spare Mary the trips to the creek. It is also likely that by now he had cut down some trees, sawed and adzed them into boards, and constructed some kind of shelter for people and animals above ground. But of this there is also no record.

What we do know is that Charlie teamed with Frank Hays, a bachelor carpenter who lived two farms to the North in a perfect partnership of a strong back and good carpentry, competence and perfectionism. And during the last years of the century, they set about building each other's house in turn. We also know that the little Hasbrook family finally moved into their new house in October 1901.

It must have been quite a moment. To literally rise out of the ground after eight years and step into a beautiful new castle, with a living room, kitchen and bedroom downstairs, two big bedrooms upstairs, a fireplace and porch with four columns. Crossing a real threshold at last, Charlie and Mary must have felt the glow of accomplishment; little Tressa, now almost nine, must have thought she was entering the most beautiful place in the world.

LAST DEFENSE

It was good times out there on the prairie. Those that had survived the intervening years—who hadn't run off, or died of sickness or cold or injury, or gone mad with the loneliness—were all now qualified as legal landowners according to the terms of Land Rush. The Hasbrooks were now not only settled in their new house, but seven harvests had given them a sense of real prosperity—which they answered by buying land, farm machinery and furniture . . . and making more babies. Merrill came along in early 1902, Audrey in 1904 and Hazel in 1907.

Across the road, Miss Lillie married Nelson P. Hill, twenty years her senior, and the source of her first widowhood. Will Neel also married, and his new wife became Mary Hasbrook's best friend. And as one continued up that road west to the new little village of Bison, or east to Marshall, or north to Enid, everywhere you saw signs of a community emerging: barns, schoolhouses, and churches.

But this wasn't Paradise, even if it may have felt so to these newly emerged subterraneans. Trapped between two great mountain ranges, the passageway between the tundra to the north and a tropical sea to the south, the Midwest has some of the strangest weather on the planet. In summer, as Charlie worked the plow and Mary tended the babies, the temperature often broke 100 degrees, with a misery index—thanks to the high humidity—of 130 or more. Spring rains brought flooding. Winter saw ice storms so heavy they would drag trees down. Like a Biblical plague, locusts were always threatening to explode their populations and chew off the landscape—as they had in Kansas in the 1870s. Summer storms brought lightning that searched the landscape for chimneys and the peaks of barns.

And then, of course, there were the tornadoes.

It was always a precarious existence. Early in the new century, a prairie fire broke out a few miles away. Driven by the prevailing wind and fueled by the long rows of dried corn and wheat stalks, the fire marched with a terrible relentlessness towards the little farmhouse, destroying every field and building in-between.

Standing by the house looking out at the distant wall of smoke, feeling the wind in his face, Charlie's heart must have sunk. Now he had two choices: stay and fight the fire or grab the family, abandon the house to the flames and run. As was his character, he chose to stand his ground.

We have only a few family memories describing what he did next. But as the options were limited, we can make a good guess. Mary would have gathered the two children and put them either in the house, the dugout, or down in the creek bed (though the last two choices would have been risky because of the overhead trees. Charlie would have then sent her into the house to gather all of the bedding and linens and carry them out to the well, where Charlie would have doused them with buckets of water.

Then, as Mary hung the wet sheets, blankets and towels from the windows, porch and eaves of the house, Charlie would have rounded up the frightened animals and put them in the paddock (if there was one) or tied them to the pillars of the house. Next, he would have gathered up a sheaf of grass or wheat stalks to make a torch, lighted it and headed out to the perimeter of the mown lawn, about one hundred feet from the house. There he would have set the tall grass alight, running back and forth to put out any intrusion by the flames onto the lawn.

That done, with the encircling fire slowly pulling away into the wind, the air thick with smoke and the choking sweet smell of a million bonfires, Charlie would have stood for a moment and waited. Then, too nervous to simply await his fate, he would have gone back to racing around, checking every detail, drawing up new water from the well to throw against the house, calming the animals, yelling orders to Mary on what to do next if his strategy failed.

The fire, stretching to the horizon, turning the burning midday sun to a lurid orange, moved inexorably towards them. And Charlie's little backfire in turn crawled towards it. Three hundred feet from the house, in an inferno of thick smoke, the two fires met . . . and the twenty-foot tall flames suddenly guttered out.

Then, a few seconds later, Charlie must have been able to look edge-wise down the entire length of the fire, perhaps a mile or more, as it passed—watching as, foot by foot, it turned brown stubble and red dirt into smoking black and gray ash.

The danger had passed. But not Charlie's sense of duty. As soon as he knew his farm and family were safe, he jumped onto Old Prize—we don't know if he took the time for a saddle or not—and took off in a gallop.

He either rode around the end of the fire, or down the creek bed through it, to Frank Hay's farmhouse, which now lay directly in the path of the flames. We don't know what precautions Hays had already taken, but we can probably assume they weren't much—probably saddling his horse and gathering a few possessions. Charlie must have been shouting even before he got to the house, even as he dismounted and leaped onto the porch.

As he had with Mary, Charlie ordered Hays to grab every bit of linen in the house and soak it with water. The fire was very close now. The two men flung the wet sheets and blankets over the low eves and across the face of the porch and dangled them from under the double-hung windows.

The fire was almost upon them. Grabbing a handful of grass, Charlie told Hays to do the same. They may even have lit them from the fire itself, and then run back to the house. There was no time left. So they lit the grass growing right in front of the river rocks that were the foundation of the house.

The backfire inched away from the house. The prairie fire was now upon them, singeing their faces and clothes, blistering the paint on the house . . . and then it died, starved by the back fire just fifteen feet from the house.

I can imagine the two exhausted men, faces and clothes wet and blackened with the soot, sitting on the porch, surrounded by Old Prize and any other animals they might have saved, panting and chuckling and shaking each other's hands.

Frank Hay's house is gone now; time having accomplished what the fire could not. But the story remains, passed through the genera-tions as a combination history lesson about the hard life on the prairie and a moral lesson about duty and friendship. Rarely noticed is the symbolism of the event: in the Hasbrook family, Charlie himself was the backfire.

THE PRICE OF PROSPERITY: THE HASBROOK HOMESTEAD

By 1910, after fifteen years on the farm, the Hasbrook family was finally enjoying some prosperity. Charlie now owned three-quarters of the section, 480 acres, most of it under cultivation. He hired an itinerant German builder to construct a big barn, complete with a gothic cupola on the top. Mary raised the family healthy and strong, and in free moments tended a fruit orchard along the road to the house, as well a truck garden beyond the house.

In the late summer, as many as twenty-five men would converge on the farm to assist Charlie in running the giant horse-drawn Case threshing machine. It was as big as a school bus and twice as wide. They would arise at dawn and harvest ten acres per day in the broiling sun. Mary, Theresa and several of the men's wives would work all morning in the kitchen, then bring the piles of food out to an outbuilding, from which they would serve the men a luncheon dinner at long outdoor tables.

Just a decade out of the dugout, Charlie and Mary had joined the middle class—at least the rural American middle class of cheap overalls and expensive tractors. Charlie even had the time and money now to become a 32nd order Mason, and Mary a local pillar of the Eastern Star. The children, who once either walked (on dry days) or were driven by buggy to the Fairview District No. 102 schoolhouse, now rode their own horses and stabled them in the newly built barn by the school. Meanwhile, back at the farm, the old dugout had now long since been converted into a well-stocked root and produce cellar.

The area too was prospering. Neighbors were busily building silos and outbuildings and hiring hands to assist on their growing farms. Outsiders, waiting for the pioneers to cut the roads and build the schools, now began to buy their way into the community.

One such family, the Collins, moved into the farm next door, buying it from one of the many families that went bust in the hard new land. The Collins were Iowans, up from Texas, having barely survived the Galveston hurricane (my grandfather would remember sitting on his bed, the flood waters two feet deep in the bedroom) and anxious to start anew. They had delivered 15 children, seven of whom had died in infancy, another as a toddler, and yet another, the oldest daughter, as a young adult to influenza. The husband was a big, pompous man, with a walrus moustache, a bald head and a genius for making money. The wife was a hard rock Baptist who believed in strong discipline and quiet children.

But what distinguished the Collins clan were those children who survived: a little girl, Velva and her five strapping older brothers. Art, John, Pearl, Charles and Leslie—actually Artie, Johnny, Pearlie, Charlie and Leslie, the perverse love of rhyming names would continue into the next generation—all of the Collins boys were destined to be more than six feet tall. Only the ill-fated second son, John, who would die in the trenches in France, would fail to live well into his late eighties or nineties, still straight and tall. In an age of short-statured people, the boys were quite a sight—one not lost on the beautiful, serious Theresa. The brother who noticed her in turn was the oldest, Art. Seven years older, he would wait years, until 1917, to finally propose. After the wedding, Theresa merely moved next door.

Nine months later, my Aunt Alliene was born in the Collins farmhouse. Fourteen months after that, my mother arrived. In between, Emeline Woodley traveled from Oregon to Oklahoma to visit her son. It may have been the first time they had seen each other in twenty years.

It also may not have been the happiest of visits, at least for Mary and Theresa. We have one record of the visit: that photograph called "Four Generations", showing the formidable Emeline Woodley, a somber Charlie Hasbrook, a weary Theresa Collins and a bright-eyed baby Alliene. Looking again at the photograph I can imagine the scene: Theresa is trying to keep little Alliene happy and clean, as she puts the baby on Charlie's knee—while an irritated Emeline tells her son and granddaughter what to do. Finally, at the last moment, Theresa runs around to the back of the little group . . . and the camera catches her, her hair slightly askew, just as she finally exhales.

As it happened, as I am writing this, my Aunt Alliene, has flown out from Tulsa to visit my mother, who lives a few blocks from me. Sitting by the pool, I show her the photograph.

"Look at how tired mother looks," Alliene says, shaking her head in dismay. "Just think about it. After they moved to Enid, mother and daddy were the only members of either family that had a house in town. So besides raising the five of us, every time somebody came into town to take somebody to the hospital or stay overnight for some reason or other, we always had to put them up. And we only had three bedrooms! Mother had to take care of everybody.

"And then, every once in a while, granddad would decide that he had a duty to go out to Oregon and see Great-Grandmother Woodley. Grandmother did not like the woman—she was apparently very difficult to get along with—so Granddad wouldn't even tell her until the last minute, until after he had packed. And that meant, in the meantime, he would come into town with all of his dress shirts and bring them to mother to iron. As if she didn't have enough to do. . ."

FREEFALL

In marrying Art, Theresa teamed for life with the most amiable, but least successful, of the Collins boys. Whereas some of his brothers would go on to become millionaires, my grandfather began married life in Enid as a truck driver . . .and never went much further. As more children came along—Alliene, Nadiene, Loriene (rhyming names once again), Wanda and Lloyd—and the economy collapsed, Art began to take on more jobs to support the family. All soon failed. He had worked during the good times driving a truck for a fruit company and then a furniture store. Now he was reduced to a seven day per week, twelve hour per day job as a night clerk at the Youngblood Hotel in downtown Enid.

Then disaster struck. Late one night, while securing the different floors of the hotel, he stepped into the open, darkened elevator. . . someone had broken the rules. . .and fell three stories down the empty shaft, from the second floor into the basement. The only thing that saved him was the rubber bumper on the bottom. As it was, he was pretty busted up, with a shattered shoulder, broken ribs and one leg fractured in two places.

Theresa and the children learned what had happened from the morning paper, because Art, lying in the hospital, didn't want to worry them.

It took him almost six months to recover. The family might have starved had not the two families brought in endless supplies of food from the farms.

It is a measure of the precariousness of their situation that my grandmother, driving flats of eggs to town, accidentally missed the turn out of the Hasbrook farm onto the bridge over Wolf Creek, skidded down the steep bank and crashed into a tree. The eggs were ruined. Grandma was so traumatized by the experience that she never drove again for the remaining half century of her life.

In time, Grandpa recovered, the Depression ended, and the children married. Through it all, Art and Theresa lived a comfortable, if not an especially prosperous, life. Grandpa held various jobs over the years—mostly as a carpet installer, first for Sears, then in his own business—none of them with much growth potential. After a heart attack sidelined him in 1963, he took even lesser jobs, ending his career as a parking lot attendant. Mostly he tinkered in the garage, making little wooden items and refurbishing pocketknives. He was a kindly, if not ambitious, man.

What did grandma see in him? I think he knew how to make her happy. He teased her for sixty years, always earning a tiny smile and the happy complaint "Oh Art!" At their golden anniversary party, as they were cutting the cake, grandpa pinched grandma's bottom right in front of three generations of descendents.

The second child of the dugout, Nate, was a wholly different breed of cat. He was blessed with every prerequisite of greatness except character.

At each family reunion, Nate's children bring out the sacred relics. One is a photo of Nate that looks like the very image of a Prairie Apollo. He has thick blonde hair, parted Gatsby-style in the middle, a square jaw, high cheekbones, a twenty-inch neck and almond shaped eyes. At age twenty, Nate is so good-looking that you wonder what combination of Hasbrook genes managed to produce him. There has been nobody so magnificent since, and one doubts for centuries before.

But Nate was blessed with more than looks. The other sacred relic is his letter sweater from OSU, then called Oklahoma A&M. At Marshall high school, Nate set every possible football rushing record—some of which stood for decades. At OSU, Nate was equally accomplished as both the team captain and big man on campus. Before it was over, he also squired around the Belle—literally, for that was her name—of the Ball. Even as an elderly lady, with her fingers twisted with arthritis, great-aunt Belle still bore the elegance and feminine gracefulness that must have made her a campus heartthrob. Unfortunately, but perhaps not surprisingly, she was as spoiled as her husband.

Remarkably, looks and athletic glory were the lesser of Nate's attributes. As I've already noted, he was charming, sly, witty, and a rogue. Men loved his company, while women were both scandalized and intrigued. And that was when he was an old man, slowly dying of lung cancer. In the blush of young manhood, Nate must have been utterly irresistible.

He certainly was to his own family. My grandmother adored him and excused his every excess. Nate's younger brothers and sisters held him in awe. And even Charlie, normally a fine judge of character, developed a blind spot when it came to his son. Perhaps he was making up for his own treatment by Homer Adkins, but Charlie refused his oldest son nothing, sending him off to college with new suits and a car—a considerable extravagance even in the good times of the 1920s. An indomitable sports fan, especially when it involved his son, Charlie even traveled with the A&M coach to out-of-state games.

Unfortunately, though perhaps not surprisingly, all of this indulgence and hero-worship had its effect. It turned Nate neither into an egoist nor a narcissist, but it did leave him with a distorted sense of entitlement.

The first recorded glimpse of this other side of Nate relates to his marriage. As a schoolteacher, Belle was not allowed to be married. So Nate simply married her on the sly, telling no one, including his own family, for two years as they traveled from job to job in Eastern Oklahoma. Exactly how they maintained this pretense in the various towns in which they lived is anyone's guess—though we can assume Nate's charm played a role.

Once the truth was finally disclosed, Belle was dismissed. With his not-so-new bride at his side, Nate came home to work on his father's farm. Charlie even built the couple their own house on the property. The plan, it appears, was for Nate to take over the farm when Charlie retired. And for more than a decade, that strategy succeeded. Nate lived well enough off his share of the proceeds, even during the Depression, and in the surrounding towns he was still the legendary football hero.

But fate took a different turn, as will soon be explained. Suddenly the farm was gone and Nate, now in his mid-thirties, went looking for work. Given the times, this couldn't have been easy. And making matters worse, Belle's taste for the good life exceeded even her husband's.

Nevertheless, no doubt again due to his charm, Nate managed to land a plum job working for the U.S. government in western Arkansas, doling out Federal aid money to poor farm families. It was compelling work—on his return visits to Enid, Nate would describe how dogs, chickens, pigs and naked children would crawl out from under shacks to meet him as he drove up—and Nate took to it well.

Too well. Nate soon began pocketing some of the money himself . . . and he was caught

Had this been a private company, something might have been worked out on the side. But this was the government, and there was no way out. Nate spent a year in prison in El Reno for embezzlement. Belle, living in Enid, was supported by the family. And Nate's crime was never spoken of again. It was never to be mentioned in front of my grandmother, nor is it ever spoken of at the family reunion. Few of my cousins even know the story.

Still, it is a measure of what Charlie Hasbrook accomplished that Nate's squalid little felony was the only serious crime committed by the ever-larger Hasbrook clan in the twentieth century. The tragedy is that Charlie's own son committed it.

As for Nate, the loss was incalculable. The man whose charisma and looks could have taken him anywhere instead spent a career in various jobs, including sheet metal fabricator and shipyard worker, and finally as the owner of a cement building block company in Tennessee. Still, the experience seems to have made him a better, wiser man.

Certainly it did nothing to his charm. And even as a little boy I remember coming away feeling elevated, thrilled, for having just met a man who was special in all sorts of marvelous ways.

PROGENY

Of Charlie's and Mary's other three children, the children not of the dugout but the house, my own memories are slim. With so many great-aunts and uncles at the various Hasbrook and Collins gatherings, all merged into a generic Old Relative who seemed to know much about me and remarked upon how much I looked like one or the other of my parents.

But Merrill, Audrey and Hazel Hasbrook were distinctly different characters.

(George) Merrill, born in 1902, was Nate's perfect opposite. Comparatively charmless and uneducated, honest but dreary, he carried with him an air of perpetual disapproval. Where Nate would tease his nieces until they squealed with delight, Merrill would complain if the girls made the slightest sound at the dinner table.

Merrill, who spent much of his life working at a dairy, was married three times. His first wife, delicate and beautiful Juanita McCulloch, contracted tuberculosis—and in an attempt to improve her health, the couple moved to Southern California. There they were joined by teenaged Audrey Hasbrook, sent out, it was rumored, by Charlie to cool her relationship with a local farm boy. While Audrey was there, Juanita gave birth (the timing of which also raised my father's eyebrows) to a daughter, Vie Lee.

When Juanita died, Merrill brought her home. My mother remembers seeing Juanita's casket, surrounded by mourners, resting in the kitchen of the farmhouse. Vie Lee went to live with Nate and Belle, who were at that point childless (they would later have two children). Vie Lee, though friendly to Merrill, ever after considered Nate her true father.

Merrill married again, briefly, to a woman named Inez, then finally settled down in North Enid in a long marriage to Gladys Herrian, a schoolteacher. They had one daughter, Louise. Merrill lived into his nineties.

Audrey, like Nate a beauty and a charmer, fell in love early to Ted Olmstead—for which she was sent out West. Charlie's strategy didn't work, and upon her return, following her graduation from Phillips University in Enid, the flapper and the farm boy were married.

Of all the Hasbrook children, Audrey's life may have been the hardest. Ted proved to be a mediocre farmer—and, according to my aunts, "a mean drunk." He supplemented the growing family's meager income by making moonshine, a profession in which he was only marginally more successful, as he was regularly caught and sent to jail. Meanwhile, Audrey and the kids lived in a shack with rough wood plank floors.

One can only wonder what a college educated woman felt about such a hardscrabble life. My mother does remember the afternoon a yellow cab pulled up in front of their house and deposited Audrey, baby Teddy and a big trunk. Audrey, it seems, had left Ted and decided to stay (where else?) at her big sister's house. But a few days later, she went home . . . to four more children, a teaching career, and a marriage that lasted more than fifty years.

Hazel, born in 1907, married a schoolteacher (later a refinery worker) from nearby Douglas named Elmer Franke. When their first child, Corky, was born, Elmer had just taken the refinery job, and the couple couldn't afford a home . . .so they moved in (again, where else?) with Art and Theresa. My mother and her sisters awoke up one morning to the cries of a new baby in the house.

Like many last-born, Hazel remained childish and irresponsible well into early adulthood. In particular, Hazel was a horrible housekeeper. My aunts, who babysat her five kids, still wince at the memory of dirty diapers, urine-soaked mattresses and all manner of household filth. Worse, Hazel often 'forgot' to pay the girls for their work. Meanwhile, she was off earning a living doing odd domestic jobs and housesitting.

Still, there is more to motherhood than hygiene, and Hazel seemed to have a talent for the rest: to the amazement of their older cousins, Hazel's children all grew up to be well-adjusted and successful professionals. Hazel herself spent her last years as a museum docent and a pillar of the community.

A PIECE OF PAPER: ENID, OKLAHOMA

By the mid-1930s, all of the Hasbrook children were grown, married and gone. Mary and Charlie, having survived the worst of the Depression, were now approaching sixty and looked forward to a few more years of hard work, then turning the farm over to Nate. They had much to be proud of: the farm was prosperous, they had a dozen healthy grandchildren, and there was money in the bank.

But once again, disaster struck. And this time Charlie couldn't beat it. As in many farm towns in the Mid-West, the local farmers around Bison had developed a deep and enduring relationship with their local banker. In Charlie's case, he may have visited the local banker for a quarter century, borrowing money to buy seed and feed, occasionally mortgaging parts of the farm to purchase heavy equipment, and depositing his earnings at the end of each harvest.

Needless to say, the relationship between farmer and banker was both intimate and deeply interdependent. Never more so than in the 1930s: as farmers one hundred miles West of Bison abandoned their farms to the Dust Bowl and headed to California, as banks failed throughout the country, the little bank in Bison managed to stay on its feet. As a result, Charlie and Mary not only held onto their farm, and the two nearby farms they'd acquired in the intervening years, but managed to help feed their children and grandchildren as well.

But unbeknownst to the aging couple, unseen and covetous forces were already plotting against them to steal the farm. A decade later, now living in Enid, Charlie sat down and wrote for his descendents, as well as for his own understanding, a chronology of what happened.

"In 1930," he wrote in a careful hand, *"I received a letter from H.D. Hearn to come in and talk matters over."* H.D. Hearn was the local banker. *"When I did, he says, 'I wish you would make a list of all your personal property so we would have it to show the bank examiner, so he would not have to take our word for what you really have.'*

"I then made the list and gave it to him." Hearn next did something extraordinary, "He then copied it on a mortgage blank which we signed." Charlie, who trusted a man he'd known for a quarter century, was about to be trapped.

"'Now,' he says, 'we will have to take part of your account off the bank rolls—for the commissioners will not approve of that much from any one individual. Next,' he says, 'we will charge $10,000 off to J. L. Hearn [the banker's brother] and you may give him a second mortgage on your three farms.'"

That made Charlie uneasy, "I told him I did not mind giving it on the two places, but I did not like to re-mortgage the homestead."

Then Banker Hearn played his trump card. "He says, 'Look here Charlie, the bank is in a mighty strenuous condition. I do not know what the outcome will be. You owe the bank a lot of money, and you are not the only one. J.L. Hearn is having to carry the bank and if the examiner thinks his security is not enough they will close the bank.'

"Well, I says, then J.L. might chase me out by paying off the first mortgage and leave me holding the sack. He says, 'You need not fear J. L., all he wants is to tide the bank over the depression.'

"Well, we both signed the papers. Mind you, we were borrowing no more money. Just trying to do all we could to help save the bank and ourselves . . ."

Six months later, the bank closed, taking the local farmers' money with it. A stunned Charlie Hasbrook drove over the Banker Hearns' house and called him outside. "[I] asked him what the outcome of the J.L. Hearn mortgage would be and said he did not know what the creditors of J.L. would do." It seems that J.L. too had gone bust. "He said he did not know what the creditors would do, but I need not fear J.L."

In fact, J. L., before declaring bankruptcy, had signed over the Hasbrook mortgage to yet another Hearn brother, Edd. The farm was slipping away fast; the mortgage being passed from brother to brother faster than Charlie could chase it.

Then, a few days later, Banker Hearn suddenly died. Though the details are sketchy, the coincidence has always been too great to assume natural causes.

The Depression was now in full force—and even as he was fighting to keep his extended family alive, Charlie struggled to regain ownership of his farm. But success always just eluded him. After a few months, he eventually reached an agreement with Edd Hearn to use profits from the harvest to pay off the interest on the mortgage. Charlie was to cover the rest of the debt by giving up one of the other farms.

This took Charlie several years—only then to be told that Edd Hearns had transferred the mortgage months earlier to one of Charlie's own tenants, Mrs. Loisa Hammer, who had long coveted it. *"[Edd Hearn] said it was out of his hands and that she would not take the one farm in payment. I then offered every imaginable proposition but could reach no settlement."*

It was over. Charlie tried to fight the case in court, but history was now against him. The second wave of the Great Depression was already underway, sending a tidal wave of bankruptcies and foreclosures through the increasingly unforgiving courts. The hearing, in Federal Court in Oklahoma City, was held on September 8, 1938.

"There were 73 cases almost identical with mine," Charlie wrote sadly, *"and the Judge ruled against them all as fast as they came in."*

The family homestead was gone.

PART TWO

GOOD BONES

Granddaughter:
Silicon Valley, California

Nadiene had planned to sleep in that Saturday morning.

The high school senior had spent the night before at a school football game and dance and had barely gotten home before her midnight curfew. Now, the clock read 7 a.m. and her Aunt Hazel was shaking her awake. What was she doing here? Where were her parents? She noticed that Hazel was wearing a coat and hat.

"We gotta get going," said a voice from the other room, "It starts in an hour." Nadiene recognized the voice of her Uncle Bud.

"What's going on?" asked Nadiene, sitting up and shaking out her thick, wavy hair. "Why the hurry?"

"Just get dressed," said Hazel, not sharply, but as if she was distracted by something else. "I'll tell you on the way."

But there were no explanations. Instead, the three of them rode in grim silence in Bud's dusty Ford pick-up. They headed south along the long paved highway, then turned east at the familiar grain elevators of Bison and down the dusty red dirt road.

Nadiene had taken this route her entire life. She had long-since realized where they were going: Either the Hasbrook farm were she had spent much of her childhood, or the Collins farm, where she was born. Which one, and why?

Only when Bud crossed the bridge over Wolf Creek and turned back up the connecting road did Nadiene know for sure: Grandfather Charlie's place. And when they drove past Grandmother Mary's apple grove, and pulled up to the farm—and saw that its grounds were jammed with scores of parked trucks—did she understand that something important had happened.

And when Nadiene saw, beyond the parked trucks, that all the furniture from the house—the bed she slept in every summer, the kitchen table, the living room chairs—was lined up in the yard, did she suddenly realize that the farm, the place that three generations of Hasbrooks had seen in their mind's eye whenever they heard the world home, was lost.

Nadiene had always assumed that the farm would belong to the family forever; that even if she never lived there, at least Nate or Merrill, or one of Charlie's other grandchildren, would. No one had even told her that the farm was in trouble . . . and now strangers were greedily inspecting the private contents of the house that her grandfather had built with his bare hands, casually bidding on the farm equipment that had kept her family fed when times had been at their worst and her father had been injured. Now all of those things by which Nadiene had defined herself, whose permanence she had always assumed, were about to be scattered across the countryside, never to be seen again.

Bud and Hazel, shaking their heads, walked on towards the house. But Nadiene, tall and slim, the wind whipping at her dress and hair, stood rooted in place. Tears welled in her eyes, but she didn't wipe them away.

Instead, her jaw set. And her fists clenched. *I don't know how I'll do it, she said to herself, but I'll get this place back. I swear to God.*

GONE

Before the day was over, much of the house furniture, as well as all of the farm equipment was sold, as were the farm animals. Not long after, Mrs. Hammer's daughter married a farmer—and the newlyweds moved into Charlie's and Mary's house. And for almost seven decades, the Hasbrook Farm was their Farm. Meanwhile, the Hasbrooks, like the Collins before them, became a town family.

Forty-five years after Charlie rode Old Prize onto the land, he put Mary into the car, took a look back at the house, the farm, Prize's grave, and the old dugout cave, then drove away to their new home in Enid.

It was a pleasant little cottage, a few blocks from the hospital and the busy downtown. Best of all, it was just a block from Art and Theresa's home. The elder Collins had already had the same idea. Much richer than the Hasbrooks, they too moved to a house just a few blocks away from their eldest son. Nadiene, my mother, loved visiting her maternal grandparents, where she was always allowed to make herself at home. The senior Collins' house was another story: there, the children were ordered to stay away from the good furniture and not make a mess.

But in one area, both elderly couples were in accord: if they spotted any of their grandchildren misbehaving on the way home from school they would call ahead to make sure the child was properly punished. The senior Collins' had done that since the girls had been in elementary school; now Charlie and Mary joined the surveillance. Looking back, my mother says that was one reason why she married my father and got away from Enid.

The war came and the local boys, including several of Charlie and Mary's own grandsons went off to fight it. The granddaughters remained, but they were older now, busy with the many soldiers who passed through the local army bases—two of them even found husbands among these young men.

The war ended, but the peace brought its own changes, including two great-grandchildren, one of them Linda, the daughter of Alliene, the baby in the second Four Generations photograph. And even as family members and neighbors returned home, others were leaving: Theresa's second daughter, Nadiene, who had seemed too busy with boys to settle on one, suddenly chose a most unlikely husband and took off for California.

The pioneer couple was getting old now, crossing into their eighties. Mary's health declined first. She died of a stroke on a hot summer day in late July 1949. Without her, Charlie found he didn't have much to live for.

In the summer, he sat on the porch in a rocking chair; in the winter inside by the stove on a hassock. Already a small man, the years had made Charlie even smaller, deepening the vertical lines on his face, but leaving his wavy white hair still too thick to comb. Theresa fed him three meals per day and carefully watched his diet. Otherwise, he spent his days listening to the radio, maintaining his enduring love of ball games and horse races. When he heard that my parents had lived in Baltimore without going to see the Preakness, he was visibly disappointed.

Perhaps because of his daughter's attention—and Victorian modesty—he disappeared once to Tulsa to have prostate surgery. Only after the surgery did he send a postcard to my grandmother to say where he was.

That was he lat long trip. Once he had willingly driven 15 miles through snow and sleet storms to attend Enid High School football games; now, though the field was two blocks away, he was content to read the box scores in the next morning's paper. Some of his happiest moments came from visits by his oldest friend, Will Neel, who now lived 50 miles away in Okarche.

In February 1950, he was invited out to Audrey's farm for a nice dinner. There, he happily indulged himself in a big, heavy meal of meat, biscuits and gravy and pie—all of Charlie's favorites, which Audrey, resenting her older sister's iron hand, had decided to cook for him. My grandmother was bitter about it for years, but I suspect Charlie was happy to get out from under her strict regimen. And he was always happiest out of the city and on a farm.

After dinner Charlie, complaining about having trouble breathing, stretched out on the couch . . . and never awoke.

He was buried beside Mary in Memorial Park Cemetery in Enid. In the years that followed, the Oklahoma Land Rush and its heroic Boomers grew in the eyes of history. Today, even as Charlie's and Mary's gravestone wears away, their freshly inscribed names can be seen on a brick in the courtyard of the Cherokee Strip Museum near Enid's Government Springs Park and the pond where a young Charlie Hasbrook founded the city.

Big World

Though my mother wrote regularly to my grandmother, often to her three sisters, and occasionally to her only brother, the years that followed had taken her far from home. And whereas the others had mostly married and settled less than a few hours' drive away, my mother had found a man who had been little more than passing through and who would rarely ever return.

And my mother, to the dismay of her family, had been happy to go. Though she was the prettiest daughter and had suffered no shortage of suitors and beaus—from local boys to soldiers heading to and from the

War—she had steadfastly refused to marry, saying that she had never found a boy interesting enough to hold her attention.

That was worrisome; but when one sibling after another married and settled down, and my mother remained single at 26, there was real fear in the family that she would never marry and become a sad old spinster, or worse. The war had ended, and there were fewer soldiers passing through Enid; while the local boys who had survived to come home were now, armed with their GI Bills and VA loans, pairing up with less judgmental local girls. Yet, my mother seemed indifferent.

And then my father arrived—and then suddenly the family's one fear was replaced by another. My father was cocky, brilliant, dangerous and troubled. Already in his young life he had been all-but abandoned by his disintegrating family, buried a drunken father, ridden the rails with hobos, dated a Hollywood starlet, and gone off to war to fly 30 terrifying missions as the bombardier-navigator in a B-17.

Now he was stateside once more, running from his demons and, as always, searching for the next adventure. Killing time, deciding whether to become a civilian again or stay in the rapidly shrinking military, he had washed up at Vance Army Air Corps base in Enid, for the moment still a captain, and put in charge of the bar at the Officer's Club. Restocking booze was a half-day job at most, and my father, whose attention span was what you'd expect from a dyslexic with a genius IQ, quickly found himself bored to tears, and stuck in a Podunk town in the very navel of the Mid-West.

He might have stayed drunk for the duration of this posting, but he was always wary of alcohol—it had, after all, killed his own father at age 34—and so the days were mostly dry and endless. It was a mark of his desperation that when a buddy landed a date with a local girl who didn't want to go out alone, my father agreed to go along on a blind date in order to serve as wingman.

My mother hadn't wanted to go out that night. She'd already suffered through two dreary dates already that week, and it had been a long day at the switchboard enduring the hot weather and a nasty supervisor. But when her friend called and prevailed upon her, my mother reluctantly agreed to go—on provision that she could leave early.

The first meeting of my parents was as novel and unpredictable as their forty-two year marriage. As was proper my mother, dressed and ready, waited inside my grandparents' house—and when the appointed hour arrived, she heard a car pull up outside, and awaited a knock at the door. And waited. And waited. But the knock never came.

Finally, in frustration, she broke with protocol and went out on the porch, then down onto the brightly lit front lawn. A convertible Ford was parked, still running, in front of the house next door, its headlight beam raking across the grass. There seemed to be a commotion in the drainage ditch that ran alongside the street and through a culvert under the driveway. Then she spotted her father, who appeared to be kneeling in the ditch, shouting to someone.

"Daddy?" she asked "What's going on?"

Her father, still kneeling, pointed towards the culvert, "That young soldier spotted a raccoon running in there. I think I see it."

Young soldier? My mother walked across the driveway. She could just make a figure, clad in khaki, all-but climbing headfirst into the narrow tunnel.

"Hello?" she asked.

The figure extricated itself, then slowly rose to his feet—as he did the headlights illuminated a long face with high cheekbones, thinning wavy hair and shockingly pale blue eyes. My father looked up at the unexpected sight of a self-assured Mid-Western beauty and broke into a big, crooked grin. "Hey," he said, with a voice that suggested that he was already family, "Are you Nadiene? I'm Pat."

If it wasn't love at first sight, it was damn close. My mother found my father endlessly interesting—an opinion that never changed over all of their years together. And for my father, who had been handed from family to family for most of his life, my mother was an island of stability and calm in a volatile, and often lethal, world.

But my father was about the last thing my mother's family had been praying for. He was too wild, too fast, and too worldly—and almost overnight they went from hoping my mother would find a man to fervently wishing she dump the man she'd found. Though my grandparents were more silently disapproving in their mid-Western way, my aunts and uncles each in turn took my mother aside and tried to talk her out of the match.

As was her way, she listened to them politely and took off with my father anyway. And whereas, with a few exceptions, none of my aunts and uncles ever moved far from Enid, my father took my mother far away: to the Hollywood film community in Palos Verdes, to a frozen winter in Minnesota, then on to Germany, then Morocco, and then to Germany again.

A DUTIFUL WIFE

I was conceived, my father believed, in an inn in the Italian Alps; I was born at the Air Force base in the Bavarian village of *Furstenfeldbruck*, and spent my childhood in Munich, speaking German (thanks to the maid) before I spoke English. My father was the district director of counter-intelligence for the Air Force Office of Special Investigations—a job that consisted mostly of chasing down Polish and Russian agents trying to sneak undetected into post-war Germany, but sometimes—especially when he slipped under the wire into Poland— was extremely dangerous.

Through it all, my mother fought to assert the normalcy she had known in Enid. She would make sure my father had a good dinner before he went out on one of his night missions—even making sure he had the bullets for the little FN .32 automatic that fit neatly under his suit jacket. One night she kept up a friendly conversation at a small din- ner party with a woman who didn't know—as my mother did—that her husband was late because he was trapped in high grass on the far side of the border fence, unable to move because of Polish guards nearby. And if she fretted and feared for my father's safety, my mother, like my grand- mother before her, fought hard to never show her worry.

Inevitably, this life changed her. My mother now wore her once long and wavy hair in a stylish short cut, and dressed in elegant Italian wools—and her beauty, combined with her unmannered simplicity, made many of the hard-bitten spies in my father's office secretly fall in love with her. She didn't think twice now about talking to a shop-clerk in German, or wandering through the Kasbah in Casablanca. And when my father was caught by the French government working with the Moroccan revolutionary party, declared persona non grata and given 72 hours to leave the country or be arrested as a spy, my mother quickly packed up their belongings and raced with my father to Gibraltar. They spent Christmas in a Madrid hotel—and my mother still managed to find a scraggly little tree and decorate it.

Oklahoma was now far away, and though my mother dutifully wrote each week to my grandmother, the attractions of home began to fade. When we returned, now a family of three, to the States—my father had been posted to Fairchild Air Force base in Spokane, Washington—we stopped only briefly in Enid as we were passing through.

It would always be like that. Two years later, we paused a few days in Enid on the way to Washington, DC to what proved to be my father's last assignment in the Air Force. Then, over Christmas 1962, in the midst of bad blizzard, we spent two nights at my grandparents before racing on to California to visit my father's adopted parents in Palos Verdes, the headed up to the Bay Area where my father successfully interviewed for a job with NASA.

It was only the next summer, seventeen years after my mother left home, that she finally returned for an extended—that is, week-long—stay. We were moving to Mountain View, California and my father's new job.

My father, who long ago had learned about the family's early opinion of him, seemed to revel in his notoriety. Newly retired as a much-decorated Major, with a job in the Space Program awaiting him, nothing made him happier than to drive up to the little house on Washington Avenue in Enid in our brand new Thunderbird, with a case of liquor in the trunk, wearing his aviator glasses, and a Tiparillo clenched in his teeth. He spent the week relaxing on the porch, politely but ominously refusing to discuss any of his career for national security reasons, and most of all watching in amusement as my mother had to deal with all of the old family dynamics: the power struggles, the envies, pointed comments and raised eyebrows.

For my part, I learned for the first time that I had an extended family: nearly a dozen cousins, all of them older than me, and generally paying me attention only long enough to tell me not to follow them, or to trick me into doing something stupid. At one point I ended up suspended momentarily upside down from a barbed wire fence, a barb embedded in my calf. Nearly a half-century later, I still have the scar.

Though my cousins had little use for me, I found their very existence enthralling. There was no real family on my father's side; my drunken, brawling grandfather had been dead for thirty years, and my father had little contact with either his re-married mother (who terrified me the only time I met her) or his half-sister. But now, suddenly, I realized the power of blood; that I was part of something far larger than me that stretched generation upon generation back through time. Suddenly, unexpectedly, I had a source of myself.

In the next few days I met a seemingly endless number of great-aunts and uncles, whose names and faces I quickly forgot. Except for one: my great-uncle Nate, my grandmother's next younger sibling. He was my mother's favorite, and, I quickly realized as I listened to him tease her, that she was his. Nate was the one Oklahoma in-law with whom my father could truly unwind. My great-uncle was surpassingly handsome, elegant and very witty in a slightly racy way. He was like no Hasbrook (his family) or Collins I had ever seen; utterly different from his plain-clothed, plain-spoken and generally humorless older sister. It was as if a Manhattan boulevardier had been plucked off Fifth Avenue and dropped against his will into the geographic heart of America and told he could never leave. Nate and my father sat on the porch well into the night, and to the roar of crickets and the flicker of fireflies, they drank whiskey, smoked and told dirty jokes that I strained to hear and memorize. And Nate laughed and laughed with the jagged cough that had already begun to kill him.

Nate was something altogether unexpected and new, and though I was too young to detect the message he presented, in the years to come I would look back and realize that this was the first time that I noticed that my mother's family was not quite what it appeared to be. After all, how could this ostensibly God-fearing, decent Midwestern family, that belonged to the Grange and the Daughters of the Eastern Star, paid its taxes and collected Easter Seals, prayed in church every Sunday and kept no liquor in the house except as 'medicine', have produced a worldly roué like Nate Hasbrook?

GOLDEN

We returned to Oklahoma a few years later.

The occasion was my grandparents' fiftieth wedding anniversary. Thus, it was not only a gathering of immediate family, but my great-aunts and uncles and their progeny (most of whom I'd never heard of, much less met) and old friends from the days when the oil boom had made Enid the fastest-growing town in America.

In those long gone days, the first two decades of the 20th century, Enid had been the Silicon Valley of its era, not the fading prairie metropolis, left behind by the interstate that it was rapidly becoming. And these aged men and women standing around me, looking uncomfortable in their suits and starched shirts, were the new arrivals who had never left. They had found their brief moment in history, settled in and then let history pass them by. As such, they were a glimpse, now in the mid-1960s, of the world already far gone. Most had been born in pioneer shacks, taught on a kitchen table, and known neither electricity nor indoor plumbing until their early adulthoods. No generation had ever come so far in a single lifetime, and despite their isolation in the American heartland, they had the self-assurance of people who had thrived, suffered and endured through unimaginable changes, and had lost all fear of the future.

But whatever interest I had in these elders quickly disappeared in the face of an even more arresting apparition. My father and my Uncle Bob—he was a veterinarian, a giant man with a kindly face and a devastating sense of humor—had been sent off to pick up the special guest at the Golden Anniversary. This woman, I was told, wasn't just a friend of my grandparents, but of my *great-grandparents*. Indeed, she was all-but the last of her generation, one of a handful of survivors to have not only participated in the Land Rush—there were no doubt still-surviving children who had ridden in wagons—but to have actually rode it. Not only that, but she had ridden it *alone*, a young single woman in a buggy flouting every convention of the age.

It was Lillie A. Gibson. And her appearance caused a considerable stir—and not for the expected reasons: Miss Lillie, a wizened crone in her nineties, arrived at the party in a tight mini-dress, bright orange hair, and a gash of claret-colored lipstick. My father told my mother afterwards that on the ride to the party Miss Lillie had shamelessly flirted with both men—and even squeezed my father's thigh with her long fingernails. My father found the whole thing hilarious; at ten, I thought she was the strangest creature I'd ever seen. *This* was what a pioneer woman looked like?

But even then at that young age I could hardly miss the sheer indominability of Miss Lillie. She was tough, perhaps even tougher than those spies who had worked with my father. From what I heard my relatives say, Miss Lillie had already buried several husbands, and it now appeared to me that she was quite prepared to bury one or two more. In all, she even made those raw-boned, hard-bitten Dust Bowl survivors around me look a little soft around the edges.

And yet, Miss Lillie A. Gibson had lined up with those multitudes of others on that September morning in 1893, and when the cannon had fired, she had urged her horse and buggy forward and raced along the same path as Charlie Hasbrook. She had been my great-grandparents' lifelong friend and neighbor, and no doubt had been in attendance—perhaps holding my grandmother—when my great-uncle Nate was born. She was not only a link to that departed world, but a surviving member of that generation. And if the rest of that crowd was anything like her, I had misread my family history completely.

PRODIGAL

I visited Enid only once more in the next thirty years.

I was nineteen years old, lean and cocky, the happy inheritor of my old man's wanderlust, and I had gotten into my head to drive across America in my little fiberglass dune buggy, serve on the staff of the Boy Scout National Jamboree, and then see America. It began with a hair-raising four day, 3,000 mile marathon that at one point had me sitting in a corn field along Interstate 80 in Nebraska rolling a bent push rod tube on a flat rock. I did my week in Pennsylvania, drove down to Virginia to watch a childhood friend play in the American Legion World Series, then met up with my California buddy Craig and we took off back across the country.

We thundered into Enid late on an August afternoon. The dune buggy's headers popped and snarled and turned heads as we cruised menacingly through the old neighborhood. Craig and I, with our long hair, sunburned faces, torn jeans and tie-dyed t-shirts, looked every bit a grandparent's worst nightmare—*this is what happens when your children move to California.*

But I was their grandson, after all—not the youngest anymore that honor now went to my kid sister—but certainly the prodigal. And family was family, blood was blood, in a way that no West Coast suburban boy could ever fully understand, and so we were welcomed, fed and given a place to sleep.

That evening after dinner Craig and I decided to hit the town and check out the local girls. My grandparents came out on the gravel driveway to see us off. As we climbed in, we were surprised to discover my grandfather behind us trying to climb in around the roll bar into the narrow back seat.

"Oh Art!" said my grandmother with disgust, "Get yourself down off of there. Those boys don't want to go out on the town with an old man like you."

I can still recall my grandfather's crestfallen face as we drove off. It's the last memory I have of him.

INFLECTION

That visit to Enid unexpectedly reignited in me a tiny flame of interest in my mother's family history that would never again extinguish.

I'd long been curious about my father's family. With its long and sad Irish narrative of famine, starvation, war, suicide and self-destruction—making *Studs Lonegan* seem upbeat by comparison—it was hard to resist. On the other hand, the story of my mother's side of the family tree—the Hasbrooks and Collins—seemed tame and even a little boring. Yet there was something oddly appealing about its apparent plainness; something almost too good to be true that kept turning my attention back towards it.

Perhaps it was being the son of an intelligence officer and criminal investigator. Or maybe it was because I was now a newspaperman. But somehow the edges of the story seemed just too smooth, the joints just a little too tight and precise. What was that odd story about my great-great-grandmother and her murdered husbands all about? Nobody seemed to know. And what of Miss Lillie? And that impossible combination of my grandmother and my great-uncle Nate? How did they fit into the sedate family tableau?

In the story of any healthy family there is almost always one remarkable individual who serves as a stop-gap between a crippled, dysfunctional past and a hopeful, healthy future.

These individuals are almost always extraordinary, not least because they not only have to defeat those destructive forces, but often must carry the scars from them as they do so. Difficult as it is to live an honorable life, have a successful career or raise children well, those tasks become almost impossible when the people who raised you have failed at all of those tasks. The easiest path is to simply follow them off the cliff.

And yet, every day in a thousand families, these individuals unexpectedly appear, sometimes after a dozen generations of degeneration. Somehow, against all odds, they find their way . . . and set off a transformation, a redirection, so complete that history itself changes.

Those who follow in subsequent generations have little or no idea what came before, or just what sacrifices were made to create the comfortable image of themselves and their families they currently enjoy. The happy and healthy extended family they know is what they assume it has always been—and it seems impossible that it ever could have been anything else. Indeed, sometimes the only clue is that the family, long often after it has forgotten why, still reveres the memory of an ancestor whose biography, if read by anyone else, would seem undistinguished, even prosaic. Somehow the memories of the children of these extraordinary individuals, the people still proximate enough to events to appreciate what their mother or father accomplished, manage to survive as a kind of reverence that is passed down from generation.

My own father was one of those individuals. His life had been one of lifelong abandonment, passed from one reluctant relative to the next. He had hit the road the moment he could escape and lived a life fraught with risk: a lumberjack, a razor-blade swallower in the circus sideshow, a tramp riding the rails, an officer in the 8th Air Force. But when he stood outside my mother's house that night in 1946 he had already decided to break the chain of suicide, adultery, violence, religious fanaticism and alcoholism that had characterized his family for the previous half-century. And in marrying my mother, the very antithesis of the smart L.A. girls he'd dated, he made the smartest decision of his life. My mother saved him, as he was the first to admit, and in doing so had turned the trajectory of the Malone family on a very different path.

I knew all of that, or at least I had begun to understand it by the time my father died—at age 68 he had doubled the lifespan of his own father—in 1988. And to my two sons, who never met him, their grandfather seems larger than life: not just because of the stories I tell them, or the medals on the wall, but also I think because of the awe and affection that comes into my voice (and my wife's) whenever we speak of him. Their children may only know their great-grandfather by name, but I suspect they'll still understand that he was somehow very important.

What only began to dawn on me as I entered adulthood was that Charlie Hasbrook was also one of these heroic figures. In one of those ironies that seem to characterize real life, my father had married my mother in no small part because she represented the stability he had never known, the close family he had only seen from afar, and the structure that even the Army Air Corps had failed to provide him. He had seen in her a way to break from the crazy past and create a sane future—not knowing that, just two generations before, her family had been just as mad, bad and dangerous as his own . . . perhaps worse. So complete had been the break that almost no record—other than the odd anomaly, such as my great-uncle Nate—had remained.

In that respect, my father had been tricked, but he never seemed to regret his fate. And, as a man whose career was one of forever solving the puzzles of other people's characters, he surely must have understood that had my mother been the perfect embodiment of sanity, stability and rectitude they never would have been compatible; he would have frightened her, and she would have bored him to death. It was the tiny residue of wildness in her blood that made my mother a willing accomplice to a life of travel, adventure and risk. She saved him, and he in turn, in a small but crucial way, liberated her.

MARCHING ORDERS

After my father died and my mother had taken the time to grieve and put her life back together, I asked her what she wanted to do in the years she had left to her.

She had spent almost seven decades being a dutiful daughter, a supportive wife and a dedicated mother. If the actuarial tables and the family history were anywhere accurate, she still might have two or more decades ahead of her—time enough to make her own mark.

She didn't hesitate. "I want the farm back," she said. "I want to get it and I want to restore it. And I don't ever want us to lose it again."

She was my mother; her request was my duty. But where to begin? To me the farm was a strange and ominous cave in a creek bank and a big barn door. My great-grandfather Charlie had lost the farm during the Great Depression under suspicious circumstances—and ever since it had been in the hands of the family that had taken it.

Moreover, even if somehow I did manage to obtain title to the place, what was left? The last I'd heard the farm buildings had been abandoned for more than a decade. Squatters and collectors had destroyed or run off with most of the architectural fixtures. And the latest report from one of my aunts who had ventured out to the farm had sadly noted that cows had wandered into the house, even climbing to the second floor, smashing the stairs and railings as they went. The porches on the house had collapsed, the main spar beam of the great barn had snapped and the whole structure was starting to buckle. And worst of all, part of the roof of the dugout had fallen in, allowing rain and snow to accumulate inside. Was there anything worth saving?

Still, I had to try. With the help of one of my aunts, I obtained the phone number of the old farmer, the man I had seen in front of the house thirty years before, and called. When he answered, in a tired drawl, I introduced myself and asked if he might consider selling the old Hasbrook farm. No, he replied, surprised by the very question, he would never sell the place because he planned to leave it to his daughter and grandkids. His words seemed final.

I delivered the bad news to my mother. She pondered it for a moment, and then announced, "It doesn't matter. We'll find another way. Or we'll just wait him out. He's older than me, so I'll just outlive him."

This was just about the toughest talk I'd ever heard from the lady who had once made sure I wore a jacket on cool days and who had driven me to Little League practice. So I did what I was told. We subscribed to the Garfield County legal record, and though I was myself busy with career, marriage and my first child on the way, I dutifully stopped by mother's house once per month specifically to peruse the latest issue to see if the farmer had died and his property gone into probate.

At the same time, at my mother's insistence, I had a credit search made on the farmer's daughter and grandchildren. It produced one ray of hope: the farmer's descendents were so mired in debt, and the farm itself so encumbered, that it seemed impossible that, once the deed was in their hands, they could do anything but sell. "Good," said my mother, "We'll be ready when it happens."

It was all getting a little strange and disconcerting. Here I was keeping watch over the impending death of an old man, while gathering a list of family creditors so as to pounce upon the survivors. Meanwhile, my mother, now a sweet and beloved grandmother, had become, at least when it came to regaining the Hasbrook farm, as hard and relentless as a hired killer. What was happening here?

About this time, a package arrived at my mother's house. A distant cousin, Ben Wilkerson, our only relative in Northern California, had recently died and his widow had mailed to my mother a packet of materials he had wanted her to have. I had reluctantly met the man a few times when he had visited and my parents had insisted I at least drop by and say hello.

Every family has one relation for whom ancestry charts and family trees become a kind of monomania. This obsession almost always makes them a bore and a burden on their contemporaries and hero to the generations that follow. This cousin was that relative. Ben was kind and genial man, but his visits were an endless exegesis on second and third cousins I had never heard of and cared even less about. I always made a polite, but early, escape. But now, as I leafed through the documents, photographs and yellowing Photostats, I finally appreciated both the man and his purpose.

What my cousin had left us were not answers, but all of the right questions. I saw the faces of my great-great-great grandparents for the first time; saw a photograph of my great-great-grandfather's grave showing his early death from homicide. There was the newspaper interview with 'grandmother' Woodley when she was in her eighties, as well as her application for a veteran's pension in the name of her murdered second husband. And there was even a contemporary account of the trial in that case, which took place just miles from my family's vacation home in Oregon.

I had no choice now: I had to learn the whole story. Now it was my turn to take on the case, to reconstruct what had really happened on those two lonely Oregon farms twenty years apart and more than a century ago. To learn what had driven Charlie Hasbrook back to the prairie to reset the family narrative and start everything anew.

And I had far more skills and tools than my cousin to do the job.

And so even as I was shadowing and tracking the owners, awaiting the moment to make our move to regain the Hasbrook farm, I was also on the case, reconstructing the family history that had brought us there.

I also knew when and where to start looking for answers: Saturday, September 16, 1893 outside Hennessey, Oklahoma, where Charles Hasbrook began the day as part of the largest land run in American history, and finished by digging the cave that would become his—and my—family's first true home.

THE HUNT:
THE HASBROOK HOMESTEAD

Throughout the 1990s, my mother and I opened the monthly Garfield County newsletter and looked for the surname "Pryor", perversely hoping for the good news of a man's death. This was pretty pitiless attitude—one not that far removed from the people who had stolen the farm in the first place—but then again, this was Charlie Hasbrook's homestead, and if his children had never inherited it, perhaps his great- and great-great-grandchildren could.

As the months and years passed, it began to be like a game, a monthly excuse to stop by my old house—in the topsy-turvy world of Northern California, it was my mother who lived in the modernist glass house and I in an historic Gold Rush farmhouse—and see her. And after my sons were born, it became an excuse to take by her grandchildren as well. My children grew taller, my mother older, and my hair grayer, but the news out of the courthouse in Enid, on the site of the tent where Charlie had once stood in line to register his claim, never changed.

And then suddenly, it did, long after we'd given up hope. The little newsletter carried the news of the farmer's death. The announcement was so long awaited, and now so unexpected, that we momentarily didn't know how to react.

Indeed, I wasn't sure we even *should* react.

It was one thing to dream about buying the farm and restoring it; and something altogether different when we faced the reality of actually doing so. In particular: what exactly would we do with the farm if we actually bought it? My mother had left Oklahoma fifty years before and had no intention of ever going back for more than an occasional visit. My wife and I were all-but native Californians, as was my sister, and my kids were suburban Silicon Valley boys. Not only did we have no interest in living in Oklahoma, but beyond the occasional Hasbrook or Collins family reunion, we never even considered vacationing there.

So, were we really contemplating spending what would likely be as much as a million dollars to buy and restore a farm we would rarely even *visit*?

Yes, my mother informed me, "That's exactly what I intend to do. If I live long enough, I'm going to restore the farm. And if I don't, I expect *you* to finish the job."

That made the farm my responsibility too—and that in turn meant I had to justify this crusade to myself. When this project had begun I was a newlywed in my early thirties, with no kids, a rented house and a fairly leisurely life writing books and newspaper articles. Now I was in my late forties, with two children and a big mortgage.

Moreover, I had just accepted the job of editor of the world's largest circulation business and technology magazine—which meant I had jumped almost overnight from a quiet life working in my home office to a daily sixty-mile commute, managing a staff of twenty people producing a $20 million product for nearly a million readers. On top of that, the Internet Bubble was just starting to inflate, so with every issue we were finding ourselves scrambling to create more copy to keep up with the every-growing number of advertising pages. Looking back it was the most pressure-driven and chaotic period of my adult life.

But even more than that, I had already seen what it was like to restore a historic house: years of contractors, permits, ugly and expensive discoveries every time you opened up a wall, the ever-present threat of litigation if a worker got hurt and most of all, the endless money sink. That was what our Silicon Valley house—perhaps the oldest American house in the area—had been like. The first contractor had wasted two years and cost us $200 thousand in shoddy work. We had been saved by Tim Lantz, our second contractor—but he had been so obsessive and meticulous about historical accuracy and purity that the work stretched out four more years.

In the end, we had been so broke that we finally moved out of the house we had been renting and moved into the historic house—even though the entire family (including my wife, four year old son, and newborn baby) had to sleep in the dining room and I nailed the windows and doors shut each night. With gaping holes and nails in the floors, we had to monitor the children at all times, and mosquitoes and an occasional bird flew in through the open upstairs windows.

And, for all the massive amount of work that our house needed, it had at least been continuously inhabited for the previous 140 years. By comparison, the Hasbrook homestead—Charlie's place—had been abandoned for nearly twenty years. I had heard horror stories from various relatives that squatters—'hippies', as they called them to my amusement—had taken over the house for several years and trashed the place; followed soon after by collectors, who saw any abandoned building as an opportunity, and who had torn away trim, ginger breading and doorknobs. The barn was reportedly in equally bad shape, filled with yards of rotting cow manure, the red siding gone silver and splitting, and the great roofline betraying a cracked main beam. As for the dugout, my relatives only shook their heads sadly.

Thus, to our first question was added a second: even if we did buy the old farm, would there be anything left to save? And as the years passed, and winter storms, spring floods and summer heat waves came and went, I would imagine in my mind the structures on the Hasbrook farm slowly sinking into the earth, clapboards popping free, rain dripping through rotted shingles—and worst of all, mud bricks dissolving and falling to the floor of the dugout. With each new winter, I felt evermore depressed: it was as if I was in a race with Charlie's place—it towards total, irredeemable collapse and me towards finally getting my hands on the farm and bringing the place back to life. It was a race I was losing; indeed, I hadn't even left the starting line.

And yet, despite all of this, two things finally convinced me to keep going and join my mother in one last push to regain the farm.

SILICON VALLEY

The first had to do with a very different sort of Land Rush. While Enid had been slowly dying, through the combination of a missed interstate highway and the general economic malaise of small-town middle-America, Silicon Valley was enjoying one of the greatest booms in American history.

My father had never made a lot of money from his career; he had retired as a major from the Air Force, and that retirement money, combined with his salary from NASA, had given us a comfortable life—one that, economically at least, hardly felt the impact of his two heart attacks and second retirement. But where my parents had made some real money was in real estate.

I once wrote, in my early newspaper days, that Silicon Valley real estate was like a train leaving the station. Until the late sixties that train was still waiting at the siding; and even in the early seventies it was still slowly lurching forward. If you were smart enough or brave enough to jump on-board in those days, that train carried you to great wealth.

My parents were both. Somehow, my mother had inherited Charlie Hasbrook's eye for property. And this, combined with my father's near-reckless sense of adventure, had combined to make them a brilliant investing team. With what little money they had, they bought one house or property after another. Each time, they enhanced the value of the new property with their own (and my) sweat equity. I helped paint houses, installed sprinkler systems and rolled out lawns. I remember one Thanksgiving, in the rain, atop the roof of one of our rentals, snaking out the sewer line because the renters and their dinner guests had stuffed too much paper in the toilet.

My parents dealt with unwatered gardens, holes in plaster walls, broken windows, dope growers, late payments, and even deadbeats sneaking out in the middle of the night (a big mistake when your landlord used to run surveillance on the KGB). Through it all, the rents paid the mortgages and all the time the value of the houses kept climbing. Then my parents started leveraging the smaller houses into bigger ones. And though outsiders assumed that my father was the dealmaker, I knew it was my mother who got the fire in her eyes at the prospect of another house purchase.

By the mid-Eighties, each of the houses my parents had purchased for less than $25,000 were now worth $500,000 . . . and the real boom was yet to come. But even then, my father had the satisfaction of knowing that the abandoned child had made good—and even more important, no matter what happened to him, that my mother would always be financially comfortable.

I remember walking out of a San Jose diner after breakfast with him one morning. My father was telling me that he'd had an audit done on all of their assets. He stopped and shook his head in amazement, "Jesus, son, can you believe it? I'm a millionaire."

Ten years later, after he was gone, just about everyone who owned a home in Silicon Valley could give themselves that label; and my mother, whose own home was worth more than a million dollars by itself, now had a net worth several times that.

Those years had been good to me as well. I had gone from a daily newspaperman's salary to the editorship of a national magazine—with a commensurate jump in salary. But, given the ever-increasing cost of living in the Valley, that would have kept me permanently ensconced in the middle class. But, during the long years of freelancing, whenever I could do so without conflict with my writing, I tried my own hand as an entrepreneur. I had spent my entire adult life writing about and judging these complex and remarkable individuals, and it seemed only proper that I test myself in the arena of a new company creation.

I was more lucky than smart: the start-ups into which I put heart, money and time almost all failed. Meanwhile, the opportunities that essentially fell in my lap—an unsolicited request to advise a young on-line auction company with just three employees, an offer to co-write a book with a local executive I'd never heard of before—rewarded me beyond all my fantasies: the latter company being Siebel Systems, which eventually sold for several billion dollars to Oracle, and the former, as you may have already guessed, was eBay. I didn't become billionaire like some of the men and women I worked with, but I did well enough to finish the work on my own house and—briefly— see a level of financial security known to few freelance writers.

All of this—the Internet bubble, my magazine career, the skyrocketing real estate values in Silicon Valley—was going on at the same time that the farm suddenly became potentially available for purchase. My mother and I had been immersed so long in the economy of Northern California that we had little idea of what property values were like in Oklahoma, other than that they were likely much lower. But just how much lower staggered us—and suddenly made any potential price for the farm not only reasonable, but a downright steal. Our initial inquiries had determined that good farmland outside Bison was going for about $500 to $750 per acre. In our Sunnyvale neighborhood, where a single available acre would be quickly developed with five houses or twenty apartments, the price was about *1,000* times that. In Silicon Valley, seven hundred and fifty dollars wouldn't even buy the land under the sidewalk out front; and a thousand dollars was what local executives were paying per month just to have a T1 fiber optic line brought to their homes.

We quickly realized that even if we paid absolute top dollar for the entire 320 surviving acres of the Charlie Hasbrook's farm, the entire cost would still be less than it would take to buy almost any home (outside of a double-wide or a run-down old pre-War bungalow in a dangerous neighborhood) in the San Francisco Bay Area. Suddenly, we felt like tycoons—at least by late 20th century Oklahoma standards.

Buying the Hasbrook farm now seemed like less an act of dangerous speculation and more a reasonable diversification. We might not make any money on Charlie's Place, but we probably wouldn't lose much either.

A Visit and a Vow

If the first impetus to buy the Hasbrook Farm was financial, the second was emotional.

My mother was intent upon buying her grandfather's farm because of the vow she had made as a teenager. This to her was vindication, a setting things aright, of completing the circle.

But what about me? Charlie and Mary Hasbrook died before I was born. I had never lived in Oklahoma, nor ever cared to. And I had visited the farm exactly once in my life, as a nine year-old. I was nearly fifty now, with a wife and two kids. The money my mother wanted to spend on the farm was part of their inheritance, as it was my sister's and mine. And my sister found the whole notion absurd. It was my mother's decision to make about how she wanted to spend her money, but should I be actively supporting her in this boondoggle? Serving as her advisor? Hiring agents?

And that was only the beginning. After mom was gone, Charlie's Place would no doubt fall into my hands . . . along with that unbreakable codicil that I was to maintain its upkeep and to guarantee that it would never again be let out of the family's control. That meant regular expenditures on the farm, and a schedule of annual, even quarterly, visits to Enid, and property tax payments *forever*. Was I really ready to taken on that open-ended responsibility? Were my kids? And *their* kids?

It was in search of an answer that, in the spring of 1999, I boarded a plane and flew back to Oklahoma. I spent a day outside Tulsa with my Aunt Alliene and Uncle Delbert, then, in search of my past, drove a rental car to Enid.

The ostensible reason was research on an essay I proposed to write. As contributing editor of my bimonthly magazine, Forbes ASAP, I had devised a special edition, to be called, arrogantly, "The Big Issue." When I became editor, I inherited my own creation. The editorial strategy of the Big Issue was to convince the best writers in the country to tackle a single topic, such as *Time* or *Truth*.

"The Big Issue" proved to be something of a landmark in modern magazine publishing, nominated for a National Magazine Award and presenting essays by everyone from Arthur Miller to Muhammad Ali, and from Kurt Vonnegut to George W. Bush. Many of these essays have been reprinted in collections and college textbooks ever since. Others have quite rightly become famous, such as Peggy Noonan's eerie prediction of 9/11 and Wolfe's essay "Sorry, Your Soul Just Died."

For my staff, it was a chance to connect (and sometimes learn the unhappy truth about) their literary and cultural heroes. But for me, the Big Issue was the ultimate challenge—not just as an editor, but as a writer. I allowed only two of us, myself and my senior columnist Owen Edwards, himself a former editor of Cosmopolitan, to write for the Big Issue. And both of us agreed that the prospect of rubbing shoulders on those pages with Nobel Prize winners, former Presidents and famous authors and poets, was especially intimidating. This was the Big Leagues and we were ever-mindful that we needed to bring our 'A' game.

The Big Issue essays were due in the summer, but Owen and I both began worrying about our contributions the previous winter. And it was on one of those chilly nights that I suddenly realized that the essay I needed to write was about Charlie's Place, about the technological transformation of American society and culture, from that September morning of the Land Rush through the life of my grandparents in their house in the boomtown of Enid, Oklahoma to my own life in yet another boomtown a century later and more than a thousand miles away.

And so I found myself checking into a motel in Enid, interviewing the city manager, and hanging out in the pharmacy off the town square where my mother and grandmother, each in their turn, had hung out with friends and drunk malts (and which, tellingly, was going out of business).

I next visited my grandparent's house, now in one of the poorer neighborhoods of Enid, and was given a tour by the new owners, a couple from Mexico who had taken advantage of a low-income loan program to move in. Despite their comparative poverty, I computed that, just in their cable television, home computer, programmable thermostat, and a myriad of cheap consumer products, their house not only had more electronic technology than all of Enid (including the Air Base) had when my grandparents were alive, but that the little house even had more computational power than NASA used in the Apollo missions—thus proving the point of my essay.

The couple was very nice and gracious, but I didn't stay long. Little remained of my grandparents, who had moved into the house when it was new and lived there for more than a half-century. All that really survived was the shape of the house and detached garage, the drainage trench in front where my mother had first met my father, and the gravel alleyway that ran alongside—just a palimpsest of the past, a shape that I didn't need to see to remember.

That afternoon, I found myself driving down the long red dirt road for the first time in thirty years. Strangely, I knew, without a map, where to find the farm. I parked my rental car by the locked gate, climbed over the fence and walked along the waist-high grass that had once been the driveway. Mary's apple trees, the dozen or so that had survived nearly a century, now stooped and gnarled, still lined the path. It was nearly one hundred degrees. The chatter of the locusts was almost deafening, though occasionally through its throb I could make out the gobble of a wild turkey somewhere off in the trees.

Cows from a neighboring farm had recently bedded down along this driveway and in the yard around the house—and, though I wouldn't discover it until I was back in the car, their ticks were clinging to the tips of long grass blades hungry to leap on me as I passed.

To my enormous relief, the farm house was still standing—though missing windows, chimney and the back porch roof. Inside, everything my relatives had warned me about proved to be true. The squatters and collectors had done their damage. So had the cows—a third of the stair treads had broken through, and the second floor smelled of manure and rotting insulation. I walked across that floor, where my mother had spent summer nights in her childhood dreaming of a bigger world. Carefully as possible, I stepped from joist to joist, fearful of falling through at any moment.

Grateful at last to be back downstairs, I turned a corner and nearly collided with a giant garden spider, its abdomen the size of a marble, that dangled in the middle of a web stretching across the old parlor. After that, I was relieved to head outside, despite nearly stumbling down the crumbling front steps.

Still, despite all of the decay, I had seen inside. What I couldn't get out of my mind was a single mark. It was on one of the stair treads where it met the riser: a tiny slip of the saw, a scratch made by the teeth of a crosscut blade. My great-grandfather had made that mark, as he and Frank Hays had every other saw cut and augur hole and hammer mark in the construction of that house. They had done the job with every last ounce of skill they could muster—that's why the house had taken so long to build, and why it still stood almost thirty years after being abandoned.

I made my way through the high weeds and the endless wild melon vines, past an abandoned van, an outbuilding (perhaps the oldest structure on the farm) so overgrown that I thought it was a thicket at first, and the windmill. A forty foot tree had grown right up the center of the last, and its branches had slowly twisted the steel frame into a corkscrew.

Beyond, the great barn loomed as impressively as ever. But on closer inspection, the siding was all silvered now, having lost every trace of paint, and many of the clapboards—and all of the big doors—were gone. So too was most of the glass in the windows. Enough of the shingles were missing from the great roof that I could, in places, see right through the building to the sky beyond.

When I tried to enter through the big doorway on the southern end of the barn, I found my way blocked by a rotting mound of hay and manure. But peering in, I could make out at least one of the big cross-beams that had cracked in the middle, enabling the walls on both sides to begin to slump. I couldn't see far enough into the darkness, but the swaybacked, hundred-foot long roof peak told me that, as reported, the main beam of the barn was in imminent danger of collapse.

By this point, all I had was a very large collection of reasons to abandon our dream of buying and restoring the farm. The place was just too far gone; another ten winters and there would be nothing left but piles of splintered wood. I remembered what a nightmare it had been to restore my own house—and that had been a suburban palace compared to these country ruins. Whatever optimism I arrived with had evaporated in a matter of minutes. I wasn't even sure I *could* still restore the farm even if I wanted to. And that was assuming we could even buy the place.

In my mind, I rehearsed my phone call to California: "Sorry, mom. It's too late. There's no point in even trying."

Even as I thought this, I unconsciously began walking towards the creek. My heart knew where I was going before my head did. I had to find the dugout; the little door into the creek bank.

Cottonwood saplings and high weeds blocked the way down the bank, blocking my view. But at last, as I came around an old, lightning-blasted trunk, I looked up and saw the patch of hard dirt . . . and then the doorway. A cynical old newspaperman, I still caught my breath at the sight.

The door was gone, but the old frame, still holding the rusting halves of hinges, remained. Odd; I had remembered the entrance being in the open, not sheltered by tall trees and hanging so precariously over the creek. Nearly a foot taller than Charlie, I had to duck my head to cross the threshold. And that was the moment, not without trepidation, when I entered the Hasbrook dugout for the first time in my life.

I found myself in the empty vault, no bigger than a walk in closet, the peak just inches above my head. Light poured down through the empty chimney hole—the only breach in the old mud bricks—and filled the dugout with a shaft of light. I stood a long time there, inspecting the old walls, looking back out through the doorway at the trees and far creek bank. It was all becoming overwhelming.

Could this really be the place where my grandmother spent her childhood? Raised in a cave, struggling to keep her family alive during the Great Depression, running a de facto boardinghouse for her ne'er-do-well relatives, and secretly supporting her own father's guilt . . no wonder she looked so tired and sad.

And Nate: he had been *born* here, his nursery resembling nothing more than a cemetery vault. Where had he learned his sunny optimism and élan? And why, when he had the chance to help others in circumstances almost as miserable as his had been, did he choose to steal from them?

But most of all I began to be overwhelmed by the poignancy of this little place, with the realization that this was where *I* began, and my children too. This was the tiny tomb in the midst of the vast prairie that held our hearts—and no matter how far away our lives took us, this room would always remain at the center.

I noticed something hanging from the wall, and reached over and touched it. Muslin. That's when I started to choke up; something I hadn't done in many years.

As I sat on the bumper of the car, picking ticks off my jeans and looking back at the distant farmhouse and barn, I knew that I would now do anything to get the farm and to save it, if only to preserve the dugout, my door into the earth.

I called California that night to tell my mother I was in the project for keeps.

BUBBLE MEMORY

Not long after, I embarked—like thousands of other people in high tech—on the strangest period of my professional career.

After twenty years chronicling Silicon Valley and high tech, I prided myself on knowing the industry as well as anybody. And yet, the Internet boom—the 'dot.com bubble'—blindsided me. I had spent the previous decade publicly predicting that the emerging Internet economy would bring about a huge jump in wealth and productivity, but when it finally arrived, the boom outstripped even my most optimistic predictions.

But that was the least of it. There came a point near the end of the 1990s, at the absolute fevered zenith of dot.com hysteria, when I started to doubt my own sanity. Having spent most of my life in Silicon Valley,

I was used to its frenetic pace, its overnight billionaires and skyrocketing companies, its four year cycles of boom and bust.

But this was something altogether crazier. The highways were jammed morning and night with new arrivals, all chasing after the brass ring of dot.com stock options. Every billboard, every bus bench, every second of commercial time on television and radio carried ads for one internet start-up or another—and when they ran out of space there, companies started hiring planes to fly overhead, barges to float in the Bay just off the freeway, even flatbed trucks to sit in the gridlock bearing advertising messages.

There was no escape. To get away from the madness I caught a Giants baseball game at the team's brand new park—and found that every sign on the stadium, every cup holder at every seat, even the wrappers on my hot dog, carried dot.com advertising.

Meanwhile, almost everyone I knew was either diving into a dot.com start-up company or finagling to get stock. I knew a dozen paper billionaires, and many times that many others who had a net worth, at least on paper, of a hundred million dollars or more. The national media was swarming over my old beat, and I found myself being interviewed almost as much as I interviewed others.

Meanwhile, at the magazine, advertising was coming in so fast that we simply couldn't generate enough editorial to keep up—against all of my standards, I found myself serializing chapters from new books I didn't like, hiring freelancers whose work I didn't respect, and signing on columnists whose gibberish had to be completely reworked. I was paying my reporters salaries three times what they should have been earning with their limited experience, giving them wildly inflated job titles—and they were still being recruited by other, even more desperate, competitors willing to pay and promote them even more.

But the worst of it was that my twenty years of experience as a business reporter seemed to be doing me no good at all. Actually, it was even worst than that: everything I knew seemed to be leading me to the wrong conclusions. A little voice in my brain was screaming that none of these new companies had viable business models, that none of these overnight fortunes were real, and that instead of a boom Silicon Valley was on the brink of catastrophe.

Yet, when I expressed these concerns to my peers in the media or industry, most of them—except, tellingly, the old timers—merely laughed. And every time I anxiously predicted that the Bubble was going to pop at any moment, it just grew bigger. I sat in on presentations by young entrepreneurs before venture capitalists in which nobody in the room had any real business experience . . . and yet the start-up team not only was deemed worthy of millions of dollars of investment, but actually saw that number then doubled by the VC's "for marketing."

The absolute nadir came when my younger staffers, out of pity, began to treat me like an old man, out of touch with the new realities of the business world. One by one they quietly counseled me that I needed to get with the times, to recognize that all of the traditional rules of business—market share, revenues, profits—were obsolete; that is was a new world being created by the Internet economy.

The worst of it was that I began to think they might be right. Maybe all of the rules had changed, and I was just too Old School to accept it. After all, whatever my gut told me, the reality was that so far I had been wrong, and the kids had been right. The stock market was still climbing into the stratosphere, new companies were being born and new fortunes being made every day, and only fools weren't reaching for the brass ring.

And so I soldiered on, never knowing for sure whether the world had lost its mind, or just me—and afraid it might be the latter. Ironically, there were moments when the one thing that kept me tethered to reality in the midst of this anarchy was the Hasbrook homestead.

Once my mother and I had agreed to actively pursue the farm, we found a real estate agent in Enid. Apparently Gary Young was somewhat controversial around that part of Oklahoma—during our years together he would lose his license then successfully sue to win it back—but I found him to be brilliant, shrewd, and most importantly, tirelessly dedicated to helping us buy back the farm. And he had to be: in the end, it would take almost five years.

As for me, what had begun as a novelty had now become a lifeline. I found myself looking forward to Gary's regular update calls, the slow drawl of his voice as he told the latest anecdote—"Welllllll, Mahk, I jest got back from settin' on the porch of Pryor's daughter's place and drinkin' lemonade . . ."—a welcome respite from the superheated Master-of-the-Universe atmosphere of my own life.

In easily the single most surreal moment of my professional career, I found myself racing up the East Side of Manhattan, in Steve Forbes' limousine, to the Bloomberg studios to appear on the *Charlie Rose* PBS interview show—to be followed by dinner at Elaine's with Tom Wolfe, Stanley Crouch, John Steele Gordon and Uma Thurman's father (with a George Plimpton drop-in)—and taking a cell phone call from Gary Young in Enid asking whether I'd be willing to negotiate separately the mineral rights to the Hasbrook farm.

Looking back, it was almost a relief that the farm negotiations went nowhere during this period. I'm not sure I could have handled those seesawing negotiations while everything else was going on. Instead, as I raced about, putting out an endlessly inflating magazine, dealing with workers on my house (or more accurately, dealing with my wife dealing with subcontractors), running around the country making presentations on the Big Issue, speaking at conferences, appearing on television news shows, negotiating with younger employees with a sideways sense of their own value, and massaging the egos of world-class writers and celebrities, it was a fortnightly pleasure to crack open a beer from the minibar in some hotel room and listen to Gary Young describe his meetings with the Pryor's attorney at a golf tournament the day before, or with an appraiser outside of church that morning, or just the on-going conversation with Pryor's daughter over lemonade on her front porch.

DOWN CYCLE

How strangely the roles had reversed. When Charlie Hasbrook had ridden in from the farm that first day to file his claim, Enid was, for a brief moment, the center of attention for the entire country. By the time he built the farmhouse, Enid and the rest of Garfield County was, thanks to oil, the hottest boomtown in the nation, the heir apparent to the Klondike and the Comstock, the Silicon Valley of its day. It was a town of overnight riches, bordellos, gambling and crime. It was where the man some believe was John Wilkes Booth came to die. Postcards carried panoramic photos of forests of oil derricks covering the landscape. And locals still remembered the Doolin-Dalton gang robbing area banks just a year before. Bill Doolin was, in fact, killed in Stillwater, just a few miles from the farm, about the time the Hasbrooks moved into the dugout.

So popular was life in the old Indian territory that it sparked nearly a century of popular imagery from that era, from most of the traveling Wild West Shows of the late 19th century (Oklahoma's Pawnee Bill and Miller 101 Ranch shows were Buffalo Bill's biggest competitors) through movies such as *Cimarron* (the first Academy Award best picture) to, of course, the musical *Oklahoma!* and beyond.

By the time Teresa and Art, my grandparents, were a young married couple, living in the town's newest housing development, Enid had settled down in a more peaceful prosperity—yet remained one of the fast growing metropolitan areas in the country. The city even had its own home-grown automobile company, the Geronimo Motor Car Company.

It was an exciting place to be young and ambitious, and as in many boomtowns, doors of opportunity were opened to people who would normally be left behind. For example, in the first years of the new century, a number of African-American communities had sprung up all over the territory as aging ex-slaves and younger refugees from a Jim Crow South took advantage of the open landscape to build their own towns. These new arrivals also congregated in one district, Greenwood, of another local oil-boom city, Tulsa, where they created one of the most prosperous black neighborhoods in the U.S.

But by the end of World War I, Oklahoma's boom was over. There was still oil in the ground, but most of it was now owned or leased by big companies, such as Phillips Petroleum (which had thanked Enid by building Philips University within the city limits). The post-war downturn hit the region hard, and that, combined with a crisis in the farming industry and an enduring drought that would eventually create the Dust Bowl, sent tensions rising. In 1920, Tulsa's Greenwood district saw one of the worst race riots in U.S. history.

Oklahoma missed most of the Roaring '20s, at least the good parts. My great-aunt Velva Collins, who would live into the 21st century, may have been the family flapper, with her rolled stockings and marcelled hair—but the life she dreamed of living came out of magazines and Clara Bow movies, not from the increasingly dreary world around her.

But Oklahoma most certainly didn't miss the Thirties, as much as its residents might have wished they could. Indeed, there were times when the state seemed the very focus of everything that went wrong during that decade.

Oklahoma had it all. There were the runs on failing banks—or, as Charlie Hasbrook discovered, other forms of financial chaos. And, of course, there was the Dust Bowl: my mother always remembered the day when the sky to the west went black and she and her classmates were hurried home from junior high school. When she arrived her parents were already sealing every window and door in the house—but even with these precautions, once the dust cloud, which turned afternoon into night, passed by, the bottom corners of every window and door were filled with a pile of talcum-fine red dust. West of Enid, where the true high Prairie began, the landscape was devastated—and the residents, left with nothing, soon packed up with their fellow 'Okies' and began the great migration to California.

And if all of that misery wasn't enough—and perhaps just because of that misery—Oklahoma soon became a battleground between a new breed of outlaws and the unprepared local constabulary. At one time, Bonnie and Clyde, Machine Gun Kelly, Ma Barker and her sons, and Pretty Boy Floyd, along with an uncounted number of lesser criminals, were all racing across the state, robbing banks, shooting policemen and hiding out on back roads and in isolated farmhouses. The beleaguered population sometimes cheered these outlaws on, then turned around and cheered their bloody demise. In the low decade of the 1930s in Oklahoma, murder and mayhem became popular entertainment. And the most popular entertainer in America was Oklahoman Will Rogers— until he tragically died in a plane crash.

World War II saved Oklahoma from this downward spiral . . . but at a cost. The local boys went off to war, and many didn't return—and even among those that did, many didn't stay long, but used their GI Bills and training to go find work in the more exciting locales they'd seen before being shipped overseas.

By the 1950s, Oklahoma had finally escaped the thirty years of continuous crisis that had overwhelmed it—and, thanks to the Interstate Highway System and oil, it would slowly come back to prosperity in places like Oklahoma City and Tulsa—but it would never be the same again.

BOOM AND BUST

By comparison, Silicon Valley—then called Santa Clara Valley—was a sleepy farming region when Oklahoma was enjoying its boom. The entire south Bay Area was a vast carpet of fruit trees punctuated by a few small cities such as San Jose and Santa Clara. Life was seasonal, the weather pleasant—and if no one got particularly rich, there wasn't much poverty either. It was one case where the promotional hype—the area was billed as "The Valley of Heart's Delight"—almost fit the reality.

But about the time the good times began to fade in Oklahoma, they arrived in Santa Clara Valley. It was an unlikely confluence of events that made this change possible: A university, Stanford, built by two grieving parents. A president of that University, famous for inventing the standard IQ test, whose son, Frederick Terman, turned out not only to be an electronics genius but perhaps the most influential teacher/mentor of the century. Two local boys, the Lockheed Brothers, who had made a fortune in aerospace, decided to come home and build rockets. Another genius, this one even greater, but infinitely more difficult, William Shockley, who also decided to come home and build a company after winning the Nobel Prize. And perhaps most of all, thousands of GIs who passed through San Francisco on the way to the war in the Pacific— and decided that this was they place to which they wanted to return.

If the Roaring '20s largely missed Northern California (landing instead on Hollywood and Southern California), the same could be said of the Depression that followed. Though no corner of the United States—or indeed the world—escaped the Crash, it seemed to land lighter and last less time here than most everywhere else. That's why the poor Okies headed west and didn't stop until they crossed the Sierra Nevada.

The boom that Silicon Valley touched off in the mid-1960s has never really ended but merely hesitated every four or five years to catch its breath before roaring on. It has spread to cover the world, not least of which (as I discovered on my visit) my grandparents' little house in Enid. It has produced more wealth, extended more lives and rescued more people from poverty around the globe than any single event since the Industrial Revolution. It also reset the clock on all of our lives; speeding it up, imbuing it with the expectation of perpetual change and improvement, leveling us and interconnecting us in ways we never could have imagined

This is the world, and at its very epicenter, where I grew up: mad optimism, an acceptance of failure, and a complete historic amnesia. The secret to success in Silicon Valley—and increasingly the entire electronics world—is to always assume you are going to win and to never entrust your fate to anyone.

It is also about risk and an odd way of looking at that risk: what the rest of the world saw as taking huge chances was, in the mind of true Valley entrepreneur, the very opposite of that; betting everything, running your own career, starting your own company . . . all of those things were ways of *reducing* risk by taking your fate out of the hands of others.

Looking back, I now see that this was what drew my parents to the Valley: they were classic risk-averse risk-takers, no different from the captains of industry I spent my days interviewing. And it wasn't just my swashbuckling father, but also my quiet, even more fearless mother.   It was she who had abandoned her family and Oklahoma to run off with a dangerous man. And it was my mother who would turn to my father every few years and announce *Let's buy another house* even when they couldn't afford it . . . a decision that had made them wealthy.

And now, at an age when half of her peers were dead and the rest were puttering in gardens and moving into convalescent homes, my mother had decided take her boldest, craziest move yet—and who was to say that it wasn't as brilliant as the ones she'd made in the past? She wasn't the first entrepreneurial personality I'd seen who, contrary to the accepted view, had grown more audacious with age.

I was my parents' child, and I had even married a fellow Valleyite, who, despite being very different in personality from my mother, was just as much a risk taker, and just as unafraid of failure. So too were my boys. And the day we were attacked in our boat by a hippo on the Okavango River in Africa and, in the aftermath, as I watched as my wife calmly packed her broken nose with the help of my boys—my youngest himself with two black eyes—and none of them the least bit frightened by the experience, I felt like I was living with a different species of humans. I didn't know if I could have survived in that dugout on the Cherokee Strip, but I had no doubt the rest of my family would have done just fine. And I knew that every one of them, including my octogenarian mother, would have lined up with Charlie Hasbrook on the starting line that day in 1893.

Silicon Valley also teaches one other lesson: *never look back.* The past might have lessons to teach, but you don't have time to learn them . . . besides, the future will provide lessons enough. Memories and experiences are only tools for succeeding in the present. Even my mother seemed to subscribe to that rule: the return and restoration of the Hasbrook Farm may have looked like an exercise in nostalgia, but in my mother's mind it was anything but that. Rather, it was the final fulfillment of an unkept promise, a rebuilding of what had been wrongfully abandoned, and most of all, a legacy that would live on into the future.

For her, it only mattered if the farm *looked* right once again. And if that meant running a 200 amp line in to run air conditioning in the house, or adding another bathroom for convenience, so be it. She was an entrepreneur and the Hasbrook farm was to be her start-up, built from the debris of what came before. And if it cost her small fortune to restore the place, and even if we had no idea what to do with the place when we were done, well, once again, so be it. We'd figure it out as we went along.

What became apparent to me during our years of conversations about what we'd do with the farm if we ever got our hands on it was that whatever serious historic preservation took place would be largely up to me. That's because, for as long as I've lived and worked in Silicon Valley, historical amnesia is one rule that, perhaps to my loss, that I've never been able to follow.

Not having grown up, like my cousins, with my relatives and my past ever-present around me—and thus never feeling trapped by history—I have always been endlessly curious about both. Though I spend my days in the eternal near-future in an endless search for the Next Big Thing, it is the past that has always seems to me a happier, richer place. It's not a coincidence that I bought one of the oldest houses in California and filled it with 19th century antiques. I type this on the latest laptop computer, linked to a broadband hub in my home . . . that rests atop a 1870s Eastlake library table.

From the beginning, however it was disguised; history has always been my business. The old saw that journalism was 'the first draft of history' had always been a truism to me, and I used every sidebar, profile and feature to record the near past for the sake of the near future. My rookie book, the first comprehensive history of Silicon Valley, was more like an old man's book, though it was written before I was thirty, the summation of an era that in fact had barely begun. A quarter century and nearly a dozen books later, after having covered the high tech revolution as long as anybody, I was starting to see—not entirely welcomed—the title of "the Silicon Valley historian" attached to my name. It was a prestigious-sounding title for a job with few applicants.

But if history was my albatross in a place where forgetfulness was a virtue, there were still moments when a little perspective went a long way—and never more so than as the new Millennium began. By now, whatever my employees and peers were saying, *all* of the warning sirens were going off in my head. Nothing in Silicon Valley seemed logical anymore: there were just too many new companies with no real products, no real sales and absolutely no profits. People I knew who had no knowledge of how daily business worked were making millions advising people on what stocks to buy. Mere children were being handed giant marketing budgets and spending them on meaningless Super Bowl ads. We were due for a long postponed bust—and this one might be the worst high tech had ever seen.

Then, one afternoon, I found myself conducting a telephone interview with the two men who had done more than anyone to explain the forces driving this new world: Gordon Moore, the chairman of Intel Corp. and the man who had devised Moore's Law, the single best indicator of the pace of the modern world, and networking genius Bob Metcalfe, whose own 'law' of networks brilliantly explained in a single equation why the Internet had transformed the world.

Inevitably, the conversation got around to the current economic bubble in tech. Moore, the most admired man in technology, said simply that he didn't understand it, that it didn't seem rational, and that he was getting as far from it as he could before it blew. But when? I asked.

So far, every prediction of a bust had overrun by the next leap in stock prices. Metcalfe, the eternal joker, laughed and said: April   2000.

History (especially if I write it) will record that Bob Metcalfe was the only person who got it right.

I was shaken by that conversation—and not entirely sure why. But I turned to my wife and said 'let's exercise and sell every stock option we've got *right now*.' It seemed a little crazy—after all, the market was still climbing to nosebleed heights and the economy was roaring—but after talking to those two men it seemed a whole lot less crazy than the status quo. Given all of the lock-out periods and vesting requirements for the options, it would take more than a year to liquidate everything—and even then I knew that by the time I got to the last of those shares they would be all-but worthless.

Then, over the complaints of many of my younger staffers, I ordered a drawing of a guillotine to be put on the cover of the magazine, its blade bearing a list of the absurd numbers of competitors in each of the hot new markets (". . . 400 auction sites . . . 1,500 e-commerce shoe sites . . . thousands of mom-and-pop operations selling vitamins and drugs . . ."). Then I hunkered down in my own psychological dugout and waited for the crash. My own Land Rush was over.

FULFILLMENT

It was nearly two years later when Gary Young called with good news: the Pryor family had unencumbered the farm from its many layers of debt, settled with the IRS and nearly all of the family members were ready to sell.

It is cold-blooded to say, but I knew (given that family's financial history) that the other two grandchildren, hungry for cash, would prevail on the more nostalgic third grandchild to sell. I told my mother to be patient, that they would come around.

Meanwhile, I had other things to worry about. My days of limousines and nearly-unlimited expense accounts were long over. Thanks to both the dot-com bubble bursting and 9/11, Silicon Valley had suffered a double-whammy and sunk into its worst depression ever. The national media had declared the Valley over, packed up and moved on to its next story. Fortunes had been lost, and an entire generation of young people had seen their dreams evaporate. Now many were packing up and moving home . . . so many that at one point in 2002 there were no U-Haul trailers left in the Bay Area; all had been rented by locals to escape.

At home I was struggling to find a paycheck. We weren't poor by any means. We'd managed to get about three-fourths of our stock sold in time—thanks to our early start it was more than most people we knew—and had immediately put it into real estate and restoration work on our still-unfinished historic house. Rather, it was daily living that was proving difficult: I'd always assumed that I could survive by balancing on the three legs of books, newspapers and magazines. But unlike every tech downturn before it, this one swept away the media as well. No one wanted business books, all of the big locally-based magazines (including my own) were dead, and all of the local newspapers were dying. Restoring the Hasbrook farm, which had seemed like pocket change three years before, was now looking like a crushing financial burden. I spent my days (and many nights) at home in my office hunched over my computer searching for writing gigs and taking anything that came my way.

For years I had casually discussed in my writings the importance of liquidity, easily dropping the phrase "cash poor" to described troubled companies. Now I got my own lesson on how one could be wealthy and broke at the same time.

Luckily, thanks to pensions, and the sell-off of the assets that she and my late father had so shrewdly acquired over the years, my mother could still afford to take on the farm by herself. But now she was facing a whole new set of problems.

My mother had been sixty-eight when we first agreed to pursue the Hasbrook farm. Now she was eighty-two, comparatively young by Hasbrook and Collins standards, but she was becoming visibly frail. She survived a bout of breast cancer, and by the Millennium celebration— her childhood goal had been to live long enough to see the 21st century— she regained her strength, thanks both to a new gentleman friend and daily three mile walks with a neighbor lady.

But then she began to weaken again, and by the time Gary Young called with the news, my mother was looking very much like an old lady in her final days. So now, even as the prize was finally being dangled before us, it seemed that I no longer had the money and my mother no longer had the time. And when Gary called again to inform us that the owners had changed their minds and decided to turn down our offer of twice the market value for the farm and were demanding *four times* market price—they had gotten it into their minds that, being Californians we must be from Hollywood and had secret plans to create a film studio—I told both Gary and my mother that it was time to walk away. I'd been through too much craziness in Silicon Valley; I didn't need it now in Oklahoma.

I would have walked away forever, despite all that I now felt about the farm and its history. I would have bundled up all of my notes and old photographs and family genealogies and tossed them into the closet to be rediscovered by my boys or one of my grandchildren if they were ever curious. And I would have spent each winter checking the weather reports on the Enid News & Eagle web site and then lie in bed imagining the shingles being slowly stripped from roofs, clapboards from walls, and saddest of all, bricks falling from the dugout's ceiling. And I would have sadly awaited word from a relative who had driven past the farm that the house or the barn was down or that the creek bank had slumped into a crater.

Then, one afternoon in the spring of 2004, Gary Young called again. No solemn drawl this time; instead he was almost giddy. "They'll take your offer, Mike. They want to keep the oil and mineral rights until the old widow dies, but they'll take your offer." Gary paused to catch his breath, "Whew! I can't believe it! After all of these years, we finally got the farm!"

I thanked Gary, told him that no other agent on earth would ever have fought this long and hard just for a piece of red dirt in the middle of nowhere, offered to buy him a steak at Cattleman's restaurant the next time I was in Oklahoma City, and then hung up to call my mother. She answered the phone with a thin voice. "Well, I'll be," she said, "I'll be." I jumped into my car and drove over to her house. She was sitting on the leather couch, a little white-haired lady surrounded by walls of glass.

We had a cup of tea and reminisced about all that we had been through during the previous dozen years.   We talked about all she remembered from her childhood, and what she had seen of the farm during her most recent visit after a Hasbrook family reunion. And I told her what I thought it would take to restore the place—if it could still even be done.

Finally, I asked, "So what do you want to do, mom?"

She looked surprised, "Why, *buy* it of course. And fix it back up. And if I don't live long enough to complete it, then you take over from there and finish the job."

RENEWAL: THE HASBROOK BARN

I already knew my first step: call Tim Lantz.

After having worked with him for more than five years on our own house, my wife and I simply explained Tim by saying that it took a nineteenth century man to restore a nineteenth century house.

Tim was, and is, a lot more complicated than that. Six foot four, with a ponytail down to his cowboy belt, an NRA Lifetime Member cap covering his balding head, a walrus moustache and heavy forestry boots, Tim cut a singular figure when working on jobs in Silicon Valley suburbia. He drove a V-10 Dodge Ram with undersized wheels on the front, dualies on the back under the built-in steel boxes, and, inevitably some sad dog in the front seat—old, blind, abused, forgetful, incontinent— that he hadn't had heart to not to accept from a neighbor or relative. An old country hippie, Tim mostly played C&W on his radio and sometimes reminisced about his old days hanging out with biker gangs.

Despite working in Silicon Valley, Tim lived in another century— which is how we described him to the curious. Tim's house was three creeks back up in the mountains west of Hollister, itself the last old-time town in the South Bay. There were winter days when the creeks ran high—too high for the truck to ford their shallows—and he never got down off the mountain. Even on good days, thanks to the gridlock created by the Dot.com Bubble, his commute was often an hour each way.

As for his house, it was a case of the cobbler's children: forever unfinished, it had no electricity, and plastic sheeting covered a leaky roof. His endlessly tragic dogs were forever at risk of being eaten by coyotes or mountain lions. And one day, he brought my kids, as a pet, a scorpion he'd found wandering through his living room (Ms. Scorpion was pregnant, but luckily for us, ate her young—we kept her for eight years). Despite all this . . . actually, *because* of it . . . women found Tim hugely attractive, and he was never short of lady friends.

None of what I just said, however, captures the essential feature of Tim Lantz. It is that he was a genius. I don't mean that in some mythic sense of someone inhabiting a more rarified plane than the rest of us; but rather that unique combination of talent, focus and monomania that makes a person's expertise in a particular field seem all-but super-human.

As an editor I've dealt with more than my share of geniuses, including both their good and bad sides. And Tim was all that. Just a few years before working with us, he had won the gold medal from the National Trust for Historic Preservation for one of the most remarkable feats of the era. During the Loma Prieta earthquake a three story Queen Anne historic Victorian house in Los Gatos had literally fallen into its own basement. Tim and his team of workers—most didn't stay with him long because he was too much of a perfectionist—managed not only to lift the entire structure up and restore the first floor, but even tackled the giant jigsaw puzzle of putting every stone in the face of the house front *back into its original position.* That accomplishment, and the subsequent award, rightly earned Lantz national publicity.

Anyone who read that story closely would have gotten a glimpse into what it was like to work with Tim: that same obsession with detail also meant that Tim always preferred to glue together the splinters of an original two-by-four than buy a new one; and his obsession with authenticity also meant that Tim almost always came to loggerheads with more practical, or at least more pragmatic, owners. And finally, Tim's perfectionism almost always meant that he never finished most jobs, that he and the owners would eventually part in either frustration or exhaustion after years of working together.

That's what finally happened to us and our historic Silicon Valley house. The kitchen wasn't finished, the basement was untouched and there were a thousand details yet to be done ... but broke, exhausted and ready to move on with our lives, my wife and I finally said to hell with it, thanked Tim for saving us, and told him we were done. Lantz was even more relieved than we were. Only our youngest son, five years old and also named Tim (he assumed he was named after Lantz) was broken-hearted. The next morning—the first weekday morning in his life that big Tim wasn't there at the breakfast table—he burst into tears.

We had gone on with our lives, and so had Lantz, buying and restoring several house of his own in the south County town of Hollister, taking on some restoration jobs on Victorians around Silicon Valley, and even opening an antique tile shop. He had known about our early efforts to buy the farm, and so he was only moderately surprised when called to tell him the news.

"I want to hire you," I told him over the phone, "You're the only guy in the world I trust for this." I explained to Tim that I needed him to hop on a plane as soon as possible for Oklahoma City, rent a car and drive up to Enid to meet Gary Young. Then, the two of them, accompanied by a contractor Gary recommended named Dave Dopps, needed to get out to the farm and conduct a restoration appraisal. Young, I told Tim, thought very highly of Dopps, but the latter had made his career building shopping centers and knew almost nothing about historic restoration.

"Check the place out," I told Tim. "Tell me what I can save and what I can't. Check out Dopps, too. If he's up for the job, I'll hire him—and then I'll hire you to supervise him."

Three weeks later, Tim was on a plane, and I awaited the news. He didn't call until the evening of the day he was scheduled to visit the farm. And when he did, it sounded like he was calling from a bar, and his normally deep voice was even more muffled than usual—suggesting that he and the other two men had already celebrated the day with a few beers. What I only learned later was that Tim had earned those beers and more: while crawling under the farmhouse, he had run nose-to-nose into a big, black, six-foot king snake. Man and reptile had tumbled out of the crawlspace in opposite directions.

"So, doctor, what's the diagnosis?" I asked.

"Let's take it one structure at a time," he half-shouted over the honky-tonk. "The house: fifty-fifty. Your call. It's pretty much a wreck. Either restore it, or tear it down and build a precise replica; it'll cost you the same either way."

"I don't want a copy. My great-grandfather built that damn house with his own hands. We'll fix it up."

"Like I said: your call. But it'll take a lot of work. We've got to get all of the shit out of there and see how much detailing is left, and see how much original plaster we can save. And we gotta keep the elements out of there—a few more years of rain and snow blowing through the empty window frames and the holes in the roof and the place'll be gone. So, we seal the place up. We keep the crappy '50s siding on their for now, board up the windows with some vents in them for air circulation and seal the roof with plastic tarp. . .Oh yeah, I found where Charlie kept his valuables."

"Really?"

"Yeah, hidden under the front porch I found a box buried in the ground."

That old rascal. "Anything in it?"

"Nope. Empty. Sorry. But I'll bet that's where he hid the jewelry and money whenever the family left the farm."

"So why not just restore the house first?"

"I'll get to that in a minute."

"Fine. What about the dugout?"

"I don't think we can touch it. It's basically a national treasure. The trouble is that your great-grandfather lined the entrance with flat river rocks, the same rocks he used in the foundation of the house. Problem is that they've begun to weather and deteriorate. We can't really replace them, and there's no real consolidant I know of that will stop the damage."

"So what do we do?"

"Replace the old door with a new one using contemporary boards, rebuild the chimney on top, and then . . . I don't know. Maybe we just enclose the entire damn thing in a big steel box with lights in it. Like an archaeological site."

"That sounds bizarre."

"Yeah. Maybe we'll come up with something better. Right now we'll just cover it with heavy plastic sheeting."

It was almost as an afterthought that I asked, "And the barn?"

"Ah," Tim replied, suddenly sounding like a man who had just fallen in love, "The barn. Let me tell you something, Mike, that barn may look like every other abandoned old barn you've ever seen. But in fact, it's some kind of architectural masterpiece."

"You're kidding."

"No, I'm very serious. And I don't think Charlie built it. By the looks of it, it was built by a professional. It's almost like a Pennsylvania

Dutch barn. And you can see exactly how they built it, wall by wall, on the ground then lifted it up. It's really amazing. You could write a whole monograph just on its construction.

"By the way," Tim continued, as if going through a mental checklist, "Did you ever notice that cupola on the roof the barn?"

"Yeah."

"Well, there's something wrong with it. Was it ever bigger?"

"I dunno."

"I'm pretty sure it was and I think your great-grandfather cut it down for some reason. But when he did he also screwed up a very sophisticated ventilation system—and that hasn't helped the barn age well."

"What does that mean?"

"Well, it's a mess. It hasn't had paint on it for fifty years; the siding is pretty rotted away at the bottom. And the big pile of cowshit has burned up most of the posts on that end of the barn. Just like the house, the perimeter foundation—which was narrow and made from local dirt mixed with cement—is in collapse in at least twenty places. But the big thing is that two of the three main beams holding the whole barn up are cracked; and one of those is broken. That's why the roofline is starting to bow."

"Jesus. So do we even try to save it?"

Tim laughed, "Oh *hell* yes. Are you kidding? You can't let a structure like that be lost. We *start* with the barn."

The next day Tim left Dopps with his marching orders, my mother wrote the first check, and the restoration of the Charlie's Place was underway.

But the project nearly ended even as it finally began.

MATTERS OF THE HEART

The work on the Hasbrook farm began in the fall of 2005. Thanks to the Internet, we were able to track the progress of Dopps and his crew as they went along. About once per month I would receive an email with a Shutterfly link that would enable me to slideshow my way through several dozen digital photographs of each step of the project. Most of the photos were well beyond my understanding of rough carpentry—ten shots, say, of how epoxy consolidant was used to square off the rotting end of a siding plank—was pretty dreary viewing. But at least once in every set of new photos, Dopps would step back and take a wide shot of the house or barn, or best of all, the entire farm. These were the shots we lived for; while the detailed architectural shots were designed for Tim's sign-off as supervisor of the project.

Unfortunately, Tim didn't always see the photos, or the project diary and invoice that accompanied them. Almost from the beginning it was apparent to me that the Lantz/Dopps arrangement wasn't going to work. Both men seemed to have tremendous respect for each other's abilities. Tim, who set almost impossible standards for every one from subcontractors to clients, even said of Dopps, that he "doesn't know much about historic restoration yet, but he's a good man and he knows how to build"—high praise indeed, considering the source.

Dopps in return would say, years later, that the single most important thing he had ever learned about historic restoration had come from Tim Lantz. They had been inspecting the barn, trying to determine how best to save it from collapse, when Tim had turned to Dave and said, "Just remember, it doesn't have to be perfect. After all, they didn't build perfect in the first place. It just has to be right."

But the biggest compliment that Dave Dopps gave to Tim Lantz was that—sometimes to my chagrin—as the months went by, Dopps increasingly *became* Lantz. He had spent most of his life in Kansas City, and had raised a family and built a career there. But the children had grown, the marriage ended—and when the new love in his life refused to leave Oklahoma, Dave had made the decision to move to Enid. He had only been working there for a few years, mostly rebuilding office buildings and shopping centers, when one of his new professional acquaintances, the realtor Gary Young, had called and asked if he'd be willing to meet with a contractor from California and go look at an old farm house.

Dopps had gone mostly out of curiosity. And meeting a six foot-four inch hippy-biker with a ponytail down his waist, had only made the visit even curiouser. But as he followed Tim around the weed-choked farm, and explored with him abandoned and tumbled down buildings, listening to Lantz's growing enthusiasm about the singular construction of the barn, the challenges of preserving the cave, Dave Dopps began to fall in love for the second time in his middle age. And as the months turned into years, with both the owners and his supervisor more than a thousand miles away, and with the house and barn increasingly becoming his sole work, Dopps understandably began to take emotional possession of the farm. In time, he began to fire one subcontractor after another as being insufficiently careful and committed to the project . . .until the work crew was little more than Dopps, his son Cody and a hard-working laborer named TK. Just like Lantz. And, just like Tim, the quality of the work grew ever better, even as the pace slowed to a crawl.

It was Dave Dopps' project now, and someone had to go. The result was that though neither Dopps nor Lantz wanted to confront the other, neither had much interest in maintaining this relationship. This was particularly true with Dopps, who, once he began to become obsessed with, even to identify with, the project became less and less willing to submit to Tim's oversight. After a few months he stopped routing Tim in on his monthly reports—and my demands that he do so merely resulted in a month or two of dutiful reporting before he lapsed into his old ways.

Tim, for his part, was not only frustrated with this apparent insubordination but with the very nature of trying to manage an operation from a half-continent away. Tim was the ultimate hands-on contractor, and this kind of remote, virtual project management was utterly anathema to his personality. I figured he wasn't going to put up with this situation for long.

So I knew a break-up was coming, but more important matters were taking precedence—so all I could do was try to keep the participants on board as long as I could, hoping that Tim could impart as much of his wisdom as possible and that Dopps would listen and learn enough before the divorce.

The other matter that now took all of my attention was the rapidly deteriorating health of my mother.

Unlike my father, my mother had always been the very embodiment of good health. She had never smoked, rarely drank more than a glass of wine, and since my father's death had walked several miles each day with Mildred Lincoln, a long-time neighbor. She was one of those rare people who actually listened in health class as a teenager—and when her gym teacher had told her class that they should drink at least six glasses of water per day, I suspect my mother was the only one who went home and did just that . . . *every day* for seventy years.

Because my mother religiously scheduled her annual physicals, a mammogram in 1999 spotted the very earliest sign of a cancerous tumor, and surgery stopped it in time. Tellingly, the day she went back to the hospital for a check-up, the waiting room nurse walked right by her three times in search of an eighty year-old woman, before in exasperation calling out her name. My father had looked seventy at sixty, my mother looked sixty at eighty.

But soon thereafter, my mother began to slow down. My wife noticed it first, but my sister and I dismissed it as the natural process of becoming an octogenarian. Certainly my mother's attitude hadn't changed, and when she joined us on a brief vacation at our house in Southern Oregon, she was happy to join me in a long stroll down the beach.

We walked more than a mile along the sand, and my mother did such a good job of keeping my pace that I forgot I was walking with an 81 year-old. We walked quickly, even into the light wind. And we even made swift work of the fairly steep hike up the hill back to the beach road.

But then, as we started up the beach road, with its brief incline, my mother suddenly faded. It was as if her legs suddenly had given out and would no longer support her weight. We stopped, I took her arm and we waited as she caught her breath and regained her energy. We walked on, but only another hundred yards, and she had to stop again.

There was no place to sit, we still had another five hundred yards of a comparatively gentle uphill slope, and it was starting to get dark. So I held my mother up and we took slow steps forward, waiting whenever she felt weak. I briefly considered leaving her and running on ahead to get my truck and return for her—but there was no place to put her, and I was afraid that if I left my mother standing she might fall. So we made our way along, one hundred feet at a time, stopping for a few minutes, then pressing on.

As was my mother's way, she continuously apologized for her weakness: "I don't know what's gotten into me, why I'm so tired. I usually walk much further than that at home every day with Mildred." When I suggested that perhaps I had set too fast of a pace, she demurred—she would never let her son be responsible for her infirmity, "No, no, I think I just overdid it on that last hill. I went too fast."

We at last reached the roadside gate to my house. The lights were on inside, but my family hadn't yet noticed us. I opened the gate for my mother and walked her through, then left her for a moment to turn around and latch it . . . and turned back just in time to watch in horror as my mother took two steps and then tumbled onto the lawn.

As I lifted her to her feet—astonished at how light she had become—my mother seemed more embarrassed then hurt. But in the weeks to come, after we returned to California, her sore shoulder didn't improve. She finally went to an orthopedist for an X-ray—and was told that in the fall she had torn her rotator cuff. That arm and shoulder were already fragile from having most of the lymph nodes removed during the cancer surgery; now, to my endless guilt, she could no longer lift that arm above the horizontal. The doctor recommended against surgery—she wouldn't need to throw any sliders in her future—but put her on a course of therapy. And though some of the mobility did return, my mother's right arm would never be the same again.

Soon, however, my mother's sore shoulder would be the least of her worries.

That Christmas, it was apparent even to my sister and me that our mother was looking very old and fragile. Her skin was gray, and she was beginning to sleep a lot, dozing off at odd times, and beginning to lose her usual desire to up and about in the world. My wife's mother, who had lived a much more self-destructive life, was going into her final decline at the same time—and by comparison, my mother looked pretty good. But when we were alone with her, it was obvious that she was now a fraction of the robust woman she'd been just two years before.

One day in March, when I stopped by to visit, she said off-handedly, "You know, when I went to that birthday party last night the strangest thing happened: all of a sudden, I had no strength in my left arm. None. Everything else was fine, but it was as if couldn't even lift my hand. Then, a minute or two later, it just went away. Isn't that odd?"

A little alarm went off inside my head, but not loud enough to send me into action. A pinched nerve? A hidden injury from the same fall? Her heart? I told my mother to call me the very next time that happened.

Two weeks later I got the call. "It happened again," she said, with a kind of surprised disbelief, "I couldn't even grab the doorknob and turn it, my arm was so weak. And then it went away again, just like last time."

"I want you to make an appointment to see your internist as soon as possible," I told her.

She called back to say that the appointment had been set for the next week. I got off the phone relieved: that little alarm was ringing loudly now.

Two mornings later, at 8:15 a.m., I had just walked into my house from dropping the boys off at their schools. The phone rang. It was my mother, speaking in a frail, quavering voice, "Mike? Will you take me to the hospital? I was barely able to get out of bed. I think I may be having a heart attack."

I grabbed the keys and ran. As I started to climb into my pickup truck, my wife yelled for me to take the car instead, otherwise I'd never be able to get her into the passenger seat.

It was the one smart thing I did that morning. My childhood pal Craig, now an operating room nurse and reserve sheriff in Montana, and who has been like a second son to my mother for forty years, lit into me a few days later when I called to tell him what happened: "Are you out of your mind? There's a goddamned fire station two blocks away from your mom's house. You drove right by it. They've got oxygen, a defibrillator and trained responders. . .All you had to do was call 911, but instead you decide to drive her by yourself four miles to the hospital. Are you f----ing nuts?"

Well, I was a little that morning. My mother was still in her nightgown, leaning heavily against the back of a couch as I burst through the front door and ran across the atrium to her. She was so weak that I all-but carried her to the car—and as I threaded my way through the morning traffic, about all that she could manage to say was, "You'd better hurry. I think this is pretty bad."

Five minutes later I tore up the driveway loop at the emergency entrance of El Camino Hospital. An orderly met me with a wheelchair and they rushed my mother inside. By the time I rejoined her in the one of the treatment rooms, my mother was already on oxygen and being hooked up to an EKG.

Fifteen minutes later, I had the diagnosis. It was indeed a heart attack. Once they had her stabilized, they moved my mother upstairs to the cardiac ward. I called my sister and my wife with the bad news.

Two days later, my mother was wheeled into surgery and two stents were placed in the blocked blood vessels of her heart. They were only partially effective: though the emergency had now passed, my mother's heart was now only running at about 80 percent efficiency—it seemed that her life of busy activity were now forever behind her, and that her fate was to be a quiet, slow fading away.

But that was only part of the bad news. Blood tests had also found that she was anemic. "Has your mother not been eating?" the nurse asked accusingly. "No," I replied, "She eats three balanced meals a day." But I knew the nurse didn't believe me.

Two days later, the culprit was found: colon cancer. The only good news was that it was both early stage (it hadn't penetrated the colon wall) and of low-grade malignancy. But the tumor had to go. Soon.

My mother went home a week later. Two days after that I drove her to her (new) cardiologist's office in a professional center just across the street from the hospital. The doctor was an older Egyptian man. And though he was courtly and professionally gracious, as I watched him look up from the brand-new cardiograph printout, I could tell that he was already psychologically distancing himself.

"I am afraid," he said to my mother very carefully, choosing his words, "that removing your tumor—which would be a simple task with a healthier person—will be *difficult* in your current condition. Your heart function is much reduced . . . and I'm afraid that it will not be able to withstand surgery."

"What does that mean?" my mother asked.

"It means that you essentially have two choices: Go home and use other non-surgical means to slow the cancer—which may mean that you have a couple of years. Or take the risk of surgery, though the odds are very high that you will not survive the surgery."

My mother stared at the wall for a moment, then nodded to the doctor, "I'll think about it."

"I understand," said doctor. "And please let me know what you decide."

We drove home in silence. I had never discussed with another person their imminent death and I had no idea what to say.

We sat for a while in my mother's living room, its spare walls and Danish modern furniture so different from my own antiques-filled house. We discussed trifles, doing our best not to address the life or death matter at hand.

Finally, my mother shook her head. "Well," she said, with a mix of disbelief and finality, "This is something isn't it? What do you think?"

I tried my best to recapitulate what the doctor had said, trying to explain the long odds against my mother in a sufficiently clinical way that the sheer awfulness of the choice wouldn't choke me up. When I finished describing her options, I asked very carefully, "Do you have any thoughts on what you want to do?"

My mother looked at me in surprise, "I'm having the surgery, of course."

SECOND CHANCE

The four of us—my wife and I, my sister and her longtime boyfriend, Tony—accompanied the gurney down the long hallway from the surgical prep room to the ominous double doors of cardiac surgery.

My mother was already sedated, a hairnet on her head, and a sheet covering her up the neck—a funereal sight in itself. She was too groggy to tell us much more than that she loved us. And we told her we loved her. And as the orderly wheeled her off, we knew we'd never see her alive again.

We sat solemnly in the waiting room for the next three hours. There wasn't much to say. And when at last the door opened and a serious-faced doctor called out our name, we assumed the worst.

The surgeon was a young man, as they all seem to be these days—especially after you pass fifty—and he looked weary. Then . . .unexpectedly, amazingly . . . he made a tired smile. "Well, you'll never believe it," he said. "Before we worked on your mother's colon, we decided to put in one last stent. Just to see if it would help that weak heart of hers."

Now he grinned. I felt my shoulders involuntarily lifting. "And damned if it didn't work. The moment that stent went in place, your mom's heart just locked in. It started working like a teenager's.

"After that, the colon surgery was a breeze. She went through it like someone half her age."

My sister and my wife wiped their eyes.

FINAL WORDS

Two months later my mother was back walking three miles per day with Mildred. She was out almost every evening, especially on the weekends, with her gentleman friend Bob, making sandwiches for my boys when they came over to swim in the pool, attending weekly meetings and mah-jongg games . . . and most of all, my mother was once again focused on the restoration of the Hasbrook Farm.

Tim Lantz was largely out of the picture now. For a while, I pounded on Dopps to keep Tim in the loop, but in the end I had to go with the guy on the ground in Oklahoma. Nevertheless, before he signed off, Tim undertook a series of actions that probably saved the project.

The first was the decision to clean up, but then seal, the farmhouse from the elements and then move on to the barn. In doing so, he probably saved the former from sliding past the point of being salvageable, and the latter from full structural collapse.

Just as important, when he discovered (via a photograph) that Dopps and his crew had, in a pique of curiosity, stripped the cheap vinyl siding off the farmhouse to look at the wooden clapboards underneath, Tim went ballistic. He ordered the crew to immediately paint the entire house with white sealant to keep the old, dried board—exposed for the first time in a half-century—from absorbing half of the humidity in the state of Oklahoma.

Inside the house, Lantz was just as unyielding. Though most of the old walls were falling off the underlying lath, Tim insisted that Dopps re-attach it wherever possible.

But all of this paled against the contribution that Tim made to the restoration of the great barn. Dopps, as I've already noted, was a builder, and most often a rebuilder—but he was not a restorer. And left to his own devices, he would have undoubtedly done the prudent and reasonable thing with the barn: tear out the old foundation and pour a new one, replace with new lumber the scores of rotting and broken boards (some still sitting in the mud) running vertically along the bottom of the structure, and put on a new roof of thick modern shingles.

But there is nothing reasonable about historic restoration. And that, I had learned over the previous decade, was the reason that Tim Lantz was not a particularly reasonable man to work with. Restoration is instead about obsession, purity and only the most painful compromises. That's why Tim's solution to the problem of the barn—in his mind the only solution—probably seemed crazy to Dave Dopps when he first heard it. But I insisted that he follow it to the letter. I had let Tim down many times over the years with my willingness to cut a corner here, to use modern materials there . . .but not this time, and not with Charlie's barn.

What Lantz demanded, and what Dopps accomplished long after Tim was gone, was to maintain the barn's *historic* integrity. What this meant was that instead of tearing out the narrow old foundation, which was in collapse at numerous points around the perimeter of the barn, Tim required that the pieces instead be epoxied back together—and that a new and wider foundation be poured into a hollow dug beside and *under* the original foundation. Just to do that, Dopps had to first construct special clamps, forms and jigs to hold everything in place as the epoxy dried (in the bitter cold of winter he and his crew had to set up plastic wind-breaks and heated the materials with lamps) and the newly-poured concrete cured.

And that was only the beginning. In studying the old foundation during his visit, Tim had noticed that it was slightly pink—obviously with no available sources of sand, Charlie Hasbrook had mixed his cement with the local red dirt and river rock. So he ordered Dopps to do the same. "No one may ever notice," Lantz told me, "But somehow, it'll *feel* right. It'll fit in with the building and the landscape better."

As for the siding on the barn—simple 1x12s, ten feet long, clear-grained fir, nailed vertically to underlying studs with no insulation, then painted just once a century before—Tim was equally unyielding. Unless a plank was completely splintered (and sometimes even then) it was to be saved.

This absolutism seemed problematic, especially regarding the lower course of boards that ran along the foundation mudsill. As I said, these were in particularly sorry shape, as they are on most old barns. Nearly every one of these more than one hundred boards was rotted away on the bottom end from a combination of wear, dry rot, and ureic acid. But Tim was adamant: each of these planks was to be removed and restored to its original squared-off form using a combination of epoxy consolidants and a little artistry. In the end, that process alone would take Dopps and his crew several months.

Finally, there was the matter of the roof and the cupola. Having restored everything from Mexican ranchos to elaborate multi-story Queen Annes, Lantz knew his business when it came to 19th century roofing materials. And one of the things he understood was that modern shingles, even reproductions, look very little like their historic counterparts. Because of that, before he departed, Lantz insisted (to put a polite word on it) that the barn and house roofs be covered with thin, split cedar shingles—which, as it turned out later, could only be procured at some cost in Washington State and shipped in by railroad.

The cupola, meanwhile, had troubled Tim almost from the first moment he saw a photo of the barn. It assaulted his sense of symmetry. "Are you *sure* that's the way it originally looked?" he asked. I checked with my mother, and she assured me that it had looked that way as long as she could remember, which was the mid-1920s. Aunt Alliene, eighteen months older than my mother, confirmed it.

"No, no, something's wrong," said Tim on hearing the news. "It's too small. It can't do what it's supposed to do. It has to act as a heat ventilator for the hay, drawing the air up and out through the roof."

Finally, a few months later I had a phone conversation with my uncle, my mother's only brother. Though the baby of the family, he would die a year later. But when we spoke, he was still robust and full of humor.

"So Mike," he said in his dusty mid-Western twang, so much like my grandfather's, "What're you going to do about the barn?"

"We're going to restore it."

"Good. Good. You going to fix that old cupola while you're at it?"

"Fix?"

"I mean, are you going to take it back to the original? 'Cause you know, it was about twice that tall when that German barn builder built it for grandpa. It was before my time, but I've seen pictures, and it was a pretty impressive looking sight."

"Really?"

"I suppose that's why grandpa cut it down. He never said as much, but I always figured that it was so imposing-looking and ostentatious that Charlie was embarrassed by the thing. I'll bet the neighbors kidded him about it. Whatever the reason, he cut it down—probably back before World War I—and that's the way it's been ever since."

"In that case, Uncle Lloyd, we'll restore it back the way it was."

"Good, Mike. That's good to hear."

Sadly, my Uncle Lloyd never saw the true cupola on the barn.

I told Tim what I'd learned.

"Ah," he said, "that explains it. We climbed up there and you could see where the bottom had been sawed off and the whole thing dropped down. And lemme tell ya, this was one time that Charlie Hasbrook didn't do us any favors. I'm sure the part he cut out had big vents in it—those old barn-builders knew what they were doing—and by getting rid of them, Charlie trapped heat and moisture inside the barn and accelerated its decay."

"So, we put the old cupola back?"

"Oh yeah. But it'd be better if you find a photo. Otherwise we'll have to guess and risk not being historically accurate."

TOPPING OFF

It took me two years to find that photo. Almost magically, it appeared just weeks before Dopps was planning on constructing the replacement cupola. The tiny print, likely from a Brownie box camera, was part of a group of old photos sent to my mother from one her cousins in hopes that one of them might be useful to the farm restoration.

She couldn't have been more right, nor the photo been more useful. It was winter shot, showing Charlie standing in ankle deep snow at the big sliding doors at the south entrance to the barn, wearing a cap and a heavy, plaid coat. Sitting at his feet was a dark German Shepherd—"Old Shep", my mother instantly remembered when she looked at a blow-up of the image. But the most important part of the photograph was the top: there, every detail delineated by the light frosting of snow, was the original cupola in all of its glory, nearly unique for that region of the country.

We quickly sent the print to Oklahoma, and Dave Dopps, now with the image in hand, built an exact reproduction.

The cupola was set atop the barn in early spring, 2008, at about the same time as the shingles arrived. Thin, split cedar, the original shingles on the barn had been obsolete for years in Oklahoma, replaced by much thicker and more durable versions. So we had to order them—6,000 square feet of shingles—from Washington State, to be shipped by train.

When they at last arrived and were trucked to the farm, the shingles were hoisted up by a group of eight men, who lined up across the great roof and nailed course after course over two full days. It was an indelible image—and the photograph taken during that work is, to my mind, the most enduring of the many hundreds taken during the restoration of the farm. My mother framed it and put it on a dresser to remind her of the task she had taken upon herself.

Little did we realize that in treasuring this image, we were repeating history. Only later after the barn was done, did another of my aunts, Wanda, sent my, mother a collection of photographs showing another group of men lined up a century ago across the same roof, nailing down shingles under the ghostly and empty frame of the cupola. Like grandfather, like granddaughter, Charlie too had obviously been drawn to preserve that brief and distinctive moment.

I wasn't there to see the crane lift the cupola and place it in its cradle atop the barn. Indeed, I hadn't actually set foot on the farm since that day, as a magazine editor, I had climbed the fence and visited the farm. Since my wife and I were helping my mother with her business affairs, it was our task to oversee the Hasbrook Farm restoration by remote control—the occasional phone call, comments by relatives who had passed by the farm, and the monthly diary and two dozen on-line photos.

Dopps was kind enough to send me over the years literally hundreds of close-up photographs of rotting beams, sistered studs, and replaced joints to prove that he was busily at work . . .but I still found myself studying the one or two long shots included in each group that showed the barn, its broken back now mended, standing against the frosted trees, or the house, stripped of its porches, but now restored to its original siding and undercoated a brilliant white above a newly-mowed green lawn. I would study these photographs, even print them out and scrutinize them with a magnifying glass, trying to imagine the buildings both finished and in three dimensions.

But those were difficult days for me—in less than twelve months I'd gone from a Media Executive to a poor freelance writer struggling to cover the mortgage in a market where almost all of my clients had disappeared. A flight to Oklahoma—a casual decision a few years before—was now all-but out of the question.

But my mother did make it back to the farm. Indeed, just three months after her heart surgery, she insisted on going to the Hasbrook family reunion. And my sister and Tony agreed to take her.

The reunion was held at a hall in downtown Enid, and when it ended a convoy of Hasbrook descendents, young and old, drove out to the old family homestead. It was the first time (other than a few others who, like myself, who had sneaked onto the property) that most other Hasbrooks had walked on the farm in more than a half-century.

Dopps had cleaned up the place as best he could for a busy worksite, even mowing the grass an extra time and constructing a walkway and steps to his work trailer for the older visitors. But there was little he could do about state of the house and barn: braced by boards, stripped of porches, windows covered by plywood sheets, plastic sheeting on the roof, the two structures both looked in many ways *worse* than they had when they had just stood there rotten and abandoned.

But in the end none of that really mattered. On that hot, muggy August day, all that counted to those assembled visitors was the simple fact that the family homestead was now back in the family's hands . . .and that the processes of decay and disintegration had now, if only slightly, been reversed. And many tears were shed at that realization as the evidence stood before them.

No one that day as more affected than my mother's cousin Vie Lee,

Merrill's daughter. Of all of the people there that day, she was the only one who had ever lived on the farm, spending most of her summers there and then moving in with my grandparents to attend school in Enid the rest of the year.

Vie Lee was the cleverest and most accomplished of all of the Hasbrook grandchildren, and she and my mother, to whom she had the closest relationship, would often as girls take a blanket out on the wide and level bank beside the Dugout and lie there until late into the night looking at stars, talking about boys and school, and dreaming of their futures.

Unfortunately, that future did not turn out anything like Vie Lee had planned. In a fairer world she might have been a corporate executive or a successful professional. But circumstances and some bad choices had led her into a long and unhappy marriage to a bitter alcoholic—and then, after his death, to second marriage to an old Enid High School acquaintance who quickly became an invalid.

Now, diabetic and frail, Alzheimer's disease beginning to gnaw away at her fine mind, Vie Lee was pushed across that same lawn in a wheelchair by her middle-aged son. She said very little that day, but there were tears behind her dark glasses. And when she had a moment alone with my mother, she said softly, "Nadiene, I wish I could be buried here."

TWISTER

From out distant outpost in California, we cheered the news of the restored cupola being placed atop the barn. Until then, the quotidian work of restoring the farm had been a slow and comparatively uninspiring process that stretched out month after month, seemingly without end. We tried to be patient, having gone through this sort of thing before, but it was hard sometimes not to get frustrated—especially after Dopps began to strip away his crew and began to work more slowly with his dedicated team.

But the placement of the cupola was an undeniable milestone in the restoration of the Hasbrook Farm. There was no denying it—and the thrill the news gave each of us suggested that we had all been unconsciously waiting for this moment for a long time. And we weren't alone: Dave

Dopps betrayed his own obsession with the farm by immediately (and without our knowledge) calling the *Enid News & Eagle* with the story.

A few days later, *Eagle* readers opened the paper to see a huge front page photo of the freshly painted red barn, with the new cupola perched on top. Now all of Northwest Oklahoma knew what we were up to. I was a little annoyed by this invasion of our privacy—and as an old journalist angry that I'd been scooped on my own story.

But within the month, on a crazy Saturday afternoon, I suddenly found myself thankful that at least we had some record of our efforts before it was lost forever.

* * *

On that May afternoon, I had been sitting in my home office, pounding out an editorial for the *Wall Street Journal,* when I impulsively switched on the television to check the news . . .

The first image I saw was a map. And at the very center of that map was the word HENNESSEY. The next thing I saw, on the news roll beneath that map, was the word TORNADO.

Oh my God.

It took several minutes of frenetic switching back and forth between news channels to get the gist of the story: Multiple tornados had been spotted touching down in the area around the towns of Hennessey and Bison, Oklahoma—and they were heading east from Highway 81 towards Marshall. I felt my stomach instantly knot: the farm was nine miles east of Bison off Hwy 81. My mother's birth certificate says "Marshall, OK" on it because that is the nearest town.

The tornados—and there now eight of them—were heading straight towards the farmhouse and the barn with its shiny new cupola. More than a century after it had been built, after sixty years of waiting to get it back, after five years and three-quarters of a million dollars spent on its repurchase and restoration . . . was the Hasbrook Homestead now, under my watch, about to get scraped off the face of the Earth?

A horrifying image appeared in my mind of splinters of fresh-painted wood scattered over miles of countryside. How could I tell my mother that she had lost the farm again? How could I ever restore it now?

And then the worst thought of all: after all of these struggles, was the farm about to disappear *without me ever having seen that damn cupola*?

For the next three hours, I sat stricken at my desk, with one hand hopping from channel to channel, following the live coverage from an incredibly heroic Oklahoma City helicopter reporter who seemed to be darting between the emerging tornado cells—while with the other hand, scrolled across the Google Map of the farm, trying to mentally overlay the two images.

I tried calling Dave Dopps, whom I knew had to be at least as worried as me. We had corresponded many times, but it was the first time we had actually talked. I caught him with one leg in his home storm shelter, the rest of him leaning out to watch the news coverage on his garage TV, tornado sirens screaming in the distance, his wife nearby telling him to get inside. "I don't know anything," he said plaintively, "but they're really close to the farm."

I called my farmer-renter, Eddie Mack, who leased the fields at the farm. The only time we had ever spoken was when Eddie, a little confused about where I lived, had called to tell me that the wheat harvest was in and asking where he should ship my half. I had visions of thousands of bushels of wheat stacked up on my suburban Sunnyvale lawn— and very carefully told him that he should just sell my half along with his share and send me the check.

I caught Eddie in what appeared to be a howling rainstorm. But he had no news either, other than that "it's pretty dark over that way." Eddie added that he had an uncle who lived not far from the farm, but had been unable to get through either on his home phone or cell.

It wasn't until four o'clock that the phone rang with news. By then I was past sorrow. Eight tornadoes; and if the maps were accurate, they had all-but lined up to take turns ravaging the Hasbrook Farm. It was all over, our dream had been still-born.

It was Dopps on the phone. Unable to stand it any longer, and against the protestations of his more prudent wife, Dopps had jumped into his truck and braved the still-swirling wind and rain to drive south to Bison and then out the sodden, debris-strewn road to the farm, all the while dreading what he would find.

"*Nothing,*" he said. The phone line was still crackly, and I almost misunderstood the implication of that word, but Dave's excitement was unmistakable, "The farm is perfect. As near as I can figure, the tornados passed on both sides of the property—yet I don't even think a twig was broken on the homestead. It's the most amazing thing . . . but you know what they say: the Indians always believed that a tornado will never touch down at the fork of a creek. So maybe Charlie Hasbrook had another reason for picking that spot."

I thanked Dave for the news, and the risks he'd taken getting it—then I hung up and got drunk.

Reunion

The near-brush with the tornados, even though it was a likely once in a century event, finally convinced me that I needed to get back to Oklahoma.

My wife was of the same opinion. My mother, though still quite healthy, still busy, and still walking several miles each day was beginning to lose her ability to keep track of her finances. The multiple bank accounts, lines of credit, etc. required to manage her houses, the farm and property were beginning to overwhelm her, so Carol stepped in. Over the course of a week, she managed to work her way through a mountain of cancelled checks, bills and tax documents, and finally reconciled all of her mother-in-law's finances. And when she was done, she announced, "I've got to sit down face-to-face with Dopps and plan the rest of this project."

We chose as the occasion for our visit the annual Hasbrook reunion in Enid, which we had attended only once before. It was scheduled for the first weekend in August—perfect, because my mother was (as always) planning to attend, and my sister was buried in a new job at Oracle and would not be able to get away to accompany her as she had in the past. It would also be a week after our younger son, Tim, would finish Boy Scout camp; and our older son, Tad, would be done with summer school.

As is my nature, I immediately began to plot an even more elaborate trip to Oklahoma. Like many dads, I had begun fatherhood by convincing myself that I could be a useful father by merely cheering on my children from the bleachers or from the back of a school cafeteria. And like most fathers, I found myself, year by year, kid by kid, being drawn deeper into the institutions of childhood. In my case, that meant twelve years as a Little League manager, from little 4 year-olds who would lie in the outfield grass during the game and watch the clouds, to veteran 17 year-olds with goatees who would drive themselves and their girlfriends to night games.

But even more important, as an old Eagle Scout, I found myself drawn back to Scouting when Tad turned eleven. Over the years, my role in the troop as assistant Scoutmaster evolved into overseeing the older Scouts, the high schoolers, helping them advancing through the final ranks to their own Eagle . . . and just as important, to keep Scouting interesting enough for these young men in the face of such distractions as girls, cars, SATs and college interviews.

Towards that end, I began devising an annual trip for these Scouts that would be so singular that they would remember it for the rest of their lives. The year before, with five Scouts including my two sons, we had travelled to the UK to hike the 192-mile Wainwright Walk across Northern England. Every one of the boys who were heading off to college the next year listed that hike as one of the most memorable experiences of their childhood.

Needless to say, that set expectations pretty high for the next year—and I was already scheduled to take both my family and my mother to Oklahoma for the family reunion.

The only solution was the combine the two. It took three months planning, but the result was extraordinary even by Scouting standards: our group of suburban Silicon Valley teenagers and dads, most of whom had never been on a horse beyond posing on a Shetland Pony at a McDonald's, were to ride 55 miles up the Chisholm Trail, from El Reno to Bison, Oklahoma. Along the way, we would shoot traditional weapons, meet with an elder and 'dog soldier' of the Cheyenne nation, ford the Cimarron River, bulldog and brand cattle, and, most remarkably, drive longhorn cattle up the trail for a day. We would be joined by a group of veteran cowboys, including the most experienced long-range cattle driver in America, and even eat our meals out of a mule-drawn chuck wagon that would follow us up the trail.

Two of my Scouts planned to perform their Eagle projects while on the trail; one was to clear brush and restore the Trail markers that, fifteen years before, had been placed each mile along the path through Oklahoma; the other was to create a website on the Trail and develop a medal for those who completed fifty miles of it.

In the course of organizing the ride, and developing contacts for the two boys, I was introduced to Bob Klemme, an historian even more obsessed than Tim Lantz or Dave Dopps. In 1939, while still in high school, Klemme had listened to one of his teachers tell the history of the Chisholm Trail . . . and then announce, to the students' surprise, that the Trail itself was just a mile outside of town.

Bob Klemme never forgot that moment, and like my mother (who would have been just down the hall at Enid High) Klemme swore that one day he would do something about it. And, also like my mother, it took a half-century for him to fulfill that oath: in the mid-1980s, Klemme, now retired, set out to mark the exact path of the Chisholm Trail. Using old maps, he charted the Trail for all 350 miles through Oklahoma, from the Texas border to the edge of Kansas. And to mark it, he devised, poured and then levered into the ground—often by himself—a 200 pound, steel-reinforced cement post with the words "Chisholm Trail" in block letters embedded on one side . . .at least one for every mile of the Trail.   It took him ten years to emplace all 400 markers—and by the time he was finished, Bob Klemme knew more about the Chisholm than any living person and had been invited to join the board of the Oklahoma Historical Society.

Needless to say, in the course of our many e-mail conversations, I told Klemme the story of Charlie Hasbrook. He had read the *Enid Eagle* story, and was curious about the location of the homestead. I figured this was just an historian's natural curiosity, so I gave him directions and forgot all about it.

A few weeks later, Klemme sent an email that floored me. Did you know, he asked, that Charlie Hasbrook's name is carved on a statue just outside Enid? Not only didn't I know it, but nobody else in the family apparently knew it either, even those who had seen the monument. Klemme sent me a digital photograph of the edifice, an impressive art deco carving dedicated to the Cherokee Strip Cowpunchers Association. The monument dated from the Thirties. A second photograph, a close-up, showed my great-grandfather's name, "Chas. Hasbrook", carved on the list with a hundred others, both unknown and famous (like Tom Mix).

Cowpunchers? When was Charlie Hasbrook a *cowboy*? But if that new information was disconcerting, the next few images only added to the mystery. It was the pages of the brochure-sized Cowpunchers membership directory, dated September, 1925. As it happened, I first looked at the title page, then the page where Charlie's name should have been listed. But it wasn't there. Had there been some kind of mistake? Then I clicked open another page . . . and there, *handwritten* over a cowboy poem was "Chas Hasbrook 1932-33." What did that mean? I phoned Klemme.

The Cherokee Strip Cowpunchers Association, Klemme explained, was a social group founded after WWI by old cowboys from the region. The requirement for membership was that they had to have worked cattle on the Cherokee Strip in the years before the Land Rush.

You mean, I asked, on the Chisholm Trail? I thought of my upcoming ride and the spectacular coincidence of encountering this document at this moment.

Yes, said Klemme, exactly. He then went on to explain that the Association was basically an excuse for the old cowboys to set up a tent at county fairs or rodeos, or to hang around a cabin they built at the site where the monument is now, and to drink, smoke and swap lies about the good old days before civilization showed up.

So why was Charlie's name on the monument and why was it added so late to the original membership rolls?

We'll probably never know, said Klemme, but you did say that your great-grandfather worked on the railroad through the Strip in the years before the Run. And he probably knew all of the old members. They probably figured that was qualification enough and let him in. The Association, in its original form, didn't last many years after that, so Charlie Hasbrook was probably its last member.

I had always visualized my great-grandfather as spending those years on the farm, occasionally driving into the town to buy supplies or go to church. I had almost forgotten those years in Chicago and Charlie's love of horseracing. Happily getting drunk with a bunch of grizzled old cowboys was an image I hadn't anticipated. I assume that Mary Hasbrook wasn't too keen on the idea either.

It certainly explained why his daughter, Theresa, my sober and serious grandmother, kept an eagle eye out on Charlie in his old age. She probably didn't relax until the news came that the Association's barn had burned to the ground. Like many townspeople, she no doubt preferred the noble cowboys of legend and film to the smelly and crude real ones who hung around the Enid town square.

As for me, becoming (if briefly) a Chisholm Trail cowboy now seemed less a lark, than the unexpected assertion of destiny.

ORAL HISTORY

As I scheduled it, the ride would begin the day after the Hasbrook family reunion. We would all fly to Oklahoma City on Thursday, have a steak dinner at Cattleman's, then drive up in the morning to Enid. There we would attend Vie Lee's memorial at the Memorial Park—she had died two months before, and her son had chosen to follow the request in her will to be buried beside her first husband—meet with Dopps at the Hasbrook Farm in the afternoon and then attend the family reunion, to be held in the Enid Conference Center on Saturday. Then, Saturday afternoon, the whole family would be invited to the farm to inspect its progress.

As with most such trips, nothing went according to plan. We arrived in Enid in time for the memorial, but we had forgotten the invitation. After a quick drive through the wrong cemetery, we arrived at Enid Memorial Park just in time to see the priest leaving the gazebo at the completion of the ceremony.

Then, thanks to confused signals between my mother and hers, my cousin Linda, a retired teacher, headed out to show us Charlie and Mary's grave (as well as our own grandparents) while I drove my family in the other direction back to the hotel. I didn't even know until the next day that the memorial statue of the Cherokee Strip Cowpunchers Association—the one that unexpectedly bore Charlie's name—was also just a few yards away.

That was the least of the confusion. Our original plan was for our family to drive out to the farm that afternoon, meet with Dopps and go over all of the finances on the farm and chart out the remaining work. But we had barely time to take a quick tour of the barn and house, and then sit down in Dave's trailer and pull out the paperwork .when a caravan of cars and vans pulled up into the yard.

My cousin Linda, who was leading the parade, was nonplussed when I explained our plans. "Good lord. Mike, you've got to tell *me* these things. Our moms are getting too old to remember anything accurately anymore."

I remembered my mother and my aunt saying the same thing about our grandparents. I looked at Linda's gray hair and thought of mine: when would it be our turn?

So we rolled with it. Carol postponed her meeting with Dopps until the next day. Instead we wandered about the farm with the rest of our extended family. It was odd to see so many people there. Growing up, I had never thought of the Hasbrook homestead as *my* family's farm, but I had certainly always in my heart thought that it was owned by the descendants of Art and Theresa Collins.

Now as I watched all of these people, bearing names like Franke, Olmstead, Kelly and even Hasbrook, I had to remind myself that this farm was their family homestead as well. These senior citizens and young married couples and teenagers were passing down the same family legends—excised, I noticed, of the truth about Grandma Woodley bloodstained hands, or the beloved Nate's time up the river—but filtered through the lives of Audrey or Helen, Nate or Merrill.

Indeed, in many ways, we were the odd ones. Because my grandmother had been the eldest child, my mother and my aunts were also old enough that as teenagers they babysat many of their infant cousins— including some of the stooped old men who were exploring the barnyard with me. And my grandparents had moved to town by the end of the First World War—while some of the younger Hasbrook siblings had stayed on the farm well into the 1930s. So, in that respect, their roots here were even deeper than our own.

And, of course, there was the oddness, the elephant in the room at every gathering, that we were the kinfolk who had moved away, somehow found a reputed fortune, and then (it seemed) had come swooping back to buy the farm and restore it to its former grandeur. No doubt it was a bit of an affront to everyone else who had lived within miles of the farm for decades and never done more than sneak a quick visit over the fence once per decade. Or perhaps not. Perhaps they were just happy with the miracle of the Hasbrook homestead suddenly getting a second life. I do know that when anyone asked why we had done it, I had no ready answer, except to point to an 87 year-old woman and reply, "Because she wanted to."

But whatever the reason, the simple, unassailable fact, as obvious as the cupola and the new coat of paint on the barn, and the stacks of lumber in the farmhouse, was that the Hasbrook homestead, Charlie's Place, had once again emerged from the debris, and overgrowth and vines, in a kind of resurrection. And everyone there knew that rebirth had a beating heart—and it lay behind an open doorway, surrounded by dried mud bricks, in the creek bank behind the house.

The Dugout.

As I watched, small groups of Hasbrook descendants would break away from the others, and is if in a tiny pilgrimage, walks silently down the hillside towards that doorway. I resisted as long as I could, knowing how it would affect me, but eventually I made the walk as well.

Ducking through the doorway, and wading through years' worth of leaves that had blown through the threshold, I felt that familiar knot in my throat as I looked up at the curved ceiling that barely cleared my head. "How did they ever do it?" I heard one of my second cousins say behind me. "It's so *tiny*. And that little family, out here all alone."

Passing through the doorway on the way out, I encountered a distant cousin and his wife, walking their four year old daughter towards the dugout. "This is the cave where it all began," they were telling her. "This is where we all started."

EXTENDED FAMILY

That evening we sat in one of the hotel rooms with my aunts and two of my other cousins, and talked family—a common enough occurrence for the rest of them, but as the renegade relatives who had run off to the far end of the continent, it was a rare, disconcerting, but ultimately satisfying experience. This was what my mother had left a half century before, and as I took her arm and walked her back to her room, I could tell that she both enjoyed these visits and was happy as well to leave them, with their relationships that had been permanently set, in some cases, long, long ago.

By morning it was already becoming oppressively hot—the weathercasters were predicting 100 degrees—as we drove into the center of town. We took a small detour, past Enid High School, still an impressive red brick structure— a new generation of high schoolers were out on the field, practicing their marching band moves—then down a few blocks to my grandparents' house.

Though there were a few nice homes left, this corner of Enid had fallen into poverty and decay. Dutch elm disease had robbed the neighborhood of its one-time arboreal cover, and the new trees were still insufficient to keep the streets from baking in the heat. This once busy community now seemed almost deserted, as the demolition of old homes seemed to have left at least one vacant lot per block. What had once been a neighborhood of working class folks with big families, was now largely a repository of old people and immigrants on government support.

"Oh my," my mother whispered in dismay as we rounded the corner onto Washington Street. My grandparents' house was a wreck: the long front porch where the young suitors had sat with my mother and my aunts was long gone, as was the long drainage ditch at the front of the lawn where my mother had first met my father. The window frames that had managed to hold back all but the tiniest grains of the Dust Bowl storm, were now cracked and split. And my grandmother's garden was, simply, gone.

We only stopped for a moment. Then my mother turned away. "Let's go," she said. "I don't ever need to come back here again."

We drove to the main square of downtown Enid, with its still-imposing deco Courthouse. This was not only the spot to where Charlie Hasbrook had ridden after the Land Rush, and where he had stood in line seemingly forever to file his claim, but where my grandparents had taken my mother and her sisters and brother to watch the last of the Civil War veterans, in their long white beards, ride by during the Armistice day parades. And on the lawn in front of the Courthouse also stood the WWI memorial, dedicated to local doughboys who had died in the trenches of France, including my great-uncle John.

The Hasbrook Family reunion was held in the large, concrete and comparatively brutalist-style Enid Convention Center. It was like most family reunions everywhere: mostly the same people in attendance, all of them a little older; the oldest folks and the newest family members both bored and largely oblivious to the proceedings; the two or three women who do all of the work and the great-uncle who cracks all of the jokes; the announcement of who came the furthest to the reunion (always my mother) and who was the oldest (my great-aunt Velva, then my aunt Alliene), and the sharing of the sacred images and documents.

Missing this year was Nate's Oklahoma A&M (now OSU) letter sweater and his striking college photograph—the latter having stopped my wife and I in our tracks the first time we saw it because of the uncanny resemblance between Nate and our son Tad: the same high cheekbones and almond-shaped eyes, the only difference being Tad's height, inherited from the Collins' side, and Nate's football player-thick neck.

But what relics had been left at home this time by my relatives, were more than compensated by the items brought by one of my guests. Bob Klemme, 82 years old, but as tall and ramrod straight as a man half his age, had come at my invitation to talk to the reunion about Chisholm Trail and the Land Rush. And as we sat together at one of the tables, he handed me two documents: the first a copy of the original land claim, signed by President William McKinley, for Charlie's land stake. Left blank was the date when Charlie would officially take ownership and the time the document was signed, that event was still three hard years away.

The second, larger document was also a copy, this one dated 1872, then hand-updated twenty years later, of the land survey of one section of the Cherokee Strip. Klemme pointed at a familiar fork in one of the creeks. "That right there is Charlie's place," he said. You can see by the markings for the vegetation that there were fewer trees than there are now. Cultivation and land management are the main reasons."

I spotted the train line to the west of the farm and with my finger followed its path, roughly between the old Chisholm Trail and today's Hwy. 81, from the top of the map to the bottom. "Do you think Charlie helped mark this part?"

"You said that he was part of the railroad crew, didn't you?"

"Yes."

"Then there's a good chance he did."

Klemme gave his talk about the Land Rush. He was followed by his fellow historian, TK, who spoke about the Cherokee Strip Cow-punchers—a bit of news to most of the people in the room. Then Dave Dopps took the microphone, and the warm welcome he received reminded me that during the reunions I had missed over the last few years his updates on the status of the farm had become a high point of the annual gathering. That, and the passion with which he described the farm and what he had learned, by restoring Charlie's work, of the man himself, underscored that Dopps was now an adopted part of the Hasbrook family as well. His story of the first visit with Lantz, of the freezing winter days trying to epoxy the foundation back together, of stripping the clapboards off the widow's swaying barn, of finding the photograph of the cupola and replacing it at last . . . all were now part of the growing Hasbrook family lore.

So too was Gary Young's story. It had fallen on him that first year after we signed the papers to make the announcement in our stead at the Hasbrook reunion. Now, after a half-dozen reunions, Gary (dressed in a Hawaiian shirt and shorts, with a Bluetooth phone on his ear, he looked like a Hollywood agent) seemed to know more of my relatives than I did. Once again, he told the story of the decade-long battle to regain the farm and praised my mother for having the wisdom and gumption for doing so.

Then my cousin Dennis, that doppelganger relative each of us has who is more like us than anyone in our own family, took the microphone. Dennis, a retired Army officer and city manager of North Palm Beach, Florida, presented my mother with a section of siding rescued from the Hasbrook barn. On it was carved: *The Hasbrook-Malone Farm.*

My cousin Delores, who still lived in Enid, adjourned the reunion, inviting everyone to attend the next year's event, to be held in its biannual rotation at the home of Eddie Hasbrook (Nate's son, a district attorney) and his wife Vivien (a psychologist) at their expansive home on the outskirts of Oklahoma City. Groups posed for photographs, phone numbers were taken, the ladies put the lids on the potluck casseroles, and we headed out into the brilliant, shockingly hot sun.

THE LONG RIDE HOME: THE CHISHOLM TRAIL

On Sunday morning, Tad and I dropped Carol and Tim off at Will Rogers Airport in Oklahoma City for the flight home. My mother had left a few hours before with her older sister to spend the week at Alliene's home outside Tulsa. It was already ninety degrees, and as Tad and I drove across the city to meet the rest of the Scouts and dads at their motel, it only seemed to grow hotter by the mile.

During the rest of that day, we stopped by a vast Bass Pro Shop to get any remaining items ("Who'd of thought such a boring sport would have such a great outfitter?" Tad muttered), then out to Duncan and the Chisholm Trail Heritage Center where we met Jerrica Lockwood, the organizer of our ride, and her father, Ron Green, the legendary cattle driver.

Green, with his moustache, suspenders and canvas jeans, cowboy boots, worn felt hat and slow drawl, was an awesome sight to this group of young suburban boys who typically spent their days playing video games and texting their girlfriends, and who had never seen a cowboy outside of Cineplex.

The Lt. Governor of Oklahoma, Jari Askins, also stopped by to wish us good luck—our first hint that our Trail Ride was already becoming a regional event. Indeed, before it was over, the wire services would carry our story all over the world.

Knowing at least a little bit about Oklahoma weather, I had tried to schedule the ride in late June. But those days collided directly with the wheat harvest—something, sitting in the middle of an endless housing development, I had never even considered and Jerrica was concerned we would never be able to get enough horses or cowboys. So, instead, we set it for the first week of August and as I walked out of the Duncan Museum, I knew I had made a terrible mistake.

The entire week that followed was one of blazing, almost murder-ous, heat. Monday, the first day and the longest of the ride, turned out to be the single hottest day in Oklahoma in the 21st century to date. We rode down endless dusty roads under a cloudless sky, the sweat running off our horses, most of us semi-delirious in the heat. Like most of the others, I wore a water bladder backpack—and managed to drain it of all two gallons of water in the first two hours .. and never peed a drop. My horse was a big twenty-year old chestnut gelding named Lucky, so named because he'd been found as a newborn colt beside his mother, who had starved to death. There were moments, especially on that first day, when I thought Lucky's luck had finally run out.

The only thing worse than the dust was the asphalt: on the day we rode through the town of Kingfisher, the street temperature was estimat-ed at 140 degrees. I lifted my eyes once to glance ahead and was amazed to see the horses slipping on the molten roadway, their shoes lifting up asphalt with each step. To save their hoofs, we took to riding our hors-es across people's lawns. Kingfisher residents, the evening news having warned them of our coming, poured out of their air-conditioned homes and stood on their shaded porches and waved.

I had told the boys about the friendliness of Oklahomans compared to their neighbors back home, but even I was surprised on this trip. Maybe it was the dangerous heat or perhaps the sight of young men rid-ing past on horseback trailed by a chuck wagon drawn by a pair of mules surfaced a deep and common emotion but the hospitality of the people we met was boundless.

The cowboys who accompanied us on the ride—men who in their daily lives turned out to be ranchers, college instructors, a postmaster and even a Catholic priest—had volunteered their time. So had the men and women who met us at the end of each day's ride and taught us tra-ditional archery or performed Cheyenne dances or taught the boys how to bulldog and brand calves. Local churches and museums opened their doors to us. And one day, after we rode hot and exhausted past a tiny home cheese factory, we were surprised to see its owner show up at our camp bringing us ten pounds of curds to snack upon.

I thought of Charlie and Frank Hays, fighting the prairie fire togeth-er. And Mary giving birth in the cave and in the farmhouse. Alone on the prairie, the pioneers had no hope of help except from each other. Oklahomans had turned that necessity into a duty and then, over the course of a century, into a pattern of behavior that now defined them more than anything else.

With each day we became more accomplished riders, and more accustomed to our duties. We awoke before dawn, ate breakfast off the back of the chuck wagon, and saddled up our horses. Then we rode, a dozen miles each day—moving quietly and confidently now— ending in the afternoon at some waterhole, where we unsaddled our horses, brushed them off and fed them, then headed off to some educational activity before dinner at a campfire and then an early sleep under the stars to get some rest before our assigned 2 a.m. or 3 a.m. picket duty.

We were becoming momentary celebrities as well, especially after, at the end of the first day, as the desperately thirsty horses reached the watering hole one of them, ridden by a tall, sixteen year old Scout named Varun, decided to step off the bank into the pond. The horse quickly sunk in the mud and stumbled as it tried to extricate itself. Varun, being a new horseman naturally pulled back on the reins, exactly the wrong thing to do, and found himself flung over the horse's neck into the water.

As it happened, an Associated Press photographer from the Oklahoma City bureau was standing nearby and got the shot of a lifetime: the horse rearing and splashing water, Varun still in the saddle, his grimace of fear looking more like a grin of confidence, creating the indelible image that of a veteran rider confidently galloping through deep water as if it was an everyday occurrence. This shot, which quickly erased Varun's humiliation, was carried in newspapers around the nation and then, when picked up by the BBC, around the world.

After that, we weren't surprised when three days later, as we approached the most nerve-wracking moment of the ride, the fording of the Cimarron River, we saw a camera crew set up atop the far bank, ready to capture another fortuitous disaster. We made it that time, though Varun's horse did decide to roll on the sand along the river, with him still in the saddle.

Epiphany

It was on the fourth night that, for me, everything changed. We were camped outside of Hennessey, a town whose name already resonated in the family history. All of us had gathered around the campfire in front of the chuck wagon to listen to a Western singer sing Johnny Cash, Merle Haggard and Willie Nelson tunes. Behind him was the pond where in the morning we would soak one of the wagon's wheels that had shrunk in the heat. To our left were some grain elevators on the edge of the town and far off, to the south, a thunderstorm was occasionally brightening the sky.

As the singer played there was suddenly a loud train whistle as a freight train moved through Hennessey. A few of us men chuckled at this nicely timed bit of texture to go with the music.

And then it hit me: that was the same train line, running between our path along the old Chisholm Trail on one side and Hwy 61 on the other, that was on the old survey map that Bob Klemme had given me. That train was running along the path and grade that Charlie Hasbrook had worked in 1891. The music receded now, and I could only hear the sound of steel wheels on steel rails, taking the path my great-grandfather had set for it, north through Bison and then on to Enid and past Government Springs.

In the morning, we saddled up to the crack of a bullwhip on the hill-top above us. It was the last day of the Trail Ride, and the most important. We rode in without words, other than the occasional click of command to our horses, about a mile to a ranch run by a veterinarian who, by odd coincidence, had once apprenticed to my uncle Bob. There, we picked up about forty head of longhorn steers and drove them out of their pens into a wide meadow. Today, at last, we would become real cowboys.

We were different people from the boys and men who had started the ride almost fifty miles before. That morning we had packed up our bedrolls and saddled our horses in near-silence. When it came time to get our final instructions from trail boss Gary Townsend, we expertly lined our horses shoulder to shoulder, some of the riders even backing their horses into the formation. We were sunburned, the boys had lank greasy hair and dirty faces and most of us men had grown beards. We had scarves around our necks in preparation for the dust ahead. Most of all we had the grim determination of men who were tired, filthy and humbled by the last few days.

The key to driving cattle, we quickly learned, was to use our horses to create a moving fence, especially in places when there was no real fence in place. We rode up the dusty road on either side of the cattle, leaving two or three horsemen in back to push the steers forward. Lucky, who had been (understandably) a bit balky the first few days, was now in his element, cutting off cattle and nudging them along almost before I gave the command.

The cowboys had now given us all nicknames: Peaches, Worm, Fabio, Hollywood, Tad was Slats because he was so thin, I was Cap'n Scull from a cowboy TV show—and they would bark instructions to keep the moving horseflesh fences in place: "Move yer ass, Peaches," "C'mon close 'er up, Fuzzy", 'Mind that gap, Cotton."

Occasionally, one of the cattle would suddenly, and without warn- ing, break from the herd, bolt between two of our horses and run out into an adjoining field or yard. The cowboys would then have to gallop after it and drive the animal back to the herd. Only one of the Scouts ever joined them: Tad.

Tall, lean and rawboned, and in his long-sleeved dress cowboy shirt and straw hat, my son already looked the part. But as each day passed he grew more taciturn, more focused on his horse and the task at hand, until an outsider would have been forgiven for mistaking him for a local who had spent most of his seventeen years on a horse. Tad had found his Oklahoma.

There wasn't much time to look up during the cattle drive, but on the few occasions when I did, what had been a distant silhouette on the flat horizon slowly grew and revealed itself as the towering grain eleva- tor of Bison.

It all became clear then, as explicit to me as it was unconscious to Tad: with every mile up the Chisholm, every step of our horses, we were riding into our own past. How many times, after a long morning on the rail line, had Charlie ridden these same fields, searching for that perfect spot where he could restart his life? How many times did young Art Collins, as rail-thin as his great-grandson, ride his horse down this same road to earn some money helping a neighbor with his harvest, all the while daydreaming about his pretty neighbor Theresa Hasbrook?

We drove the cattle more than ten miles, to just beyond the shadow of the towering Bison elevators. None of the animals had been lost or injured, and by trail's end, we had the herd moving smartly along, nudging forward stragglers, cutting off mavericks before they could escape, driving the intimidated creatures along with our shouts and cowboy yells. Had the Cherokee Strip Cowpunchers Association still existed, we might well have qualified as honorary members.

Once the cattle were driven into their pens, we rode out into a vast meadow and towards a small, heavily eroded pond that turned out to be one of the most historic sites in Oklahoma, Buffalo Springs. It was here in 1876 that trader Pat Hennessey and his party of men, who had set out on the trail despite warnings that there were hostiles in the area, were massacred by Indians. Despite being under a brilliant sun, it was still an oddly shadowed and disturbing place, and that was without our knowing that the Trail Boss, who had ridden ahead, had just driven away two poisonous water moccasin snakes in the shallow water.

Back at the road, our nearly 60-mile trail ride at an end, we dismounted for the last time and said our surprisingly emotional and heartfelt goodbyes to our horses. Lucky, to my surprise, spotted me and walked, bumping his nose against my shoulder. Our horses had not only survived the heat, but also our incompetence and they had done so, with a few exceptions, with phenomenal grace and patience.

I was standing watching the horses being loaded into their carriers when Bob Klemme walked up beside me. He had driven down that morning from Enid to see the rare sight of a 21st century cattle drive.

"Well," he said, "You made it."

"Yeah. Quite an experience."

He gestured out towards the meadow, "Interesting place for you to end up, too."

"Really? Why?"

"Because that meadow is where your great-grandfather would have camped, waiting for the Run to begin."

I looked back at the empty expanse, the Bison elevator looming just beyond. "You're kidding."

"No," said Klemme, "One estimate is that there were as many as 50,000 people out there. All manner of folks. And the only thing they had for water was what was in the spring. There was real concern by the Army that people might die of thirst before the Run even began."

I pictured Charlie, sleeping on his bedroll with Old Prize tied up nearby, as I had been with Lucky. But there would have been no city lights in the distance, no hum of cars and trucks on a distant highway, just hundreds of campfires stretching as far as the eye could see, the smell of food cooking, perhaps a crying child or two, and the same train whistle I had heard. A few people might have been playing music, or shouting drunken boasts; there might even have been a fight or a gunshot. And Charlie, lying there under the stars, filled with anticipation about the morrow, might have talked for a while with Will, a dark silhouette a few feet away. They would have rehearsed their strategy for the Run—in a whisper so no one could overhear—repeating to each other what landmarks to look for, how to pace their horses, and how to reconnect and watch each other's backs during the dangerous ride to register in Enid.

Short Sprint

We climbed into trucks for the ride to the Hasbrook farm. I joined Klemme in his truck to lead the way. After telling him where to cross the highway and start down the red dirt road, I explained how I measured the distance to the farm by using the odometer.

"Don't need it," he replied, "just count the crossroads. The whole Cherokee Strip is like one big checkerboard. Goes back to the days of the Run. Each square is a section, a mile on each side. So every crossroad counts as one more mile." He pointed as we passed through just such an intersection, "You always gotta be careful though, cause there's no stop signs .and people have been colliding and killing each other out here for a century."

We passed the farm of one of my second cousins. The yard was filled with historic farm implements. "You know," said Klemme, "I've been thinking about Charlie Hasbrook and that race horse of his. What people don't realize is that most people did the Run, even on horseback, with regular draught horses. They weren't very fast, but they could keep up a good strong pace for ten or twenty miles.

"By comparison, some of the ole cowboys ended up with the best plots of land because they had those cow ponies that could get into that special trot they had and could run all day. There were a lot of complaints that those horses should be disqualified from the Run."

"Now, you said Charlie rode a racehorse. From Chicago, right?"

"That's right. Old Prize."

"Well," said Klemme, "That pretty much proves that your great-grandfather knew exactly where he was going."

"What do you mean?"

"Well, it turned out that thoroughbreds weren't much good out here. The terrain was too rough, and more important, they were bred to run very fast for short distances. After seven or eight miles, they basically just wore out. And that's just about how far his claim was from the starting line. Charlie knew the spot he wanted and made sure he got there before anyone else."

I had always imagined Charlie riding a long distance across the countryside, but in fact, it must have been more of a short sprint. Including creek crossings

"That was the hard part," said Klemme, "there were no real paths, so wagons and even horses got stuck going down banks or getting caught in the mud. Some sharp operators even staked out some of these crossings and charged the people who came behind them."

Rerouting around dense groves of trees and other obstacles, Charlie's entire run probably lasted little more than ninety minutes. And it probably nearly killed Old Prize, which may explain why its grateful owner provided the horse with a comfortable life for the next twenty-five years.

We crossed the second bridge, where my grandmother had crashed the truck and smashed the eggs. Klemme studied the thick stand of trees, almost a forest, on both sides of the road, "It's no wonder Charlie remembered this place. He sure picked a fine spot. Not many better in the whole Strip.

Bob Klemme shook his head, "You know, lot of poor folks ended up out in the open, without even any water. Most of them didn't make it."

We turned backwards onto the road that led to the farm. In the distance we could see the red barn, with its distinctive cupola, and the white farmhouse. In 1913, twenty years after he had made the Run, a middle-aged Charlie Hasbrook would have seen this view as he returned to the farm from a trip to Enid or Hennessey. He would have remembered this same view when there had been nothing but trees and prairie grass and he must have been immensely proud.

HOME AGAIN

We spent the day touring the farm buildings, exploring the creek. The year's crop of frogs had just hatched and there were thousands, enough to make the creek bank seem to move as we passed. For the first time, I walked the creek bottom all of the way to the bridge, passing under the giant, often lightning shattered, trunks of old cottonwood trees that no doubt saw Cheyenne raiding parties stop to water their horses.

We had said goodbye to most of the cowboys at the end of the trail. But the chuck wagon crew—with the mules—followed us to the homestead, and there, under the trees, cooked us one final meal. Then, with heartfelt goodbyes, they drove away, and we California scouts and dads were left alone in Oklahoma for the first time.

As the sun began to set we laid out our ground cloths and the big canvas tents that had been lent to us by the Hennessey Boy Scout troop and then rolled out our bedrolls on top of them. We were scattered in small contingents across the grass lawn. Tad and I, along with another older Scout, took the spot nearest the house, just a few feet from the roof of the Dugout, and not far from the spot where my mother and my cousin Vie Lee, not much younger than Tad was now, had stretched out on blankets and shared their dreams.

It was still hot, so I stripped down to the pair of padded bicycle shorts that I had worn under my jeans the last three days of the ride. They were disgusting, but the rest of me smelled just as bad. My new beard itched, my hair was stiff with dirt and sweat, and every muscle in my body ached. I could also feel chigger bites beginning to blossom on my ankles. I stretched out on top of my bedroll, hoping to cool down a little in the hot breeze before the bugs drove me undercover.

"Dad," said Tad's voice from a few feet away. It was one of the few words he had spoken all day. "When did you say we lost the farm?"

"Nineteen thirty-eight," I replied.

"So that means we're the first Hasbrooks to sleep on this farm in seventy years."

"I guess that's right."

There was a long pause, then Tad said with finality, "Then it's about time."

I rolled over on my back and looked up at the stars. The view, crystalline all week, was now slowly being obscured by a storm front. It just figured: record heat, and now that we were ready to leave, a cooling trend.

I knew I needed to get some sleep. Tomorrow, as planned, would be a busy day: a trip to Enid to the YMCA to get a shower, then a visit to the Mall for lunch with the local Scout Executive, a tour of a Western movie studio, then back to the farm for a final banquet, followed by a square dance with ladies and high school girls from a church group in Hennessey. Dave Dopps was even going to build a temporary plywood dance floor on the level ground in front of the Dugout.

But though we didn't know it, we were already losing the race to the incoming storm. Not long after we returned to the farm and prepared for the evening's event the sky opened up in a gush of rain that showed no sign of ending any time soon. So, we quickly decamped to a cattle exhibition hall in Hennessey and held our banquet and dance there. It wasn't nearly as evocative as the farm, but the hall had a big cement floor for dancing and it didn't smell too much like cow manure in the adjoining exhibition area. And most of all, it was dry.

Nearly forty of us, Scouts, dads, cowboys, Dopps and his wife, my mother and aunt, Klemme and, remarkably, Jesse Chisholm IV (looking uncannily like his ancestor) ate and told stories and toasted one another. At the end of the dinner, as the local girls and the dance caller arrived, and before the boys got too distracted—I stood up and held out before me a photograph I had carried with me for the entire ride. I briefly explained to the assembled crowd what had brought us all, many of us for thousands of miles, to this gathering.

The photograph, taken in 1922, showed the Hasbrook farmyard, and in the background the barn, its shape, even with a truncated cupola, familiar to all assembled. In the foreground, two little girls in dirty white shifts, one of them nearly three years old, the other just eighteen months, played in the mud.

"Those little girls were sisters and best friends, and they loved that farm," I told the crowd. Then I pointed to my mother and aunt sitting on the far side of the square of tables, "Almost ninety years later they still are. And they still do."

That was all ahead tomorrow. Tonight, I just wanted to lie on the lawn in the darkness and rest my tired muscles and bones. Overhead, the moon and stars burst forth again and again, only to be hidden once more by the next swatch of silvery clouds. Just above me, the branches of the trees swung silently in the hot wind. The barn loomed as a dark shape in the distance, the dim light just picking up the highlights of its white framed windows. Closer, and just behind me, the farmhouse, with its boarded windows and primer painted walls, glowed like polished bone. And closer still, its open doorway like a portal into the past, stood the Dugout. I couldn't see it, but I felt its pull, as I had my entire life.

What an unlikely, yet inevitable, place that I now found myself, .at the end of a more than a century-long string of events created by a hero-ic young man and an indomitable old woman _ my great-grandfather and my mother.

Charlie Hasbrook had found his own self trapped on yet another such thread. But it was defined by murder, jealously and cruelty; and even at a young age, he sensed that it would only lead to tragedy and ruin. And so, in act of extraordinary bravery, he *cut* that string, jettison-ing himself into the maelstrom, and set out to weave a new thread of his own devising.

It wasn't easy, and he encountered many failures and setbacks along the way, but in the end Charlie succeeded so well that his comfortable, successful descendents had no memory of the horrors that came before. Just as important, Charlie set into motion a collection of myths, attitudes and memories that would produce in the most unlikely of vessels, a beau-tiful, unassuming granddaughter, a woman with a will as ferocious as his own.

When my mother, as a teenager, swore to save the Hasbrook farm, she had no logical explanation why. Yet, over six decades, even as she had lived and travelled all over the world; even as she aged from a teenager to a young military wife to a mother to a widow to a grandmother; even as the farm buildings were abandoned and fell into disuse and decay, my mother never once betrayed that oath. And she had triumphed, fighting age and illness long enough to finally walk once again on the grounds of the family homestead, at last again in Hasbrook hands.

Soon, and I prayed not too soon, the Hasbrook homestead would be in my hands, my responsibility. I had no reason to keep it, much less complete its restoration, but I knew that I would do both, even if I never spent another night, like this night, on the farm. I would do so because, as the eternal tug from the Dugout perpetually reminded me: in the greater picture, this farm was more important than I was, and in preserving it I was performing one of the most important duties of my life. And someday, it would be my turn to pass that duty on.

One afternoon earlier that summer, back in California, Tad and I swung by his grandmother's house to drop off some paperwork. As had always been her habit, my mother walked us out through the atrium to the front door. But this time, as we climbed into the truck and I started the motor, Tad was surprised to see his grandmother standing next to his side door. He rolled down the window, "Yeah, grandma?"

"One more thing, Tad," I heard my mother say, "Don't ever. *Ever.* Let the farm out of our family's hands again. Do you understand?"

Tad gulped and nodded.

As we drove away, and as my mother, having returned to her usual nice-granny self, waved, Tad turned to me with a shudder, "Dad, I've *never* heard grandma speak with a voice like that. It was like something out of the Old Testament."

"Did you hear what she said?" I asked.

"How could I not have?" he replied, "It totally freaked me out—I mean, that's the lady who bakes me *cookies.*"

Good, I thought, you'll never forget.

Tad was asleep now, as were most of the other Scouts and dads. A firefly sparked briefly as it flew over me. A distant sound of a motor, which I had assumed was one of the oil pumps that dotted the area, turned out to be a tractor, its twin headlights moving slowly across the south acreage. It was Eddie Mack, working late to escape the heat. I pictured Charlie Hasbrook out there, driving a team as it pulled the plow, being led by a lantern held by Nate, or perhaps even Art Collins.

He had done it. In saving himself, Charlie had saved all of us from the awful fate of a family spinning endlessly downwards, generation after generation. A man of many weakness and flaws, Charlie had nevertheless always mustered the strength of character to make the right decisions on the big things. His family had loved him for that and that love had carried down through the generations, even to descendents who knew no more of him than an old photograph. What was this restored farm, after all, than the monument to a granddaughter's love in return? A love that now stretched forward two more generations—and with luck, for many, many generations to come.

I closed my eyes. It was about time we returned. But now we were home.

On Charlie's Place.

EPILOGUE

This column first appeared on PJMedia.com on July 20, 2010

As my mother lay dying, 4th of July fireworks were exploding beyond her hospital window. That seemed appropriate, as hers was a quintessential American life, the likes of which, in our very different world, we are unlikely to ever see again.

My mother was born on November 15th, 1920, on her grandfather Collins farm, near Marshall, Oklahoma. But her heart always lived at the adjoining farm, owned by grandfather Hasbrook, where she and her three sisters and brother spent many happy summers playing in the creek, sleeping under the firefly-lit night and hiding in the dugout cave that had been her mother's first home during the Oklahoma Land Rush.

My mother grew up in the nearby city of Enid. A child of the Great Depression, she learned to do without, especially when her father was seriously injured, and the family might have starved had it not been for food brought in from the farm. My mother vividly remembered being sent home from school one day as the horizon darkened and one of the great Dust Bowl storms poured over their community, leaving piles of talcum-fine dust in the corner of every sealed window.

When Pearl Harbor was attacked, my mother was already out high school and working. The nearby Army Air Corps base was soon filled with young men heading off to war. It didn't take them long to notice my mother.

One of the traits that most defined my mother all of her life was her beauty. It was always there. When my mother was 80, she sat in a doctor's waiting room for an hour because the nurse kept looking for an old lady, and walked right past what she thought was a 60 year-old woman. Last week, as my mother slept in the hospital bed, with hardly a wrinkle on her face, a nurse confided to me that, "None of the staff here really believes your mom is 90 years old."

Needless to say, for three years, beginning in 1942, my mother's Friday and Saturday nights were booked. The boys arrived, stayed a few months, and then left for the war, some never returning. Those who did come home were ready to settle down and start families. But, even as her younger sisters and brother married, my mother stayed aloof, awaiting the right man.

He appeared in 1945, when my mother was 25, long after mom's family and friends had conceded that she might become a spinster. My father, a cocky, troubled young captain, had finished his 30 missions in a B-17 and had now found himself stuck in the Mid-West waiting out his enlistment, and anxious to get home to California. His had been a tough childhood – passed around from family to family, he had ridden the rails, been a lumberjack, and even a razor-blade swallower in the circus. His only goal at that moment was to have a better future than his past.

They met on a blind date that each only accepted as a favor to a friend. My mother heard the car pull up, but when the doorbell never rang, she went outside—to find her father and her date down in a drainage ditch looking for a raccoon. My mother looked down to see a young man in uniform with a crooked grin; my father looked up to see a stunning young woman illuminated by the headlights of his car.

My father wasn't dazzled by good looks—he'd dated Hollywood starlets before the war—but what did impress him was how casually my mother carried her beauty; as if it was an afterthought, even a subject of amusement. But ultimately, what won his heart was the realization that behind her gentle manner was a will of iron. Unconsciously, he knew he would need that will to save him. And it did: though she never quite tamed him, my mother civilized my father—as she did two more generations of Malone boys.

My mother's family quickly went from worrying that mother would never marry, to worrying that she would. My father drank too much, drove too fast, and was way too clever and reckless for his own good. Each of my mother's sisters in turn tried to talk her out of it.

But my mother ignored them—and was gone. Off to the film colony in Southern California . . . and from there, the world.

My father chose to stay in the U.S. Air Force, in intelligence, and his work soon took the young couple to Baltimore, Minnesota, and then on to Europe and North Africa. It was an exciting life. In Wiesbaden and

Munich, my mother would make sure that my father had a good dinner and a loaded gun before he went off a mission. One night, when half of another couple came to dinner, my mother studiously pretended that she didn't know the other's husband was still crawling through high grass on the other side of the wire in Czechoslovakia. In Morocco, my mother drove my father to clandestine meetings with revolutionaries, flashing her lights outside of walled compounds and circling until the gates furtively opened.

When the French caught my father and gave him 72 hours to leave the country or be arrested as a spy, my mother still managed to write out holiday cards before they packed and dashed for Gibraltar. They celebrated Christmas that year with a tiny tree in a Madrid hotel room.

It was also a very romantic life. Every free minute my parents had they explored Europe, making friends from Nice to Rotterdam with whom they would correspond for decades after. As family lore has it, I was probably conceived in a tiny inn, high in a pass of the Italian Alps.

My parents even managed to be the scandal of the 1953 Oktoberfest—my mother, by violating the then-taboo of appearing in public pregnant with me; my father by getting crazy drunk, stealing a bunch of beer steins and then looping their handles through his belt like a pistolero. Anyone who was there long remembered the sight of a crowd of thousands of people parting as my wobbly father, clanking away and held under each arm by a Munich policeman (who also happened to be workmates of my dad) led him out through the festival gates, followed by my very pregnant mother, chin high, looking neither left nor right.

Through all of this, my mother was transformed. Gone was the small town, mid-Western girl. She cut her hair fashionably short, wore tailored Italian wools, and could bargain for a deal anywhere from a Munich butcher shop to the Kasbah in Casablanca. But in other ways, she was still the same: a half-century later, my father's German translator would confess to me that everyone in the office was secretly in love with my mother. When Mark Clark gave her a birthday kiss in a restaurant, she assumed that's what four-star generals always did.

My father finished his Air Force career in Washington, D.C. It was the late 1950s now, and my mother's world swung back and forth between motherhood by day—Little League and swimming classes and bundling me up to play in the snow; and the life of an officer's wife—elegant cocktail parties and embassy soirees—at night. It was the climax of the second act of her life.

The third act began in 1963, when my father retired from the military, took a job with NASA and we moved to California, first briefly to Mountain View, then for the rest of my mother's life, to Sunnyvale. Soon, with the arrival of my sister Edie, we were four, and settled down into the heart of Sixties Silicon Valley suburbia.

For the next quarter century, my mother, in many ways, seemed to slowly vanish, sublimating her own life and desires for that of her husband and children. Ballet and Boy Scouts, yard work and real estate investments, washing and patching clothes, and twenty five years of weekly trips to the commissary. She nursed my father back to health after his heart attacks, and dealt with having a caged lion in her home when he retired.

Thankfully, in time, with my sister and me at last of age, the old wanderlust returned with vengeance. This time, with the clock ticking down for my father, the two of them decided to take on the entire world. My father's last years with my mother were filled with stays in London, Salisbury, Paris, Carcassonne, Rome, the Greek Isles, New Zealand, Sweden, Indonesia and India—often for months at a time. In the Himalayas, they even survived an earthquake that cracked their hotel in two.

After my father's death in 1988, it would have been understandable if my mother had stepped out of her busy life and enjoyed her own long retirement. Instead, she embarked on the last great act of her life, one that astonished everyone who knew her and which in the end made everything that came before it seem like a rehearsal.

My father's death broke my mother's heart, but it also set her free. Never again would she have to compromise her freedom and will to anyone else. She began by joining, or increasing her involvement in, a myriad of social and service groups—Widow & Widowers, Chat 'n Sew, Newcomers, Community Services, the Sunnyvale Historical Society, to name a few, and volunteered for leadership positions in each of them. Soon, she had the social life of someone half her age.

Each afternoon, she walked with her neighbor and good friend Mildred, until the sight of the two of them, strolling arm-in-arm down the sidewalk became something of a Sunnyvale institution. And on the weekends, her happy dates with her thoughtful gentleman companion, Bob, gave her a reason to dress up and stay young.

My mother also established a series of goals that she wanted to achieve before she died. The first of these, a goal she'd had since she was a little girl, was to see the new century. She met that one easily—and, indeed, the turn of the new Millennium and the occasion of her 80th birthday seemed to set my mother off on a quest for ever-greater and more difficult accomplishments. In the end, she achieved every one of them—and gave everyone who knew her a lesson on what can be done even in one's ninth decade.

It had been my father's dream to rebuild Sunnyvale's founding Murphy House as one of Silicon Valley's signature Museums—and my mother had helped him for two decades to fulfill that dream. Now, more than a decade after his death, the new Museum at last seemed a possibility. And when the moment came, my mother stepped up and made the first, and still the largest, private donation to the Museum's capital fund—an amount so big that it literally took my breath away when I announced it. Her donation proved to be the catalyst for others—and my father's dream became my mother's reality: her memorial was held in the new Museum, just above the room named for her.

There was another, equally large goal. My mother's beloved Hasbook farm had been lost during the Depression. And as a seventeen year old girl, my mother had stood watching as her grandfather's farm equipment had been auctioned away, and swore that one day she would win the farm back for the family. It took her more than sixty years. By then the farm house had been abandoned, the cave left to the rain and snow, and the barn had all-but collapsed. But, she re-bought the farm, and as the local papers reported with amazement, soon a bright red barn with a shiny new cupola rose again over the Prairie.

My mother had fulfilled her promise to her grandfather. Now it was time to do the same for her grandchildren.

At the beginning of this year, my mother began to fade. My wife Carol took over her correspondence and finances—something that had always been my mother's forte. In the end, it was only through the superhuman efforts of my sister, Edie and her partner Tony, cooking endless meals, dropping by twice each day to check on her, that my mother was able to spend her final days at home. No mother ever had a more caring daughter.

My mother's last two goals were smaller, but no less important—and ultimately no less ambitious. She had always been the perfect grandmother, a part of almost every day of her grandsons' lives. The woman who had once counted her husband's bullets, now counted cookies for his descendants. In the end, all that my mother wanted was to live to see her oldest grandson, Tad's, high school, and her youngest grandson, Tim's, junior high school, graduations. She attended them both, the latter with just three weeks to spare. In the end, through sheer force of will, she stayed alive long enough for Tad to return from England to see her. My mother was able at the very end to tell us all that she loved us.

She saved her last laugh for one of her grandsons; her last tear for the other.

And she died with fireworks.

Index